Mammalian Cell Technology

BIOTECHNOLOGY

Julian E. Davies, *Editor*
Biogen, S.A.
Geneva, Switzerland

Editorial Board

Mammalian Cell Technology

Edited by

William G. Thilly
Department of Applied Biological Sciences
Massachusetts Institute of Technology
Cambridge, Massachusetts

Butterworths
Boston   London   Durban   Singapore   Sydney   Toronto   Wellington

Library of Congress Cataloging-in-Publication Data
Main entry under title:

Mammalian cell technology.

  (Biotechnology ;   )
  Includes bibliographies and index.
  1. Mammals—Cytology—Technique. I. Thilly,
William G. II. Series.
QL739.15.M36 1986   599'.087'028   85–28516
ISBN 0–409–90029–X

Butterworth Publishers
80 Montvale Avenue
Stoneham, MA 02180

10 9 8 7 6 5 4 3 2 1

Printed in the United States of America

CONTRIBUTORS

Debra Barngrover
Integrated Genetics
Framingham, Massachusetts

James Barsoum
Whitehead Institute
Massachusetts Institute of Technology
Cambridge, Massachusetts

Michael Butler
Department of Biological Sciences
Manchester Polytechnic
Manchester, England

Robert J. Fleischaker, Jr.
Vista Biologicals
Carlsbad, California

Wei-Shou Hu
Department of Chemical Engineering
  and Materials Science
University of Minnesota
Minneapolis, Minnesota

Ara T. Nahapetian
E.I. duPont de Nemours and Co.
Wilmington, Delaware

Marsha Rich Rosner
Department of Applied Biological
  Sciences
Massachusetts Institute of Technology
Cambridge, Massachusetts

William G. Thilly
Department of Applied Biological
  Sciences
Massachusetts Institute of Technology
Cambridge, Massachusetts

James N. Thomas
Genentech, Inc.
South San Francisco, California

Daniel I.C. Wang
Department of Chemical Engineering
Massachusetts Institute of Technology
Cambridge, Massachusetts

Lisa A. Weymouth
Departments of Medicine and
  Pathology
New England Deaconess Hospital
Boston, Massachusetts

CONTENTS

Does anybody really know what will come from our attempts to use fermentors instead of animals to grow animal cells and to produce physiologically active macromolecules? Probably not, but readers of this book would probably appreciate an organized review of the essential elements, particularly those affecting fermentor productivity. Further reading should bring an orderly understanding of the most important aspects of animal cells' genetics, physiology, and growth at a scale sufficient to produce pharmaceuticals. Beyond that, this book is intended for the practitioners of cell technology and the newly bred biotechnology students attracted by this mysterious blend of cell physiology and biochemical engineering.

The authors of this book are not old hands in commercial use of mammalian cells and have for the most part recently completed their doctoral or postdoctoral training at MIT in cell biology, cell technology, toxicology, or biochemical engineering. Some of their ideas are a little weird, which makes them a perfect match for this field. Collectively, however, they have devised the means to grow mammalian cells at densities (gm/l) approaching those achieved in bacterial fermentation and have devised useful approaches to maintaining fermentor control by computer-aided feedback systems or by devising simple means to encourage cells to grow with minimal perturbations of their culture environment.

At this writing, the authors have dispersed and no longer argue in the halls of the Department of Applied Biological Sciences about the best way to build an autoclavable oxygen probe or whether glutamine's role as an energy source is a fact to be used or a problem to be overcome. However, since they are all plying their trade at stimulating rates of remuneration, there is the reasonable hope that some value may be obtained by those who both buy this book and read it, for we have faithfully put down the concepts and technical aspects that we have found important in daily practice.

I wish to especially acknowledge the work of Ms. Kay Dreher in assembling this volume; her editorial and technical contributions have earned her our thanks and appreciation.

William G. Thilly

The Rationale for and Elements of Mammalian Cell Technology

William G. Thilly

1.1 INTRODUCTION

If you are interested in mammalian cell technology, the chances are you want to produce something you think can be made in useful quantities only by mammalian cells—otherwise you would be planning to make your product in bacterial or yeast fermentors or to extract it from animal carcasses. You could be a student who wishes to get a good feeling for the elements of mammalian cell use. You may be a faculty member schooled in microbial fermentation who wants to comprehend the essential differences between mammalian and bacterial or yeast cell-based production. In any case, you or your students will eventually face and try to solve the problems of mammalian cell-based production. A prerequisite is an understanding of when to consider application of mammalian cell growth and production.

Actually, there are three categories of products for which the use of mammalian cells may be indispensable. The first category is the cells themselves, as in expanding a cell population from a patient for grafting purposes. Applications involving skin cell growth in vitro are already part of medical practice in burn treatment, and one is free to imagine replacement of other tissues such as blood cell precursor populations, veins, and glandular tissue

1

as well. The use of mammalian cell technology applied to the modest potential needs for homo-grafting may well be an important adjunct to future clinical practice. Since cell densities of 25 grams wet weight per liter have been obtained in our laboratory for certain mammalian kidney lines, cell amounts approaching 1 kilogram could be generated with a modest-sized 40-liter fermentor. On the other hand, there are questions yet to be asked about the mass expansion of primary human cells in culture in terms of maintenance of differentiated functions, success in transplantation, and potential selection of cells with malignant characteristics.

The second category of mammalian cell use is in viral vaccine production. Mammalian and avian cells are widely used for producing a series of animal and human vaccines; the vaccine industry is in fact the largest animal-cell-growing entity on the planet. Recent advances in preparing vaccines by combining pure antigens from an infectious agent may supersede the traditional cell-based production of the attenuated or killed virus itself. This area is definitely one in which competing biological technologies are already active. Changes that lower the cost and raise the safety and efficacy of vaccine products are long overdue.

The third category is that of cellular macromolecules such as hormones, physiological effectors, and enzymes, which are destined for use as pharmaceuticals. Some products already considered are urokinase for antithrombitic activity, interferon for action against rhinoviruses, blood-clotting factors for treatment of hemophilia, and a host of others, each addressing some medical need. Principal among these are the monoclonal antibodies, already in wide use as analytic tools in medical diagnoses, and for which important uses as adjuncts to cancer chemotherapy are anticipated.

There are however, persistent perceptions that mammalian cells cannot be manipulated genetically like bacteria and fungi and that mass culture of mammalian cells is too technically difficult or too expensive. These perceptions hamper progress more than the actual problems we meet in practice. In this book we hope to bring together the pertinent facts of genetic manipulation of mammalian cells, which permit increasing the rate of production per cell, and merge these with the kinds of cell-growing technology that have been applied to increase the number of cells available in a fermentor. The essential message of this book is that the product of cellular output rate and fermentor cell number is the key to whether or not a particular product can be efficiently manufactured using a particular cell strain or line.

In the following chapters we have divided the treatment of cellular rate of molecule or virus production into three parts. The first part (Chapters 2 and 3) addresses questions of organization of cellular components to maximize productivity on a per-cell basis. The second part (Chapters 4, 5, and 6) examines the external cell culture medium and its effect on productivity. The third part (Chapters 7, 8, and 9) deals with productivity at the level of fermentation operation and design.

We begin the discussion of cellular processing with Chapter 2, which describes the introduction of genetic information for making a particular desired protein or set of proteins (e.g., a virus) into a mammalian cell line along with DNA sequences that increase the probability that the desired gene is transcribed and translated. The goal of these manipulations is to maximize the cells' production of the mRNA(s) for the desired product while minimizing the cells' use of energy for other processes.

Chapter 3 discusses translating mRNA into protein and successive processing to give the protein biological activity. Mammalian cells have some specific processes not shared by yeasts and bacteria in processing proteins as and soon after they are made. These steps include folding the protein correctly and performing certain customizing steps, known collectively as posttranslational processing, in order to make a biologically active product. A subsequent intracellular step involves getting a cell to package the product and pump it into the fermentation medium. Use of secreting cells simplifies purification relative to whole cell homogenates.

Having considered the genetics and subcellular physiology of mammalian cells, we turn to the question of defining appropriate environments in which they could be used most productively.

The first considerations, presented in Chapter 4, are the widely studied but still poorly understood growth requirements such as oxygen, energy sources, amino acids, vitamins, and other micronutrients. For practical purposes, we don't yet know enough about simple things such as cellular energy sources; therefore, success in large-scale application requires some additional fundamental studies in biochemical dynamics.

The second set of general environmental questions (Chapter 5) involves the use of serum, the "black box" of cell culture. What we do and don't know about what serum provides is worth a book in itself and, in fact, a four-volume series on these issues has just appeared (see Chapter 4 for discussion). Serum-free formulas for growing a number of useful mammalian cell types exist, and these offer hope for easier purification schemes, freedom from unwanted antigens, and, perhaps more important, relative freedom from contamination from serum-borne viruses and mycoplasma in drug manufacture.

A third part of the cellular environment, which we consider in Chapter 6, concerns the nature of the solid substratum to which many useful mammalian cells must attach before they will multiply or produce desired products. Some practical solutions for mass cell culture are provided by available microcarrier culture techniques, but as the chapter makes clear, our understanding of the molecular mechanisms involved is still rudimentary.

Since large-scale cell culture fermentors have been used to date only for viral vaccine and interferon production in a stirred-batch configuration, we consider approaches and elements useful in maintaining high cell densities, which have become available on a practical scale only in the last few years. Chapter 7 describes an experimental approach that matches perfusion rates and nutrient concentration to the requirements of cellular nutrition and elimination of inhibitory cell products.

Biochemical engineers make their contributions in two succeeding chapters. In the first (Chapter 8), principles of feedback control used in microbial fermentation are applied to models of cell culture behavior. In the second (Chapter 9), a preliminary but important data base on changes in oxygen utilization during mammalian cell growth in a deep fermentor is analyzed in terms of feedback control system design.

1.2   GENERAL STRATEGY IN MAMMALIAN CELL TECHNOLOGY

Many commercial firms approach us for general advice on production of an unnamed macromolecule as if there were some global strategy that would solve cell technology problems. These problems and their solutions reside, however, in the precise nature of the product and intended area of use. In several cases, sophisticated molecular manipulations have been undertaken when use of a modest-sized fermentor and available cell lines would have made more product in a month than the company could sell in a year. There are probably plans on a drawing board somewhere to build a 5000-l fermentor to use cell A to produce product B, while straightforward manipulation of the product's gene enhancer region could make an already existing 100-l fermentor sufficient for production needs. Usually overlooked—at considerable cost in developing production processes—are the effects of medium constituents on cell output and limits to fermentor operations. Sometimes the woof of biochemistry is ignored when attention is focused on the warp of molecular biology.

If there is a global strategy to recommend, it is to examine the cells, the cell environment, and fermentor parameters as each contributes to overall productivity. The specific tactics to be adopted will depend critically on the product desired. Figure 1–1 outlines the steps leading from initial recognition of the need for a product to its final distribution and use.

1.2.1   Choosing the Product

Many companies still regard their mammalian cell efforts as demonstration projects rather than product-oriented development programs, primarily because corporate management has not clearly defined a product for which there is a sufficient existing market. Exceptions to this statement are producers of viral vaccines and monoclonal antibodies, such as Centocor, Inc., in Pennsylvania or Celltech in the United Kingdom. One common theme, however, is the desire to find needed macromolecular pharmaceuticals generally required in medical practice such as preparations of serum albumen,

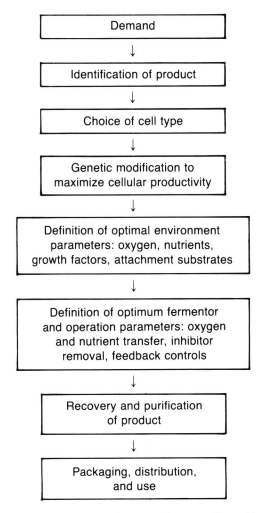

FIGURE 1–1 Diagram of the elements of mammalian cell technology.

clotting factors, and immunoglobins that will not produce untoward immune responses when transferred or injected.

1.2.2 Choice of Cell Types

The use of a product in the human body, with its attendant risk in precipitating an immune response, requires that the product have a high degree of purity and that it be coded for by a gene identical, or nearly identical, to that found in the patient. This can almost be solved by cloning the human gene and incorporating it and suitable control sequences into a cell that will produce the desired product. Reports (anecdotal) of sensitization against "pure" preparations derived from lower organisms ascribe some of the problems to transcriptional and/or translational error in which aberrant proteins result in small quantities from a single gene copy. The fact that this problem has not yet been reported in mammalian cell preparations may simply be due to lack of sufficient experiments. Alternatively, there may be lower rates of transcriptional/translational error in mammalian cells or the presence of an efficient means for intracellular degradation of aberrant proteins after synthesis.

It would seem prudent to choose cells of human origin to make products for human use, thus minimizing the risks related to introducing foreign antigens. However, it is also possible that such cells harbor specific pathogens that introduce a special standard of care in purifying and handling of the pharmaceutical.

Among human and lower primate cell types there are several strains of human fibroblasts, such as WI-38 and MRC-5, that are licensed for human vaccine production in the vaccine-producing nations. Unfortunately, human fibroblast strains can only be grown effectively for some 30 generations under present culturing conditions. A lively literature deals with this phenomenon, called "senescence" in an effort to create an analogy with aging processes, but the biochemical causes of the problem are in fact unknown.

In any case, a gram of MRC cells at the tenth doubling could be expanded with reasonable confidence some 2^{20} times to 10^6 g (1 metric ton), if necessary, before cell vitality would diminish. High-density microcarrier culture achieves about 10^7 human fibroblasts/ml or about 10 g/liter, so while most tactics try to avoid human fibroblast-based production, it is possible to use this approach.

A growing trend begun within the World Health Organization and under consideration in the United States and Canada is the licensing of vaccines produced by an established line of kidney cells, Vero, derived from the African green monkey. This cell strain appears to be pathogen-free, grows as an immortal line, maintains a stable karyotype, and has been grown in one laboratory at some 25 g/l in perfused microcarrier cultures. It can be manipulated by genetic techniques and, as an epithelial cell, it contains active cellular machinery for posttranslational processing and secretion. Vero cells would seem to be a good line to start with, assuming no available cell already making the desired product could be found.

1.2.3 Further Considerations

Once a product is chosen, its human gene isolated, and a suitable cell type identified, the rest is hard experimental work. Before undertaking a large research effort, it would be wise to calculate just how much of the product is actually needed and just what the manufacturing costs are with existing technology. This sounds simpleminded, but experience shows that this point has not always been adequately explored by management and development staff together. To help bridge this gap, I have used a simple multiplication model that lets management and separate technical groups calculate their overall production potential:

Assume a product is desired in quantities of 10 kilograms/year. Assume secondly that an existing cell, genetically engineered or not, produces 1 picogram of product/cell · day in exponential growth. A need for some 10^{16} cell · days of production is easily calculated.

This can be "easily" accomplished by a conventional stirred fermentor of suspension or microcarrier-attached cells (10^6 cells/l) of some 10^{10} ml, or 10 million liters, operating for one day. By combining our best strategies for genetic engineering, we might increase secretion of the desired protein to 1–10% of the newly synthesized protein (1,000 picograms/cell · day) or up to 100 picograms/cell · day. That would cut fermentor volume down to 10^5 liters, or about 100 times bigger than the largest mammalian cell fermentor known to be used in commercial vaccine production.

However, mammalian cell lines such as MDCK (canine kidney) and Vero (monkey kidney) have been grown in perfused microcarrier cultures at 50 and 30×10^6 cells/ml, respectively, and this fermentor operating mode could cut our megafermentor down about 40-fold to 2,500 liters.

In addition, there seems to be no compelling need to make the product in a single day, so one could forecast operating for some 100 days per year in one 25-liter perfusion fermentor, a configuration already in use in some vaccine production efforts.

If the best efforts of the genetic engineers yielded a cell productivity of only 10 picograms/cell · day, then ten 25-liter perfusion fermentors operating for 100 days would also produce the desired 10 kilograms of product.

If, however, 100 g per year was the market requirement, the combination of one cell making 1 picogram/cell · day and a single 25-l perfusion fermentor operating for 100 working days would be sufficient at near-zero R&D investment. (This assumes an efficient means of product recovery; in practice, low cellular output relative to normal secretory products and medium proteins increases the difficulty of the purification steps.)

What if a metric ton of product was needed? A genetically well-engineered producing/secretory cell (100 picograms/cell · day) operating in a perfused fermentor mode of 4×10^7 cells/ml in a 1000-liter fermentor would produce some 4 kilograms of product per day; a metric ton would require 250 continuous days of production. It would also use about $250 \times 4,000 = 1$ million liters of medium, or a medium cost alone of approximately one dollar U.S. per gram of product.

1.3 CONCLUSION

The truth is that the fundamental problems of genetic, cellular, and biochemical engineering of high-volume (1000-l), high-density mammalian cell cultures have not yet been addressed in practice. Efforts such as those described in succeeding chapters have begun to tackle some of the problems, but a more intense combination of basic science and engineering is required for general success in applying mammalian cell technology to manufacturing useful products at an acceptable cost.

Genetic Engineering in
Mammalian Cells

Lisa A. Weymouth
James Barsoum

DNA containing genes from one mammalian source, when introduced without modification into another mammalian cell, can lead to a low level of gene expression in a minor fraction, about 10^{-6}, of recipient cells (Wigler et al., 1977). However, by artificially adding other DNA sequences to a foreign gene, the genetic engineer can begin to bring the process of expression under experimental control to achieve high-level production of the desired foreign protein. Addition of appropriate DNA sequences to a foreign gene can achieve the following:

1. Provide a means of selecting those cells that have received foreign DNA.
2. Cause expression of virtually any foreign gene; for example, by adding mammalian control sequences, a bacterial gene can be expressed in mammalian cells (Mulligan and Berg, 1980).
3. Determine whether the foreign DNA will integrate into the chromosome of the host cell or exist as an extrachromosomal, autonomously replicating unit via choice of different viral vector sequences.
4. Build in the potential for increasing protein production by
   a. amplifying the number of foreign DNA copies in the new cell line, and/or

b. enhancing the expression of the foreign gene with an exogenous regulator molecule.

If the final aim of genetic engineering in mammalian cells is to achieve high-level production of a particular protein in a stable cell line that can be cultivated in bulk cell culture, the general approach taken by genetic engineering would be the following (depicted in Figure 2–1): Isolate the DNA sequence that codes for the protein of interest. Place that gene into a recombinant DNA vector designed to provide DNA sequences to achieve control over the parameters previously listed. Introduce the DNA into the mammalian cell of choice and select those cells that received the DNA. Screen the cells containing recombinant DNA for ones that produce high levels of the foreign protein. Establish a cell line that can be grown in bulk culture, and stably produces the foreign protein.

This chapter reviews what is known and suspected about the relationships between DNA sequence and gene expression in mammalian cells, which is relevant when the goal is to develop a means of producing the highest yield of a specific protein per cell. The chapter describes protocols used to introduce recombinant DNA molecules into mammalian cells, means of selecting for cells that have taken up and express the exogenous DNA, ways in which expression can be maximized and regulated, and the use of different viruses to design expression vectors for mammalian cells.

2.1 ELEMENTS OF GENE EXPRESSION

Mammalian cells will express exogenously introduced genes provided that the genes possess the proper DNA regulatory elements recognized and used by the host cell. The regulatory elements required for gene expression in mammalian cells, while not mechanistically understood in great detail, have been defined sufficiently to enable genetic engineering of DNA molecules to optimize production of the desired gene product.

In order to synthesize a protein, the cell must be supplied not only with the DNA sequence that actually codes for the protein but also with the information that governs the rate by which that DNA sequence is copied (transcribed) into RNA. This RNA transcript contains the information that determines the rate and nature of its own processing into mature messenger RNA (mRNA) and its subsequent export into the cytoplasm. In the cytoplasm, the mRNA nucleotide sequence is translated into a protein, a linear polymer of amino acids whose sequence determines the activity and stability of the protein in that it dictates the three-dimensional folding of the polypeptide, the possible insertion of the protein into cellular structures, the potential for posttranslational modifications such as proteolytic cleavage or covalent addition of carbohydrate, lipid, or other modification, and possible transport of the protein out of the cell. Since posttranslational modifications

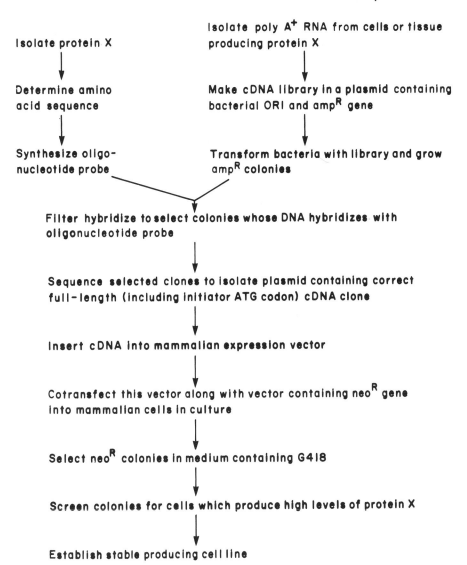

FIGURE 2-1 General scheme for cloning and expressing a gene in mammalian cells.

are required for the activity of many proteins, it often is essential that a particular protein be produced in mammalian cells rather than in bacteria where these modifications do not occur.

Not all of the original gene is represented in the final protein. Part of the DNA sequence promotes the transcription of the gene but is not itself transcribed. Also, much of the original RNA transcript is lost en route to forming mature mRNA. In turn, only part of this mRNA is translated into protein. Figure 2–2 describes the pathway to protein product formation in mammalian cells.

From the standpoint of constructing a DNA sequence that will faithfully reproduce the exact natural product desired, one does not need absolute knowledge of each of these processing steps. It is usually sufficient to copy precisely the sequence of the mRNA as DNA (cDNA) and to join this DNA to control sequences that determine the rate and precision of transcript formation and transcript processing. These control sequences can be derived from a gene that is different from the gene whose protein product is desired. In genetic engineering, it is usually easier to employ a known set of well-defined and efficient control sequences than to isolate undefined control sequences that accompany the gene to be expressed.

The yield of protein product can be increased by several means. One is to increase the actual number of DNA copies of the gene within each cell (gene amplification). Another is to use control sequences that respond to external signals, such as hormones, and thus permit protein production to

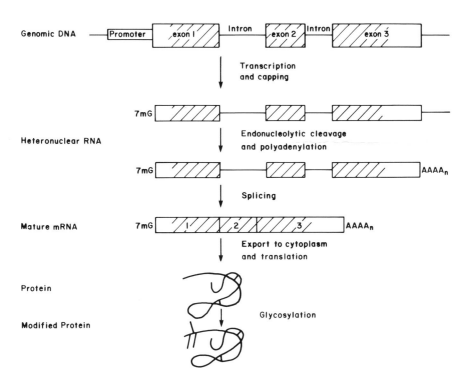

FIGURE 2–2 Pathways to protein production in mammalian cells. Large rectangular boxes represent exons. Diagonal lines mark those regions of the exons that will be translated into protein.

be increased at a set point in time. This latter feature is especially desirable in cases where high concentration of a particular protein is toxic to cells. Using an inducible promoter to control expression, cells may be propagated to large numbers under conditions where very little foreign protein is made, and then production of larger quantities of the foreign protein can be induced by an external signal just prior to harvest when long-term cell viability is no longer required.

2.2 DNA SEQUENCES REQUIRED FOR GENE EXPRESSION IN MAMMALIAN CELLS

Expression of eukaryotic genes depends upon the presence of certain functional DNA sequences, including signals for promotion, polyA addition, and RNA splicing. In order for any gene to be expressed within a mammalian cell, that gene must either already contain these expression sequences or be provided with them artificially using recombinant DNA technology. All regulatory sequences, except that segment of the transcriptional promoter known as the enhancer, appear to be so closely related that they are virtually interchangeable: They can be obtained from any mammalian cell or virus and can function in any other mammalian cell. The enhancer region, in contrast, seems to be somewhat cell-specific, and therefore should be chosen to provide activation in the particular host cell planned for use in protein production. Sequences required for mammalian cell expression are summarized in the following section, but the reader is referred for details to reviews by Breathnach and Chambon (1981) and by Nevins (1983).

2.2.1 Promoters
In bacteria, the promoter region is the area of DNA in which RNA polymerase binds so that it can initiate transcription. In eukaryotic cells, the sequences required for transcription of messenger RNA can be located many nucleotides upstream from the site where transcription actually starts, and in some instances downstream of this site. Exactly how these DNA sequences interact with RNA polymerases or alter the DNA template to affect transcription is still being investigated. The exact sequences required for efficient production of mammalian messenger RNA and how they function are the subjects of current research, so our knowledge of these expression sequences is constantly being refined.

A typical mammalian transcription promoter is shown in Figure 2–3. Research so far has shown that one region, called the TATA sequence, or Goldberg-Hogness box, is required to position accurately the start site of transcription (Breathnach and Chambon, 1981; Wasylyk et al., 1983b). The TATA box is located 25–35 base pairs upstream from the RNA initiation

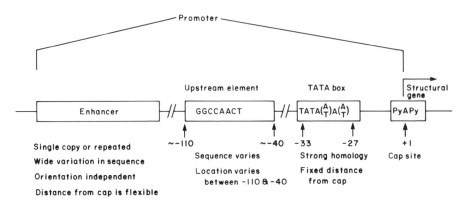

FIGURE 2–3   Typical mammalian transcription promoter.

site and consists of the consensus sequence 5'-TATAAAT-3' (Corden et al., 1980). Nearly every eukaryotic gene analyzed so far (with the exception of the late genes of SV40 and polyoma viruses and two adenovirus genes) contains some version of the TATA sequence.

Particular sequences in other regions appear to be required for efficient transcription of most genes. For example, deletion mutant mapping of simian virus (SV40) DNA has demonstrated that a GC-rich region with the repeated sequence 5'-PyPyCCGCCC-3', located 35–107 nucleotides upstream from the start site of the early gene for T-antigen, is required for transcription (Fromm and Berg, 1982, 1983). Several cellular and viral genes have been found to share a region of homology, 5'-GGCCAATCT-3', located 70–90 base pairs upstream from the start site of transcription (Efstratiadis et al., 1980; Benoist and Chambon, 1981; Dierks et al., 1983). Most genes possess some promoter element in this region of the DNA, although some show no or very little homology to the consensus sequences shown above. These control elements, located 40–110 base pairs upstream from the transcription start site, appear to increase the efficiency of transcription but do not affect the accuracy of initiation (Fromm and Berg, 1982). In some cases, their orientation can be inverted without affecting transcription (Mishoe et al., 1984).

Another element affecting rate of transcription initiation is the enhancer (reviewed by Yaniv, 1982, and by Khoury and Gruss, 1983). The prototype enhancer is the 72 base pair tandem repeat of SV40 DNA, located about 100 nucleotides upstream from the initiation site of early genes and required in cis for its transcriptional effects. Enhancers can stimulate gene transcription by as much as 100-fold. They are unique among other known transcriptional elements in that they can increase the rate of transcription independent of their orientation and at a great distance upstream or downstream of the gene that they activate (Banerji et al., 1981; Moreau et al., 1981; Fromm and Berg, 1983).

The enhancer element can function when moved as far away as several kilobases from the start of transcription. However, the level of transcription drops off significantly as the distance between the start site and the enhancer increases. Upon insertion of 200–500 base pairs of DNA between the SV40 enhancer and the start site, activation of transcription decreases to less than 10% of maximum levels, while insertions of 600–3,700 base pairs lead to an activation of only 0.5% (Wasylyk et al., 1984). Also, if an enhancer lies in the vicinity of two different promoters, it will activate the proximal promoter to the exclusion of the distal one (Kadesch and Berg, 1983; Wasylyk et al., 1983a).

The mechanism by which enhancers act remains unknown, but because their position, orientation, and distance from the gene can be altered, proposals for their role have included regulation of local superhelicity of DNA, effects on local chromatin structure, creation of an RNA polymerase II entry site, or provision of a site for attachment of the DNA to the nuclear matrix. It has recently been demonstrated that cellular trans-acting factors, probably proteins, bind to enhancer sequences in vivo and play a role in transcription activation (Ephrussi et al., 1985; Mercola et al., 1985). Experiments in which enhancer activity has been demonstrated at a low level, using in vitro transcription systems, could lead to the isolation of factors that act at this locus and eventually lead to the determination of the mechanism of enhancer activity (Sassone-Corsi et al., 1984; Wildeman et al., 1984; Sassone-Corsi et al., 1985).

Enhancers were originally found only in viruses and have been identified in SV40 (Benoist and Chambon, 1981; Gruss et al., 1981; Fromm and Berg, 1982), polyoma (Katinka et al., 1981; Tyndall et al., 1981), bovine papilloma virus (Lusky et al., 1983), retroviruses (Chang et al., 1980; Gorman et al., 1982; Levinson et al., 1982; Jolly et al., 1983; Kriegler and Botchan, 1983), and adenovirus (Hearing and Shenk, 1983; Hen et al., 1983). Unlike other transcriptional control elements, enhancers from these different mammalian viruses show very little homology. They do share a set of "core" sequences, GGTGTGGAAAG (Khoury and Gruss, 1983), that have been shown by point mutations to be required for early gene expression in SV40 (Weiher et al., 1983). Otherwise, their sequences are so different that examination of one enhancer element cannot predict the possible location of another enhancer element in a different virus.

Cellular genes were hypothesized to contain enhancers by analogy to viral genes. Conrad and Botchan (1982) succeeded in isolating fragments of human DNA that could enhance transformation by the thymidine kinase gene in an orientation-independent manner. The first direct evidence that cellular genes do, in fact, contain associated enhancer elements has been obtained in experiments demonstrating that immunoglobulin genes have functional enhancers (Banerji et al., 1983; Gillies et al., 1983; Mercola et al., 1983; Queen and Baltimore, 1983; Picard and Schaffner, 1984). Both heavy-chain and light-chain immunoglobulin genes have enhancers that lie downstream of the transcription start site.

Two features of enhancers are most important in terms of trying to produce large quantities of a foreign protein in mammalian cells. First, enhancers can operate to increase the expression of genes containing heterologous promoters. For example, the monkey virus SV40 enhancer will augment transcription by promoters from herpes simplex virus (Capecchi, 1980), adenovirus (Moreau et al., 1981), and avian genes (Moreau et al., 1981; Wasylyk et al., 1983a). However, transcription from some promoters may not be stimulated by the presence of an enhancer.

Second, enhancers do demonstrate cell specificity (consistent with the fact that enhancer sequences from different mammalian sources are not closely related). The efficiency of the enhancer from the monkey SV40 virus has been compared to that from either mouse polyoma virus (de Villiers et al., 1982) or a mouse retrovirus (Laimins et al., 1982) in monkey, human, and mouse cells. The mouse virus enhancers were slightly more active in mouse cells, while the monkey virus enhancer was significantly more active in both monkey and human cells. A mouse retrovirus sequence was found to enhance SV40 transformation of mouse but not monkey cells (Kriegler and Botchan, 1983). The monkey virus SV40 enhancer increased the expression of a thymidine kinase gene or *Ecogpt* gene in monkey or human cells by 10–20 times, but in mouse cells by only 2 times (Byrne et al., 1983).

The immunoglobulin enhancers appear to have a greater degree of cell specificity. Within the same species (mouse), an immunoglobulin heavy-chain enhancer has virtually no effect in fibroblasts but increases transcription by nearly 100-fold in myeloma cells (Gillies et al., 1983).

These results suggest that one powerful means of increasing foreign gene expression in mammalian cells is to add to the gene an enhancer element specific for the intended host cell. Moreover, since naturally occurring mutations in the polyoma virus enhancer extend the host range of the mutants to include new cell types (see review by Yaniv, 1982), it may someday be possible to mutate enhancers artificially to maximize their augmentation of gene expression in a particular cell line.

2.2.2 PolyA Addition and Termination

Almost all eukaryotic messenger RNAs have attached to their 3' end a polyA tail 150–200 nucleotides long. Transcription does not seem to stop at the polyA addition site, but rather continues some distance downstream to an undefined point. No discrete termination sites have been identified in mammalian cells, and transcription may randomly stall well downstream of the gene. The 3' end of the mature messenger RNA is generated by endonucleolytic cleavage of the initial transcript, followed by addition of the polyA tail. Polyadenylation is an early event in the genesis of mRNA and occurs before splicing.

Most genes coding for polyadenylated RNAs contain a highly conserved sequence, AAUAAA, located about 10–30 nucleotides upstream from the site of polyA addition (Proudfoot and Brownlee, 1976). Deletion of this sequence abolishes formation of mRNA. If the sequence is moved to a new site, polyA addition still occurs, but always at a distance 11–19 nucleotides downstream from the new position of the sequence AAUAAA (reviewed by Nevins, 1983). Therefore, this sequence appears to position the endonucleotide cleavage of the messenger RNA.

2.2.3 Capping and Splicing

A very early event in the production of mammalian mRNA is the addition of a "cap," $m^7G(5')ppp(5')N$, to the 5' end of the nascent RNA molecule. Since all mRNAs transcribed by RNA polymerase II in mammalian cells are capped soon after initiation, it appears that as long as the genetic engineer provides the appropriate promoter element for transcription, the transcript will be properly capped. Capping appears to be a prerequisite for splicing (Konarska et al., 1984).

With a few exceptions (histones, an early adenovirus gene, herpes simplex virus, thymidine kinase, and α-interferon), mammalian messenger RNAs are modified by splicing. That is, partial messenger RNA sequences are separated from each other in the genome. After an initial RNA copy of the entire genomic sequence is transcribed, the mature messenger RNA is formed by cutting out specific noncoding regions (called "introns") from the RNA and splicing together the specific conserved regions (called "exons") of the mature RNA.

Until recently, very little was known about the mechanism of splicing. Splicing occurs exclusively in the nucleus and requires the presence of small nuclear ribonucleoprotein particles (Padgett et al., 1983; Kramer et al., 1984). A large amount of the intron can be discarded without affecting splicing (Wieringa et al., 1984). It appears that only the DNA very near the splice junctions is required. Virtually all introns have the dinucleotide GU at their 5' end and AG at their 3' end. Surprising new mechanistic information has been revealed due to the development of conditions in which the splicing of pre-mRNAs can be studied in vitro (Hernandez and Keller, 1983; Hardy et al., 1984). Analysis of the reaction products has demonstrated that the excised intron RNA is in the form of a circle with a tail containing a branch point. These structures are now known as "lariats."

Lariats have been observed in the in vitro splicing of adenovirus major late RNA (Padgett et al., 1984) as well as in human β-globin RNA (Ruskin et al., 1984). Lariat RNAs have also been seen in vivo (Wallace and Edmonds, 1983; Zeitlin and Efstratiadis, 1984). These lariat RNAs have a branch structure in which the 5'-terminal guanosine of the intron is joined to an adenosine near the 3' splice junction via a 2'–5' phosphodiester bond. The adenosine residue is located 24 nucleotides upstream of the 3' splice junction in the β-globin intron. The RNA between these points remains as a circular structure. There is a general consensus sequence that has been observed in the vicinity of the branch point in many mammalian introns (Ruskin et al., 1984). A sequence at the 5' splice junction may base pair to this sequence to initiate branch formation. However, when sequences that include the branch point are deleted, proper splicing still occurs (Wieringa et al., 1984). Therefore, a strict sequence requirement may not be present.

Two intron-containing products of the splicing reaction have been observed. The first to form is an intermediate in which the intron has been cleaved at the 5' splice site and has formed the lariat structure but is still connected to the downstream exon. In the latter product, the lariat intron is excised and the two exons are joined. No free downstream exons are ever seen and no *linear* introns are ever observed to have a 5' splice cleavage. Therefore, cleavage at the 5' splice site and branch formation may occur simultaneously and precede the joining of the 5' and 3' exons and elimination of the lariat RNA. The lariat structure may be required for the accurate joining of the 5' exon to the 3' splice acceptor, since in all cases examined, the first AG dinucleotide downstream of the branch point serves as the 3' splice acceptor. Further work will be needed to dissect the precise mechanism and the role of the small ribonucleotide particles.

For many messenger RNAs, splicing is absolutely required for formation of stable messenger RNA and may be involved in transporting the messenger RNA from the nucleus to the cytoplasm (Breathnach and Chambon, 1981; Rigby, 1982). In fact, expression of foreign genes in recombinant DNAs could not be obtained until splicing and polyA addition signals were added to the foreign gene (Mulligan et al., 1979). There are now a few reports of naturally spliced messages (transcribed from cDNA sequences) being expressed from recombinant DNA without prior splicing (reviewed by Rigby, 1982), but it is not yet possible to predict when splicing may not be required. Therefore, when the goal is to obtain efficient expression of any mammalian gene that is normally spliced, it is wise to include splicing signals in the recombinant DNA.

Since promoters, polyA addition sites, and splice junctions share sequence homology among mammalian genes, it appears likely that these expression signals should be interchangeable among genes and among different mammalian cells. This prediction has proved true in recombinant DNA experiments. Promoters from viruses (SV40, adenovirus, or retrovirus) have been used to express a number of genes in different cell types, and promoters from cellular genes can be used for expression in cells from other mammalian species (e.g., mouse β-globin promoter functions in monkey cells; Hamer et al., 1980). PolyA addition sites from SV40, polyoma, and retroviruses have been used for many genes, and polyA sites from cellular genes can also function in other cell types; e.g., the polyA site of the rat insulin gene functions in monkey cells (Gruss et al., 1981). Splicing signals from one species can be recognized in mammalian cells of another species. For example, the β-globin gene from mouse is correctly spliced in monkey cells (Hamer and Leder, 1979) and from rabbit in mouse cells (Wold et al., 1979). In fact, Sharp and co-workers demonstrated that a 5′ splice junction from one gene (monkey SV40 virus) will correctly join to the 3′ splice junction of another gene (mouse β-globin or rat insulin) (Chu and Sharp, 1981a; Horowitz et al., 1982).

Thus, it appears that any of these expression sequences can be derived from any mammalian virus or cell and used to express a foreign gene in any other mammalian cell. This interchangeability suggests the possibility of building one prototype expression vector that could be used for a number of different genes simply by inserting new protein-coding sequences between the expression sequences. Berg's series of SV40 expression vectors (pSV2 and derivatives) have been used essentially in this manner (reviewed in Rigby, 1982).

2.3 DNA TRANSFER INTO CELLS

Recombinant DNA can be transferred into mammalian cells either through viral infection or directly as naked DNA through a variety of techniques.

2.3.1 Transfection of Naked DNA

Several methods for infecting mammalian cells directly with DNA (a procedure often called "transfection") are now available, and their efficiency is constantly being improved.

The most common method for recombinant DNA transfer is the calcium phosphate precipitation method (Graham and Van der Eb, 1973). Recombinant DNA is coprecipitated with calcium phosphate and the resulting suspension is adsorbed onto cells, after which medium is added and the cells incubated as usual. Shocking the cells after adsorption of the calcium phosphate-DNA precipitate by brief exposure to either dimethyl sulfoxide (Stow and Wilkie, 1976) or to glycerol (Frost and Williams, 1978) can increase the efficiency of DNA transfection by up to 100 times. By optimizing such methods, the efficiency of DNA transfer into the nuclei of cells measured as early transient gene expression can be as high as 10–15% of the treated cells (Chu and Sharp, 1981b; Gorman et al., 1982). However, only a small fraction of such cells will become stably "transformed," i.e., incorporate the DNA and continue to express the new gene. Typically, the number of cells that becomes stably transformed ranges from 5×10^{-4} to 10^{-6} of the cells initially exposed to DNA (Lee et al., 1981; Subramani et al., 1981; Kaufman and Sharp, 1982; Southern and Berg, 1982; Chapman et al., 1983).

Recent advances, however, have improved the chance of increasing the efficiency to 10^{-3} or better for continuous cell lines (Gorman et al., 1983). One advance has been the introduction of a new vector for rapidly measuring transfection efficiency so that the details of transfection conditions can be quickly optimized for a particular cell type. The new vector carries the *E. coli* chloramphenicol transacetylase (CAT) gene, which allows rapid quantitation of CAT enzyme activity in crude cell extracts (Gorman et al., 1982). Another advance has been the discovery of cell-specific enhancers. Using these improvements, Gorman et al. (1983) demonstrated that by choosing enhancers from the monkey virus SV40 or the avian retrovirus Rous sarcoma virus, they could obtain stable transformation of cells at an efficiency of 10^{-3} for human (HeLa and xeroderma pigmentosum cell lines), mouse (LTK$^-$, NIH3T3), and hamster (CHO) cell lines, and at an efficiency of 6×10^{-2} (6%) for monkey cells. As more is discovered about enhancers, it will become easier to design a high-efficiency transfection vector for any particular host-cell type.

A similar method frequently used to introduce DNA into mammalian cells is the DEAE-dextran method, in which DNA is mixed with high molecular weight DEAE-dextran before adsorption to cells (McCutchan and Pagano, 1968). By optimizing dextran concentration and exposure time, Sompayrac and Danna (1981) achieved an initial, purely transient infection efficiency of 25% in monkey (BSC-1) cells exposed to SV40 DNA. Since DEAE-dextran and calcium phosphate are more or less toxic to different cell types, one or the other method is usually chosen depending on the particular cell type to be transfected.

DNA can also be introduced into cells by applying short electric pulses, which permeabilize cell membranes without introducing excessive damage. This method, electroporation, greatly enhances the exchange of matter across the membrane. Uptake of DNA is rapid, and stable cell transformants can be obtained at a frequency of approximately 10^{-3} (Neumann et al., 1982). However, the nature of this technique may introduce variability in the results obtained, and it is not yet clear how efficiency of electroporation will vary in different cell types.

Gene transfers have been performed using purified metaphase chromosomes (Klobutcher and Ruddle, 1980). In order to transfer regions of chromosomes that contain no convenient genetic marker, Nelson et al. (1984) have introduced a dominant selectable marker into several different locations along the chromosomes so that maintenance of the transferred chromosome can be accomplished by maintaining selective pressure.

Recently, Okayama and Berg (1985) have developed a lambda bacteriophage vector (λMNT), which permits high-efficiency transduction of mammalian cells. A cDNA library is constructed in the lambda phage, which also contains a dominant selectable marker for antibiotic resistance. Phage particles in a calcium-phosphate precipitate are used to transfect mammalian cells and yield stable transformants at a frequency of up to 10^{-2}.

2.3.2 Microinjection

A different method for introducing DNA into cells is by microinjection: DNA can be injected directly into a cell nucleus through a glass micropipette (Graessmann and Graessmann, 1976; Capecchi, 1980). There are disadvantages: Cells must be injected one at a time, and the technique requires an expensive micromanipulator apparatus and the skill to use it. However, DNA delivery can be controlled to place a fairly precise number of DNA molecules into each cell, and its efficiency is quite high. For example, when Capecchi (1980) injected mouse (LTK$^-$) cells with the thymidine kinase gene from herpes simplex virus, he found that 50–100% of the cells transiently expressed the gene, and about 0.1% (10^{-3}) cells became stably transformed.

As when DNA is introduced by other means, the addition of enhancer sequences to the recombinant DNA can improve the efficiency of expression and transformation after microinjection. Yamaizumi et al. (1983) microinjected mouse cells with DNA containing enhancer sequences from the mouse virus polyoma ligated to the thymidine kinase gene. They observed transient expression in 20–50% of the cells and stable transformation in 5% of the cells. Using the thymidine kinase gene, Folger et al. (1982) obtained 20% stable transformants by adding the monkey virus SV40 enhancer, while Luciw et al. (1983) obtained 80% stable transformants using an enhancer from a retrovirus, avian sarcoma virus.

2.3.3 Protoplast Fusion

Another approach toward achieving high-efficiency DNA transfer has been an attempt at direct fusion between the recipient mammalian cells and the bacteria in which the recombinant DNA is grown (Schaffner, 1980). Briefly, the technique is as follows: Bacteria containing recombinant DNA in plasmid form are treated with chloramphenicol to increase the number of plasmid DNA molecules; the bacteria are converted to protoplasts and then centrifuged directly onto the mammalian cells growing in a monolayer on a cell culture plate; the cells are placed in cell culture medium and incubated as usual. Rassoulzadegan et al. (1982) have optimized this method so that when bacteria contain SV40 DNA in a pBR322 plasmid, 90–100% of the recipient monkey (CV-1) cells transiently express T-antigens. They have also shown that with this method mouse polyoma virus DNA can morphologically transform rat cells at efficiencies equal to those seen in viral infections (Rassoulzadegan et al., 1982).

Another possible method of gene transfer not yet optimized for recombinant DNA is the use of liposomes. Fraley et al. (1980) encapsulated monkey virus SV40 DNA in liposomes and optimized conditions for a lytic viral infection of monkey cells. They could increase efficiency by varying the type of lipid, presence of cholesterol, and amount of surface charge in the liposomes or by posttreatment of the cells with glycerol, dimethyl sulfoxide, or polyethylene glycol. This method may someday be exploited by adding antibody molecules to the liposomes to target attachment to particular cells, as suggested by Fraley et al. (1980).

2.3.4   DNA Transfer by Viral Infection

Since viral infection is extremely efficient, packaging recombinant DNA within a virus particle could provide one of the most effective means for introducing foreign DNA into mammalian cells. Some of the first experiments with mammalian recombinant DNA used SV40 viruses to transfer the DNA (Goff and Berg, 1976; Hamer et al., 1977). More recently, retroviruses have been used as viral vectors, because not only is infection of cells efficient, but also integration of the retrovirus-encoded DNA into the host chromosomes is very precise, providing a stable transformation efficiency of 10–80% (Cepko et al., 1984). Use of whole viruses to transfer DNA is discussed more fully in section 2.4.1.

2.4   STABILITY OF DNA AFTER TRANSFER INTO MAMMALIAN CELLS

It has become clear that mammalian cells can take up exogenous DNA and express the genes contained therein. Somewhat less clear is the exact state and stability of the DNA after uptake into the cell. From experiments reported so far (Pellicer et al., 1980; Perucho et al., 1980; Scangos et al., 1981), it appears that three different phases can be defined for the fate of exogenous DNA and its expression. The first two have been termed "transient" and "stable," so for the sake of discussion we will call the third "completely stable." Immediately after DNA is transfected or microinjected into cells, a high percentage of cells (10–100%) may express the DNA for 24 to 72 hours (Chu and Sharp, 1981b; Yamaizumi et al., 1983; Capecchi, 1980). This is called transient expression. After continued growth in selective medium, the number of cells that continue to express the genes is much lower (often only 10^{-4} to 10^{-6}, but sometimes up to 80%, as previously reviewed). These cells are called "stable transformants"; in fact, they are stable *only* if constantly cultured in selective medium. At this stage, the exogenous DNA has become ligated into large concatemeric structures termed "transgenomes" (Scangos et al. 1981), or "pekalesomes" (Perucho et al., 1980), that act as high molecular weight DNA although they are not, in fact, integrated into the host-cell chromosome. Initially, each transformed cell can contain multiple copies of different types of transgenomes (Scangos et al., 1981), as determined by restriction of high molecular weight DNA and identification of foreign gene sequences via hybridization to radioactive probes. DNA sequences contained in transgenomes are expressed and appear to be genetically linked: If two independent genetic markers are part of a transgenome, they are retained together, lost together, or amplified together (Perucho et al., 1980). As long as selective pressure is maintained, cells containing transgenomes appear stable and continue to express the new transferred phenotype for many cell generations. If selective pressure is released, however, these cells appear highly unstable and lose the transferred phenotype at a rate of 0.1–30% per generation (Pellicer et al., 1980; Scangos et al., 1981). The high reversion frequency is usually due to actual loss of DNA sequences and is probably due to loss of entire transgenomes (Scangos et al., 1981).

Over a longer period of time (e.g., 60 days), some cells eventually become completely stable transformants by actually incorporating one transgenome into a host-cell chromosome (Scangos et al., 1981; Robins et al., 1981a). After integration, each cell line stably expresses the transferred phenotype even in nonselective medium. The reversion frequency for the marker is then also stable and characteristic of the particular transformant. For the same type of cell and marker, the frequency varies with the site of chromosome integration, ranging from 10^{-3} to 10^{-6} (Steinberg et al., 1978; Robins et al., 1981b), making it possible to obtain cell lines containing a foreign gene with a reversion frequency similar to that of a normal cellular gene.

The distinction between stable and completely stable transformants is almost never made in the gene expression literature, and the reader must distinguish whether cells called stable transformants are in fact being passaged in selective or nonselective medium. If the final goal is to isolate a cell line that produces high amounts of a given foreign protein for commercial production, it appears that two choices are available: One choice is to take the time to select several high producer lines, screen them for stability, and then select ones that have become completely stable. The other choice is to maintain selective pressure to force the transformed cells to preserve their transgenomes, an approach frequently taken in expression studies. However, it is not yet clear what mutation rate is displayed by the nonselected DNA in the remainder of the transgenome. Moreover, if a cell begins with several transgenomes, it might lose all but one transgenome over time even in selective medium, and thereby change its overall phenotype.

These possibilities may explain some of the stability results reported so far in attempts to establish producer cell lines. For example, when two interferon-producing cell lines were passaged in selective medium, one retained its output, while another markedly decreased its output of interferon between passages 15 and 20 (Scahill et al., 1983). Thus, one consideration before choosing a particular approach to establish a producer cell line is exactly how stable that producer line must be.

2.4.1   Effects of Viral Vectors on Stability

The fate of exogenous DNA introduced into mammalian cells can be altered by the use of viral vectors. Some viruses integrate their DNA into the host chromosome, while others replicate their DNA separately as small extra-chromosomal units. If the goal is to cause the recombinant DNA to integrate into the host chromosome, viral vectors, with the exception of retroviruses, do not appear to make DNA integration any more specific or efficient than that already described for exogenous DNA in general. For instance, when a DNA tumor virus (such as SV40, polyoma, or adenovirus) integrates its DNA into the host chromosome of nonpermissive cells, the process is highly inefficient and occurs with much gene rearrangement and loss of viral DNA sequences (reviewed by Weinberg, 1980). In contrast, when a retrovirus infects a cell, it has the unique property of inserting a DNA copy into the host chromosome in a way that maintains the exact sequence with respect to its RNA genome (reviewed by Varmus, 1982).

It is not yet clear whether the specificity provided by a retrovirus infection is retained during a retrovirus DNA transfection. One informal report claims that it is not (a personal communication reported in Varmus, 1982). However, Copeland et al. (1981) transfected retroviral DNA containing long terminal repeats (LTRs) into cells and observed correct, colinear integration; if they used retroviral DNA already integrated into DNA as the donor DNA, they then found nonspecific insertion as with any other exogenous DNA.

2.4.2   Episomes

SV40, polyoma, BPV, and EBV viruses do not integrate their DNA into the host chromosome, but retain their DNA as separate extrachromosomal, autonomously replicating units (episomes) within a permissive host cell. Extrachromosomal SV40 DNA has been widely used as an expression vector; however, it has not been possible thus far to establish cell lines containing episomal SV40 vectors. When BPV infects mouse cells, its DNA remains extrachromosomal, at a far lower number of copies per cell than SV40, but in a stable state. Cell lines producing foreign protein from BPV vectors have been successfully established (see section 2.8.8). When either SV40 or BPV DNA is transfected into the appropriate cells, it is immediately detected in the low molecular weight episomal portion of the cell extract and can replicate autonomously. These episomal DNAs may therefore never pass through the unstable stage of being part of a high molecular weight trans-genome structure.

2.5   SELECTION SYSTEMS

When exogenous DNA is introduced into mammalian cells, typically only one out of the 10^3 to 10^6 cells takes up the DNA and expresses the genes it contains. Therefore, it is imperative to have an efficient means of selecting those cells that have taken up and express the foreign DNA.

2.5.1 Colony Morphology

One of the first methods used to select cells that have incorporated foreign DNA was based on morphological transformation of cells by tumor viruses. When a tumor virus infects fibroblasts, a small percentage of cells incorporate the viral DNA and become altered: They cause tumors if injected into animals, look more epithelioid, are able to grow in soft agar, and lack contact inhibition (Tooze, 1973). Because of their new growth characteristics, transformed cells form small recognizable piles of cells (commonly known as "transformed foci") and can therefore be picked off a cell culture plate (Elder et al., 1981).

DNA containing the transforming genes from a tumor virus will morphologically transform cells after transfection; for example, SV40 DNA transforms human cells (Aaronsen and Todaro, 1969), while the left-hand end of the adenovirus DNA transforms rat cells (Graham et al., 1975), and a DNA fragment containing 69% of the bovine papilloma virus genome transforms mouse cells (Lowy et al., 1980a). Morphological transformation of cells has been used to select cells that incorporate foreign DNA by including tumor virus transforming genes in the recombinant DNA. Recombinant DNA has been constructed and transformants selected using the transforming genes of SV40 virus (Muzyczka, 1979; Schaffner et al., 1979), bovine papilloma virus (Zinn et al., 1982), and mouse retrovirus (Doehmer et al., 1982).

2.5.2 Selection for Biochemical Transformants

An easier approach than physically picking transformed foci that appear morphologically transformed is to isolate cells biochemically by growing them in a medium that selects for the presence of a certain marker gene. Several biochemically selectable marker genes have now been cloned and are available for use in mammalian cells (see Table 2–1). Some of them are very useful but are not dominant, and therefore cannot be used for selection unless the recipient cell is a mutant that lacks the marker enzyme activity. Nondominant marker genes include thymidine kinase (TK), adenine phosphoribosyltransferase (APRT), hypoxanthine phosphoribosyltransferase (HPRT), and dihydrofolate reductase (DHFR).

2.5.2.1 Thymidine kinase. Perhaps the most commonly used selection system has been that for the thymidine kinase (TK) gene. If mammalian cells are grown in the presence of aminopterin, which inhibits the synthesis of tetrahydrofolate, thereby blocking de novo synthesis of thymidine, the

TABLE 2-1   Selectable Markers Used in Gene Transfer Experiments

Marker	Selective Agent	Dominance
Thymidine kinase	hypoxanthine-aminopterin-thymidine (HAT)	−
HPRT	HAT	−
APRT	adenine-aminopterin-thymidine	−
E. coli gpt	xanthine-adenine-aminopterin-mycophenolic acid	+
MTX-resistant DHFR	methotrexate (MTX)	+
Bacterial neomycin-resistance	G418 antibiotic	+
Hygromycin B phosphotransferase	hygromycin B	+
Bacterial bleomycin-resistance	bleomycin	+

cells become absolutely dependent for survival on the presence of a functional TK gene to obtain thymidine from the medium (Hakala and Taylor, 1959). The medium that selects for cells containing a functional thymidine kinase gene is called HAT medium, since it contains hypoxanthine, aminopterin, and thymidine (Littlefield, 1963). Several TK⁻ cell lines are available for use as recipients of recombinant DNA containing a TK gene; they include human (Bacchetti and Graham, 1977), mouse (Maitland and McDougall, 1977; Wigler et al., 1977), and rat cells (Topp, 1981). Herpes simplex virus (HSV) DNA contains a thymidine kinase gene that has been widely used to transform TK⁻ cells to the TK⁺ phenotype (Bacchetti and Graham, 1977; Maitland and McDougall, 1977; Wigler et al., 1977). The HSV thymidine kinase gene has now been cloned into a bacterial plasmid (Colbere-Garapin et al., 1979) and is therefore available for use in recombinant DNA constructions.

2.5.2.2   Hypoxanthine and adenosine phosphoribosyltransferases.

Two enzymes of purine metabolism, adenine phosphoribosyltransferase (APRT) and hypoxanthine phosphoribosyltransferase (HPRT), can be used as selectable markers because cell lines deficient in both APRT and HPRT can be selected by growth in 6-aminopurine and 6-thioguanine, or APRT⁻ and HPRT⁻ selection, respectively. Expression of the APRT gene can be selected for by growth of cells in medium containing adenine, thymidine, and aminopterin, while HPRT is selected for by growth in HAT medium. The hamster APRT gene has been cloned (Lowy et al., 1980b) and used to select cells after gene transfer (Roberts and Axel, 1982). The human HPRT gene has now also been cloned (Jolly et al., 1983) and is available for use in selection vectors.

2.5.3 Dihydrofolate Reductase

The gene for dihydrofolate reductase (DHFR) can be selected either through special medium or through drug resistance. The enzyme DHFR catalyzes the reduction of dihydrofolate to tetrahydrofolate, which is required for single carbon transfers to synthesize glycine, purines, and thymidylate. A copy of the DHFR gene synthesized from messenger RNA has been cloned (Nunberg et al., 1980), and a hamster (CHO) cell line deficient in the DHFR enzyme has been isolated that requires the presence of glycine, purines, and thymidine for growth (Urlaub and Chasin, 1980). When this cell line is transfected with DHFR-containing recombinant DNA, transformed cells can be selected through their ability to grow in the absence of these three supplements (Lee et al., 1981; Subramani et al., 1981).

The most useful selection systems, unlike those previously described, would be ones that do not require mutant recipient cells deficient in the marker enzyme activity. Work with the dihydrofolate reductase gene has been aimed toward the goal of using the DHFR gene as a selectable marker in wild-type recipient cells.

The drug methotrexate (MTX), a folate analogue, kills cells by binding to the catalytic site of the enzyme DHFR. Some cells become resistant to the drug by amplifying the DHFR gene so that more enzyme is produced per cell (Schimke et al., 1978), while others become resistant because the DHFR enzyme they express has mutated so that it has a decreased affinity for the drug. Wigler et al. (1980) demonstrated that transfer of total DNA from a hamster cell line containing an MTX-resistant mutant DHFR gene into wild-type mouse cells yielded 40 times more MTX-resistant colonies than when the donor DNA was obtained from wild-type cells. Christman et al. (1982) used the same mutant total genomic DNA along with cloned hepatitis B virus (HBV) DNA to transform wild-type mouse cells. Eighty percent of the cells selected for methotrexate resistance also contained HBV DNA sequences. Furthermore, by forcing the mutant DHFR genes to amplify in the host cell with stepwise increases in methotrexate concentration, Christman et al. (1982) caused the cells to increase their production of hepatitis B antigen. A similar mutant DHFR gene, coding for an MTX-resistant enzyme, has now been cloned by Simonsen and Levinson (1983) and has been shown to transform wild-type mouse (L) or hamster (CHO) cells at a frequency of $4-25 \times 10^{-5}$.

Therefore, mutant DHFR genes provide a gene marker that can be selected by methotrexate resistance after the DNA is transfected into any of a wide variety of wild-type cells (Simonsen and Levinson, 1983). Because the DHFR gene can also be forced to amplify its copy number after transfection (see section 2.7.1), it can serve two useful functions and may be widely used in future experiments.

2.5.4 Dominant Selective Biochemical Markers

The most useful cell selection systems are those that do not require mutant recipient cells but can be used with any type of recipient cell. Several such systems have been developed, in addition to the use of the MTX-resistant DHFR gene in wild-type cells (see Table 2–1).

One such dominant selectable system utilizes the gene for the enzyme *Ecogpt* (the xanthine-guanine phosphoribosyltransferase, XGPRT, from the bacterium *E. coli*) and exploits the fact that mammalian cells do not possess an equivalent enzyme that can utilize xanthine. Mulligan and Berg (1981) introduced a selective medium that forces mammalian cells to rely on the foreign enzyme *Ecogpt* for their survival. The medium contains aminopterin (which blocks the de novo synthesis of IMP) and mycophenolic acid (which blocks the conversion of IMP to XMP), and is supplemented with adenine, thymidine, and xanthine. Most wild-type mammalian cells, including monkey (TC7, CV1), mouse (3T6, MEL), human (Lesch-Nyhan), and hamster (CHO) cell lines (Mulligan and Berg, 1981), cannot grow on this medium. However, after recombinant DNA containing the *Ecogpt* gene and appropriate expression sequences has been introduced into mammalian cells, transformed cells can grow in this medium since the *Ecogpt* enzyme allows the utilization of xanthine (Mulligan and Berg, 1981).

The second dominant selectable marker that can be used with wild-type mammalian cells is the neomycin resistance (*neo*[R]) gene (Colbere-Garapin et al., 1981; Southern and Berg, 1982). Mammalian cells are slowly killed by the antibiotic G418, an aminoglycoside that is similar to neomycin and kanamycin but can block protein synthesis in eukaryotic cells by interfering with 80S ribosomes. Spontaneous resistance is so low it is undetectable ($< 4 \times 10^{-8}$) (Colbere-Garapin et al., 1981). Since aminoglycoside antibiotics (G418, neomycin, kanamycin) can be inactivated by a phosphotransferase gene encoded by the bacterial transposon Tn5, this gene (called *neo*[R]) was placed into expression vectors for use in mammalian cells. Colbere-Garapin et al. (1981) linked the *neo*[R] gene to expression sequences from the herpes simplex virus thymidine kinase gene and demonstrated that the vector could render mouse, monkey, and human cells resistant to the antibiotic G418. Southern and Berg (1982) linked the *neo*[R] gene to SV40 virus early gene expression sequences, used DNA transfection to produce mouse and monkey cells resistant to G418, and then showed that these cells remained stably resistant to the antibiotic after more than 100 generations in nonselective medium. G418-resistance has now been widely used as a dominant selectable marker in several systems, including bovine papilloma virus, Epstein-Barr virus, and retroviruses.

A bleomycin-resistance gene has been isolated from the same Tn5 transposon that carries the neomycin-resistance gene (Genilloud et al., 1984). It now appears that mammalian cells are killed by bleomycin, and this dominant selectable marker system is likely to be employed in the near future. Mammalian cells are sensitive to another antibiotic, hygromycin B, and the cloning of the *E. coli* gene for hygromycin B phosphotransferase has provided another dominant selectable marker for mammalian cells (Blochlinger and Diggelmann, 1984).

2.5.5 Cotransformation

Several useful selectable markers are therefore available to construct recombinant DNA molecules for use in mammalian cells. One might imagine that it would be necessary to ligate one of these selectable genes directly into the same plasmid that carries the gene for the foreign protein to be produced. However, because of a phenomenon called cotransformation, direct ligation is not necessary.

Wigler et al. (1979) discovered that if two different genes are transfected at the same time, even if they are located on separate plasmid molecules, any cell that incorporates one gene usually also incorporates the other. Apparently, although only a few mammalian cells will take up and express exogenous DNA, those that do take up large amounts of DNA. This observation suggests that one could select for the uptake of any gene by cotransforming the gene with a selectable marker gene. Wigler et al. (1979) proved this true. They optimized the selection by using a high ratio (100:1 and 1000:1) of silent DNA (φX174 DNA) to the selectable DNA (the thymidine kinase gene for herpes simplex virus). When they cotransformed cells with this mixture of DNAs, they found that 14 out of 16 clones containing thymidine kinase genes also contained the φX174 DNA sequences. Perucho et al. (1980) used several different types of DNA to demonstrate that after cotransfection a silent gene usually accompanies a selectable gene through selection, loss, and amplification.

The phenomenon of cotransformation allows investigators to transfect mammalian cells with two different recombinant plasmids and use a selectable marker carried on one plasmid to select for cells that will express genes on the other plasmid. Subramani and Berg (1983) cotransfected mouse (3T6) cells with two separate plasmids, one containing the *neo*[R] gene and the other the *Ecogpt* gene. When they selected cells for one marker and then tested for the presence of the second marker, they found that about 25% of the cells contained a functional copy of the second marker. (If the two markers were present in the same plasmid, 60–90% of the cells selected in one medium were able to grow in the second selective medium.) Dubois et al. (1980) cotransformed mouse (LTK⁻) cells with two separate plasmids. One contained a selectable marker, the thymidine kinase gene from herpes simplex virus. The other plasmid carried two copies of the hepatitis B virus (HBV) genome, including the gene for the HBV surface antigen, the foreign protein to be produced. Dubois et al. (1980) then used HAT medium to select cells expressing the thymidine kinase gene and grew 15 cell clones. All 15 of the TK-selected clones also synthesized hepatitis B surface antigens. One technique that ensures a very high frequency of cotransformation is to transfect a large excess of the nonselectable gene to the selectable gene. This assures that nearly all cells expressing the selectable gene will also express the cotransfected DNA.

The experiments described demonstrate the utility of cotransformation. A genetic engineer could construct one plasmid with a selectable marker for each particular type of recipient cell. The same selectable plasmid could then be used for all future experiments with that cell line by simply cotransforming the selectable plasmids interchangeably with any new recombinant plasmid constructed to express a desired foreign protein.

Cotransforming cells with the selectable gene and protein-coding gene on two different DNA vectors can circumvent the problem of interference of transcription of one gene as a result of transcription of another gene nearby. Interference of expression of downstream sequences due to transcription of an upstream gene has been observed when two genes, each carrying its own promoter, are closely linked and transcribed in the same direction (Kadesch and Berg, personal communication).

2.5.6 Selection by Cell Sorting

Another means of selecting cells that express an introduced gene is by sorting cells using a fluorescence-activated cell sorter (FACS). Selection by FACS can be used for any gene marker whose protein product is expressed as a cell surface antigen such as a receptor molecule. A fluorescent ligand that binds to the surface protein is used to sort the cells expressing that surface protein. Fluorescence-activated cell sorting has been used to isolate cells expressing the T lymphocyte antigens HLA and β_2-microglobulin (Kavathas and Herzenberg, 1983), HLA and 4F2 antigens (Kuhn et al., 1983), and human transferrin receptor (Kuhn et al., 1984). If the surface antigen gene is introduced to the host cell as total genomic DNA without prior cloning, the frequency of cells expressing the surface antigen is so low that FACS sorting is likely to be feasible only if a selectable marker is cotransfected with the total genomic DNA and cells selected biochemically prior to FACS sorting.

2.6 EXTERNAL REGULATION OF GENE EXPRESSION

The ability to externally regulate the expression of foreign genes within host cells would offer two distinct advantages for production of foreign proteins. First, increasing expression of the foreign gene by adding a regulating stimulus may increase production of the foreign protein far above constitutive levels. Second, the ability to turn on expression of a foreign protein at the very end of a scale-up operation might permit the large-scale production of proteins whose presence in large quantities would prove toxic to the cells (Chapman et al., 1983; Mulligan and Berg, 1981). Recent experiments in mammalian genetic engineering have aimed toward the possibility of building regulatory sequences into foreign genes to be expressed.

2.6.1 Induction by Steroid Hormones

The first types of experiments have asked if the expression of an inducible gene can still be increased by the normal inducing signal if the gene is isolated with its own promoter and flanking sequences, and then transfected into a different type of host cell. The steroid hormones form one class of signals that increase expression levels of specific genes, presumably through increasing their rates of transcription. Steroid-inducible genes from rats and humans have been isolated and introduced into mouse L cells, which contain receptors for the appropriate hormones. The genes were found to retain their inducibility. Examples include the genes for a male rat liver protein $\alpha_{2\mu}$-globulin (Kurtz, 1981), human growth hormone (Robins et al., 1982), rat growth hormone (Verma et al., 1982), which are all inducible by glucocorticoids, and the gene for the rat prostatic steroid-binding protein C3 (Page and Parker, 1983), which is inducible by androgen. Upon transfection of these genes into heterologous mouse cells, only very low levels of expression were obtained, ranging from 1–10% of that found in the normal host cell. However, the levels of RNA and protein for the foreign gene were stimulated by steroid hormone treatment, usually by 2- to 4-fold.

Although these increases are not large, they compare favorably with the increases seen in cultured cells from which the inducible gene was cloned. For example, mRNA levels coding for cloned human growth hormone in mouse cells were increased 3- to 4-fold by the glucocorticoid hormone dexamethasone, and in the original cultured pituitary cells, levels increased 3-fold (Robins et al., 1982). Robins also found that when mRNA levels increased 3- to 4-fold, the amount of human growth hormone actually produced and secreted was also induced to increase by 4-fold.

2.6.2 Induction of Metallothionein Genes by Cadmium

Metallothionein genes (see section 2.7.3) can be induced by cadmium. Hamer and Walling (1982) cloned the mouse metallothionein I (MT-1) gene, introduced it into monkey cells on an SV40 vector, and showed that cadmium could increase levels of MT-1 RNA production from the recombinant DNA by 24- to 30-fold. In this case, the final level of MT-1 RNA in the cell was similar to that found in the normal mouse host cell after cadmium induction.

2.6.3 Induction of Interferon by RNA or Viruses

Interferons are a group of proteins secreted by cells in response to a viral infection. Beta-interferon is inducible by viruses, viral DNA, or synthetic double-stranded RNA, such as poly(rI)-poly(rC). Alpha-interferon is inducible only by viruses. Human interferon genes cloned into mouse or monkey cells retain their inducibility. The human alpha-interferon gene integrated into the mouse genome has been stimulated to produce mRNA by treatment of cells with Newcastle virus, but the RNA level was only 2% of that for mouse interferon RNA in the same cells, and no human protein was detected (Mantei and Weissmann, 1982). Human beta-interferon cloned into an SV40 vector and introduced into monkey cells was induced by 10- to 30-fold, using poly(rI)-poly-(rC), to produce a final level of secreted protein of 100 units/ml (Canaani and Berg, 1982). Human beta-interferon cloned into a bovine papilloma virus vector, which replicates extrachromosomally in mouse cells, remained inducible with poly(rI)-poly(rC) by 2- to 16-fold (Zinn et al., 1982) in established cell lines. The largest induced level of human beta-interferon secreted by these cells was about 800 units/ml, which is one to two orders of magnitude less than the induced synthesis of mouse interferon in the same cells.

These experiments with cloned genes have shown that (1) a gene that is normally inducible will remain so even when it is expressed in a different host cell, and (2) an inducible gene will remain inducible whether it is integrated into the heterologous cell genome (e.g., Kurtz, 1981; Robins et al., 1982; Verma et al., 1982) or maintained extrachromosomally in the new host cell (Zinn et al., 1982; Mitrani-Rosenbaum et al., 1983). The DNA sequences responsible for the induction are described in the following section.

2.6.4 Inducible Promoters

The experiments outlined previously suggest that any gene of choice may be rendered inducible by substituting for its own promoter a relatively short piece of DNA, the promoter of an inducible gene. Lee et al. (1981) were the first to demonstrate that an inducible promoter fused to the coding region of a heterologous gene could in fact cause inducible expression of that gene. Mouse mammary tumor virus (MMTV) RNA is increased 10–20 times when infected cells are treated with a glucocorticoid hormone such as dexamethasone. Lee et al. (1981) joined the mouse mammary tumor virus promoter region to the mouse gene for dihydrofolate reductase (DHFR) in an SV40-derived vector. When DHFR⁻ hamster (CHO) cells were transfected with this recombinant DNA, they expressed very low levels of DHFR enzyme activity. However, treatment with dexamethasone caused a 3- to 5-fold increase in DHFR enzyme activity. Lee and co-workers then constructed a similar vector using the MMTV promoter ligated to the structural *lac* gene from *E. coli* coding for the enzyme beta-galactosidase, which is easily assayed

(Hall et al., 1983). They found that transient expression in mouse cells was induced 25-fold by dexamethasone, which compares favorably with the 10- to 20-fold induction normally observed in the MMTV-infected mouse cells.

Robins et al. (1982) used human glucocorticoid-responsive sequences (the 5′ flanking sequences from human growth hormone) to cause the HSV TK gene to become glucocorticoid-responsive in mouse cells. These experiments demonstrated that hormone-inducible sequences can cause another gene to become hormone-responsive, even in a heterologous cell type. (Of course, recipient cells must contain external membrane-embedded steroid receptors if induction is to occur.) Hormone-inducible sequences, therefore, appear to be transferable from cell to cell or gene to gene within mammalian systems, as are most transcription control sequences. However, since levels of expression or induction are sometimes low compared to the natural situation, other as yet undefined factors may also be important in attaining maximum expression.

The induction of expression by glucocorticoids takes place via the interaction between the glucocorticoid-receptor complex and DNA. Scheidereit et al. (1983) mapped the hormone interaction site to a 152 base pair region in the MMTV long terminal repeat (LTR). This region extends from 50–202 base pairs upstream from the transcription start site. Located in this region is the repeated hexanucleotide TGTTCT, which serves as a receptor binding site. Hynes et al. (1983) found that this segment, when moved 500 base pairs farther upstream from the transcription start site, still allowed glucocorticoid induction of a heterologous promoter. It has also been demonstrated that the receptor-interaction element can be inverted in orientation without loss of induction of the fused HSV thymidine kinase gene (Chandler et al., 1983). These findings suggest that the element at which the glucocorticoid receptor interacts may be an enhancer. However, further experiments will be needed to determine if this element can be classified as an enhancer. Ostrowski et al. (1984) found that expression of the CAT gene from the MMTV promoter can be increased by adding the enhancer sequence from the Harvey murine sarcoma virus LTR. Transcription remains glucocorticoid-inducible. This indicates that the enhancer can increase the level of expression above that observed with the normal MMTV promoter, and therefore, this enhancer may function differently from the hormone-responsive element in MMTV.

There is one report of a glucocorticoid-responsive site that lies downstream of the transcription start site. Moore et al. (1985) found that the glucocorticoid receptor binds specifically to a site in the first intron of the inducible human growth hormone gene. This site is approximately 100 base pairs downstream from the transcription start site. They found that the sequence specifically binds receptor in vitro and shares homology with the glucocorticoid-responsive promoter element in the MMTV LTR.

In most cases, induction by glucocorticoid hormones is at the level of transcription. In one case, however, that of α_1-acid glycoprotein production in rat hepatoma cells, glucocorticoid stimulation acts by increasing the stability of the specific messenger RNA (Vannice et al., 1984).

Another inducible promoter that has been shown to function with heterologous genes is the metallothionein (MT) gene promoter. MT can be induced either by heavy metals such as cadmium or by glucocorticoids. Hamer and Walling (1982) found that induction of MT expression by cadmium is at the level of transcription. They observed a 20- to 45-fold induction of the mouse MT gene after the MT gene was introduced into monkey cells on an SV40 vector.

Several human metallothionein genes have been detected in one large chromosomal cluster. The promoters of the different genes vary in their level of expression and range of inducers (Richards et al., 1984). The sequences required for induction of the human MT-II gene have been determined (Karin et al., 1984). There are two cadmium-inducible sites, although only one is required. They are located at 38–50 base pairs and 139–150 base pairs upstream from the transcription start site. The glucocorticoid-responsive site is located farther upstream (242–266 base pairs upstream from the start site). Fusion of the preceding inducible elements, excluding the MT TATA box and transcription start site, to the promoter segment of the HSV thymidine kinase gene produces a hybrid promoter that is cadmium- and glucocorticoid-inducible (Karin et al., 1984).

2.7   GENE AMPLIFICATION

Gene amplification is an increase in the number of copies of a specific gene per cell. In general, gene amplification results in production of increased amounts of the specific RNA and protein encoded by that gene. The phenomenon of gene amplification occurs throughout the animal kingdom (reviewed by Brown, 1981, and Schimke, 1984). Mammalian cells in tissue culture, selected for resistance to a specific inhibitor, have been found to contain amplified copies of the gene coding for the specific protein that interacts with the inhibitor.

2.7.1   Methotrexate Resistance

Gene amplification in tissue culture cells was first demonstrated by Schimke and co-workers (Alt et al., 1978; reviewed by Schimke et al., 1978). Mouse cells selected for resistance to methotrexate, a folic acid analogue, were found to overproduce the enzyme dihydrofolate reductase (DHFR). Alt et al. (1978) demonstrated that, in cell lines stably resistant to methotrexate, the DHFR gene was amplified to about 40 copies per cell, which correlated with the 40-fold increase in DHFR enzyme levels present in these cells. Stable methotrexate-resistant cell lines were shown to grow for over 100 generations in nonselective medium and retained both methotrexate resistance and gene amplification (Alt et al., 1978). Because methotrexate-resistant cells can be either stable or unstable with respect to their amplified genes (reviewed by Schimke et al., 1978; Kaufman et al., 1983; and Schimke, 1984), any cell line selected for methotrexate resistance must also be checked for stability, which can require several months of observation.

Amplified genes have been found to exist in two forms. The repeated genes can exist in tandem in long segments of chromosomes known as homogeneously staining regions (HSRs) (Biedler and Spengler, 1976). Genes amplified in this form are stable over long periods of time in the absence of selection. Amplified units can also be seen in small acentromeric chromosomes called "double minutes." Double minutes are unstable and are rapidly lost after removal of selective pressure (Schimke et al., 1981). It is believed that amplified genes are first found on double-minute chromosomes, and after long periods of cell propagation under selective conditions, the genes appear in the stable form of homogeneously staining regions of chromosomes. When stable gene amplification is desired, Chinese hamster ovary (CHO) cells are often the cells of choice. These cells appear to form amplified units primarily as stable HSRs.

The dihydrofolate reductase gene is by far the most extensively studied case of gene amplification. Stable cell lines can be produced with as much as a 1,000-fold increase in gene copy number and expression. As in other amplification systems, this copy number increase takes place in fairly small increments and, thus, these highly amplified cell lines must undergo stepwise selections over a period of a few months.

2.7.2 PALA Resistance

Another gene amplification system has been described in cultured Syrian hamster cells (Wahl et al., 1979). Cells selected for resistance to N-(phosphonoacetyl)-L-aspartate (PALA), an inhibitor of the enzyme aspartate transcarbamylase, overproduce the protein CAD, a multifunctional enzyme that catalyzes the first three reactions of uridine monophosphate de novo synthesis. Wahl et al. (1979) found that PALA-resistant hamster cells amplified the CAD gene up to about 100 copies per cell, enough to account for the increased levels of CAD protein. All PALA-resistant cell lines were stable, which may be a general feature of hamster cell lines.

2.7.3 Cadmium Resistance

Another extensively studied gene amplification system is the metallothionein I gene in mouse cells (Beach and Palmiter, 1981). Metallothioneins are small intracellular proteins that bind heavy metals such as cadmium, zinc, copper, silver, and mercury. They are widely distributed throughout the animal kingdom and are thought to be involved in zinc and copper homeostasis and heavy metal detoxification. Mouse liver contains two such proteins, named metallothionein I and II (MT-I and MT-II). Beach and Palmiter (1981) selected cultured mouse cells (Friend leukemia cells), that were resistant to cadmium toxicity, and found that these cells contain six times more DNA copies of the MT-I gene than normal mouse cells. In hamster (CHO) cells, MT-1 and MT-II are closely linked and are found to be amplified together (Crawford et al., 1985). The MT genes are usually amplified to a lower copy number than DHFR or CAD genes, possibly because cadmium is not as specific as the inhibitors used in the other cases. Cadmium may be too broadly toxic to many enzymes to allow higher concentrations to be used for selection.

The number of enzymes whose genes have been amplified in selection systems in mammalian cells is now quite large (see Table 2-2). These include adenine deaminase (Yeung et al., 1983), hypoxanthine-guanine phosphoribosyltransferase (HGPRT) (Brennard et al., 1982), hydroxymethylglutaryl CoA reductase (Chin et al., 1982), UMP synthetase (Kanalas and Suttle, 1984), ornithine decarboxylase (McConologue and Coffino, 1983), glutamine synthetase (Young and Ringold, 1983), asparagine synthetase (Andrulis and Siminovitch, 1982), ribonucleotide reductase (Lewis and Srinivasan, 1983), and thymidylate synthetase (Rossana et al., 1982).

The salient characteristics of gene amplification that have emerged from these studies are (1) through appropriate selection, specific chromosomal genes can be amplified to 2–1,000 copies per cell; (2) cell lines containing

TABLE 2-2   Genetic Markers That Have Been Amplified in Cell Culture

Amplified Gene	Selective Agent
Dihydrofolate reductase (DHFR)	methotrexate
Metallothionein	cadmium
CAD	phosphonoacetyl-L-aspartate
Adenine deaminase	deoxycoformycin-alanosine-adenosine-uridine
Hydroxymethylglutaryl CoA reductase	compactin
UMP synthetase	pyrazofurin
Ornithine decarboxylase	difluoromethylornithine
Glutamine synthetase	methionine sulfoxine in glutamine-free medium
Asparagine synthetase	β-aspartylhydroamate
Ribonucleotide reductase	hydroxyurea
Thymidilate synthetase	5-fluorodeoxyuridine
Hypoxanthine-guanine phosphoribosyltransferase (HGPRT)	(arose spontaneously)

amplified chromosomal genes can be stably propagated; and (3) the increased specific gene copy number leads to comparable increases in specific protein levels per cell. These facts suggest that gene amplification might be used to achieve high levels of production of a specific protein in genetically engineered cells. The fact that several different genes in different cell types can be amplified suggests that it may be possible to amplify *any* gene for which specific selective pressure can be used. In fact, Chapman et al. (1983) discovered a novel selection that causes amplification of the *Ecogpt* genes: Since the selection for presence of the *E. coli gpt* gene in mammalian cells makes the cells dependent on xanthine, they decreased the xanthine concentration in the cell medium and obtained a 5- to 10-fold amplification of the *gpt* gene in mouse cells.

2.7.4 Co-amplification

Most important, the length of the amplified DNA sequences has been found to be extremely long compared to the actual gene being selected and ranges from 20 to 3,000 kilobases (Wahl et al., 1979; reviewed by Kaufman et al., 1983). This large size suggests that by selecting one gene, neighboring genes may also be amplified. Since transfected DNA usually integrates into the chromosome in large concatemeric structures (see section 2.4), it may be possible to amplify any gene of choice by transfecting it with another gene that can be forced experimentally to amplify. This prediction has proved true. Wigler et al. (1980) transfected mouse cells with a mixture of plasmid pBR322 DNA and total genomic DNA from hamster cells that contained a mutant methotrexate-resistant DHFR gene. They used methotrexate to amplify the hamster DHFR gene and measured the number of pBR322 sequences. The pBR322 sequences were in fact increased at least 50-fold in one cell line, although different cell lines had amplified the pBR322 to different extents and with different patterns (Wigler et al., 1980).

This phenomenon of co-amplification has been used to obtain increased copy numbers and increased expression of transfected genes. Ringold et al. (1981) transfected DHFR⁻ hamster (CHO) cells with a recombinant plasmid containing both the mouse DHFR gene (with retrovirus expression sequences) and the *E. coli gpt* gene (with an early SV40 virus expression sequence). Cells selected in methotrexate for amplified copies of the DHFR gene contained 50 times more *gpt* DNA and 40–70 times more *gpt* mRNA per cell than did unselected cells. Kaufman and Sharp (1982) constructed a recombinant DNA molecule that contained structural sequences for the DHFR gene with the late adenovirus promoter and the entire SV40 genome. After transfection of this DNA into DHFR⁻ hamster (CHO) cells, the recombinant DNA was amplified by methotrexate selection to 500 copies per cell. As a result, the cotransformed SV40 gene, small t antigen, was produced at such high levels that it constituted 10% of the total protein synthesis of the cell. Christman et al. (1982) cotransfected mouse (3T3) cells with both total genomic DNA from a hamster cell containing a mutant methotrexate-resistant DHFR gene and a plasmid containing hepatitis B (HBV) DNA. One transformed clone was treated with methotrexate to amplify the DHFR DNA, which resulted in a 10-fold increase in HBV DNA, accompanied by a 5- to 6-fold increase in the quantity of hepatitis B surface antigen (HBSAg) released into the medium. With amplification, Christman et al. (1982) thereby obtained a cell line that secreted 8-10 μg of HBSAg per 10^7 cells per day, a level of production comparable to human hepatoma cells.

2.7.5   Regulation of Amplified Genes

A possible means of greatly enhancing protein production is to combine gene amplification with gene regulation to further increase gene expression. The work of Pavlakis and Hamer (1983), in which an extrachromosomal bovine papilloma virus vector containing the metallothionein gene replicated to 10–100 copies per cell and could then be induced by cadmium to increase transcription per gene copy, is one example.

Mayo et al. (1982) asked whether genes integrated into the cellular genome remain inducible after gene amplification. In their studies of the endogenous mouse metallothionein-I (MT-I) gene, which is inducible both by heavy metals such as cadmium and by glucocorticoid hormones, they used cadmium resistance to select cell lines that had amplified the MT-I gene 10-fold. They found that the amplified gene could no longer be regulated by glucocorticoids, even though long stretches of 5′ flanking DNA had been amplified. However, the amplified genes retained their normal regulation by cadmium.

Ringold and co-workers used an SV40-derived vector in which a mouse mammary tumor virus promoter is fused to the structural *E. coli gpt* gene to transfect mouse cells (Lee et al., 1981). They then amplified the *gpt* genes 5- to 10-fold by growing cells in selective medium with very low xanthine concentrations (Chapman et al., 1983). Treatment of the gene-amplified cells with dexamethasone increased the levels of *Ecogpt* mRNA by 4- to 5-fold, the same level of induction achieved for unamplified cells in the same experiment, suggesting that the amplified genes retained full inducibility.

McCormick et al. (1984) cotransfected CHO cells with the DHFR gene and the gene for human beta-interferon, which is inducible by polyribo-inosinic acid-polyribocytidylic acid. They demonstrated that the interferon gene was still inducible after co-amplification.

These experiments suggest that amplified genes, whether chromosomal or extrachromosomal, often, but not always, retain their ability to be induced by various regulator molecules. Future experiments will, no doubt, be aimed at attempting to use gene amplification to achieve high-level expression that can be turned on or further induced by a regulator molecule. This approach will be particularly important for producing proteins whose presence in high levels may prove toxic to cells (Chapman et al., 1983).

2.8 VIRAL VECTORS

Early experiments aimed at expressing foreign genes in mammalian cells utilized the monkey virus SV40 (Goff and Berg, 1976; Hamer et al., 1977). The foreign gene was simply substituted for a viral gene, the recombinant DNA was used to produce recombinant virus propagated in the presence of helper virus, and then the mixed stock of recombinant and helper virus was used to transfer the foreign gene into host cells (reviewed by Rigby, 1982). Transfer of DNA by virus is highly efficient, since with a high multiplicity of infection, virtually every cell will receive DNA. However, viral transfer has several disadvantages:

1. The size of the foreign DNA insert is limited by viral packaging constraints;
2. Since recombinant viruses are usually defective, they must be propagated with helper viruses, yielding a mixed stock of virus (except in rare circumstances where a helper cell line has been established to complement particular viral functions to produce pure stocks of recombinant virus, such as the COS cell line for SV40 virus; Gluzman, 1981);
3. The choice of recipient cell is limited to the host range of the virus;
4. If the virus causes a lytic infection, the recipient cell dies, preventing establishment of a protein-producing cell line;
5. For many viruses, such as SV40, integration of viral DNA into a cell chromosome occurs as rarely and as randomly as does integration of nonviral DNA (Weinberg, 1980; Pellicer et al., 1980).

For these reasons, viruses in the past have been used primarily as DNA vector molecules, which provide expression sequences for the heterologous protein-coding gene and often an origin of replication to provide extrachromosomal copies of the gene, and are introduced into host cells via naked DNA transfer, as previously discussed. However, the biology of retroviruses naturally circumvents many of the usual problems associated with the use of whole viruses as vectors. With the development of the ψ-2 cell line, which allows the production of pure stocks of retroviruses (Mann et al., 1983), the use of retroviruses as whole virus vectors has become an extremely powerful tool in the genetic engineering of mammalian cells.

The viruses used as mammalian expression vectors have been primarily SV40 virus, bovine papilloma virus, and the retroviruses, with some use of polyoma, adeno, adeno-associated, herpes, and vaccinia viruses. Features of some of these viruses relevant to their use as expression vectors are summarized in the following section and in Table 2–3; further details about

TABLE 2–3 General Description of Available Expression Vectors

Vector	Form Used	Host Cells Permissive for Replication	Maintenance	Advantages	Disadvantages
SV40	Virus or DNA (preferred)	Simian, human	Episomal (unstable or integrated)	Well-defined control elements; replicates to high copy number ($\sim 10^5$/cell) in transient experiments	Not stable episomally; only a small amount of DNA can be inserted if used in virus form
Polyoma	Virus or DNA (preferred)	Rodent	Same as SV40	Similar to SV40 but able to replicate in rodent cells	Unstable episomally; narrow host range; virus grows to lower titer than SV40
Adenovirus	Virus (preferred) or DNA	Human, simian, rodent	Extrachromosomal or integrated	Well-defined strong promoter; can insert large amount of DNA and still have competent virus	Virus kills host cells; often get deletions in genome upon integration into host chromosome
Adeno-associated virus	Virus (preferred) or DNA	Human, simian, rodent (requires adenovirus helper)	Episomal or integrated	Wide host range; can control whether genome is episomal or integrated	Not well-defined genome; needs helper to replicate

Vector	Form	Host range	State	Characteristics	Disadvantages
Bovine Papilloma virus	DNA	Mouse	Episomal (stable)	Morphological transformation allows selection; very stably maintained as episomes without selection; no host chromosome position effects; can insert large amount of DNA	Narrow host range; control elements not yet well-defined; cannot be used as virus
Epstein-Barr virus	DNA	Human, simian, canine	Episomal (stable)	Stably maintained as episomes; no host chromosome position effects; can insert large amount of DNA	Great variability in copy number and expression with different cell types; cannot be used as virus
Retroviruses	Virus (preferred) or DNA	Human, simian, canine, rodent, avian	Integrated	Virus does not kill host cells; wide host range; can insert up to 7 kb DNA into genome and still produce virus particles (in helper-free cells) for highly efficient introduction of genome; efficient and precise integration into host chromosomes	Low copy number

viral vectors are available in excellent reviews by Rigby (1982, 1983) and in a compendium of brief, original papers edited by Gluzman (1982).

2.8.1 SV40 Virus

Use of SV40 virus as a mammalian vector has been reviewed by several authors (e.g., Rigby, 1983) and details about SV40 virus are available in a book edited by Tooze (1980).

SV40 is a papova virus, a very small DNA virus containing only DNA and protein, that infects monkey cells. Its DNA is a double-stranded, covalently closed circle of 5,243 base pairs that has been completely sequenced. The details of SV40 gene expression are well-characterized (reviewed by Lebowitz and Weissman, 1979). The genome can be divided into early genes (small and large T antigen) synthesized before DNA replication and late genes (viral capsid proteins VP1, VP2, and VP3), synthesized after replication begins. Early genes share a promoter region and polyadenylation site; two different early messenger RNAs are synthesized with the same 5' and 3' termini and differ only by the regions spliced out of each message. The late genes also share the late promoter and late polyA site, but the messenger RNAs differ in their 5' ends (Tooze, 1980).

SV40 virus has two different life cycles, depending on whether it infects permissive or nonpermissive cells. In permissive cells (monkey cells), SV40 virus causes a lytic infection. Infection by SV40 does not inhibit synthesis of host-cell DNA, RNA, or protein. SV40 DNA enters the cell nucleus, and early genes are transcribed. The early protein, large T antigen, is required for initiation of viral DNA replication. The only cis-acting element required for replication is the SV40 origin of replication, a DNA sequence about 230 nucleotides long. Once DNA replication begins, the late viral genes are transcribed, and the newly replicated SV40 DNA is encapsidated in the three capsid proteins. About three days after infection, the host cells lyse, releasing virions. During productive infection, about 10^5 DNA molecules are produced per cell and packaged into virions, of which about 10^3 are infectious (Tooze, 1973, 1980).

In nonpermissive cells (e.g., mouse, rat, hamster), SV40 does not replicate but instead integrates into the host-cell chromosome and morphologically transforms the cells. The integration event is quite rare, occurring in only about one per 10^5 infected nonpermissive cells. Cells transformed by SV40 synthesize early but not late viral proteins. Expression of large T antigen is, in fact, required for morphological transformation of the cell.

The fate of SV40 DNA introduced into nonpermissive cells appears very similar to that of any exogenous DNA introduced into a mammalian cell. Soon after infection, SV40 DNA is in an unstable state (Hiscott et al., 1981), but once integrated, the SV40 DNA appears stable for hundreds of cell generations (Botchan et al., 1976) and does not rearrange unless placed under selective conditions that favor changes (Hiscott et al., 1980). Mutation frequency for an integrated SV40 gene has been measured as 1.2×10^{-6}, a frequency similar to that of some cellular genes (Steinberg et al., 1978). However, during the initial integration event, SV40 DNA sequences become highly rearranged and some sequences may actually be lost (Weinberg, 1980). One to ten copies of viral DNA become integrated at random locations within the genome of each transformed cell.

2.8.2 Recombinant SV40 Virus

SV40 virus has been used as a packaging vector to propagate and transfer foreign genes into both permissive and nonpermissive host cells. SV40 virus will not package DNA into virions unless the DNA size lies within a range of 70–100% of the normal 5,243 base pair DNA size. The foreign gene to be inserted is therefore limited to about 2,500 base pairs and can replace either the early or late genes of SV40. The resulting recombinant SV40 DNA is defective for infection, but can be propagated as a virus by coinfecting cells with a different SV40 virus that is temperature-sensitive in the opposite (early or late) gene region. The recombinant and temperature-sensitive viruses complement each other but also are reciprocally dependent upon each other when infected cells are grown at the high, nonpermissive temperature (Goff and Berg, 1976; Hamer et al., 1977; Goff, 1977). These conditions allow recombinant DNA to be propagated in SV40 virions, but the resulting virus stock is mixed. Gluzman (1981) established a cell line from permissive monkey (CV-1) cells by transforming them with an SV40 mutant defective at the origin of replication. The resulting cell line, COS cells, constitutively synthesize wild-type large T antigen, but cannot produce virus from the SV40 genome integrated into the cell chromosome. COS cells can be used to produce a pure stock of recombinant SV40 virus in which the foreign gene is substituted for the early genes (Gluzman, 1981).

Infection of permissive cells by mixed stocks of recombinant and helper SV40 virus leads to cell death and therefore is not useful for creating cell lines producing foreign proteins. Nevertheless, this approach has been extensively used in short-term studies of foreign gene expression in mammalian cells. The pioneering experiments which demonstrated that foreign DNA could be carried in viral vectors (Ganem et al., 1976; Goff and Berg, 1976; Hamer et al., 1977) and expressed after introduction into host cells (Goff and Berg, 1979; Mulligan et al., 1979) all utilized SV40 recombinant virus stocks. SV40 recombinant viruses have been used to help define which DNA sequences are required for expression of foreign DNA and to achieve short-term production of various proteins, including rabbit β-globin (Mulligan et al., 1979; Southern et al., 1981), mouse dihydrofolate reductase (Subramani et al., 1981), rat proinsulin (Gruss et al., 1981), human growth hormone (Pavlakis and Hamer, 1983), influenza virus hemagglutinin (Sveda and Lai, 1981; Hartman et al., 1982), hepatitis B surface antigen (Moriarty et al., 1981), and human β-interferon (Gheysen and Fiers, 1982).

Infection of nonpermissive cells with recombinant SV40 virus can be used to produce cell lines with integrated recombinant DNA, but infection by SV40 virus does not offer a higher efficiency or predictability of DNA integration compared to transfection with naked SV40 DNA. Since use of whole SV40 virus has the disadvantages of size limitation and propagation difficulties, it is much easier to introduce naked DNA directly if the goal is to integrate the foreign DNA.

2.8.3 SV40 DNA Expression Vectors

The use of naked DNA derived from SV40 as a vector (instead of SV40 virus) has several advantages. The vectors contain an origin of replication and a gene for antibiotic resistance derived from a bacterial plasmid so that the SV40 vectors can be propagated in bacteria to screen and produce large quantities of pure vector DNA. The expression sequences in SV40 have been well-characterized. The early transcription promoter possesses a typical TATA box, an upstream promoter element consisting of GC-rich repeats, and the 72 base pair repeated enhancer sequence (see Fromm and Berg, 1982, for a detailed dissection of SV40 early and late promoter structures). The SV40 vectors also contain one SV40 RNA splice site and an SV40 polyA addition signal.

Okayama and Berg (1983) have constructed SV40 expression vectors into which full-length cDNA libraries can be directly cloned. The vector itself serves as the primer for the reverse transcription reaction that converts polyA$^+$ RNA into cDNA. A late RNA splice junction lies just downstream of the SV40 early promoter, and the cDNA insert is located between this splice site and the polyA addition signal.

2.8.4 SV40 DNA Vectors in Permissive Cells

Because SV40 recombinant DNA transfected into permissive cells replicates extrachromosomally to high copy number, an episomal expression system using COS cells (an SV40-transformed monkey cell line which expresses SV40 T antigen) has been developed to achieve extrachromosomal gene amplification of recombinant DNA, and consequently, high levels of foreign gene expression. By providing T antigen, COS cells permit the replication of recombinant DNA vectors derived from the bacterial plasmid pBR322 and containing the SV40 origin of replication (only 228 base pairs of DNA) (Myers and Tjian, 1980). Replication efficiency of these vectors, called SV-ORI vectors, is enhanced by removal of a stretch of pBR322 sequences called "poison sequences" (Lusky and Botchan, 1981). SV-ORI DNA vectors lacking the poison sequence can replicate extrachromosomally in COS cells to very high numbers, from $1-5 \times 10^5$ DNA copies per cell (Mellon et al., 1981; Cattaneo et al., 1983; Crowley et al., 1983). These DNA vectors can be used to carry any foreign gene and the desired expression sequences.

Inserts as large as 8 kilobases containing α-globin sequences have been incorporated into SV-ORI vectors without inhibiting replication (Mellon et al., 1981), although Cattaneo et al. (1983) observed that the level of DNA amplification was lowered 5- to 50-fold after insertion of hepatitis B surface antigen sequences. SV40-derived vectors in COS cells have been used to obtain high expression levels of several genes: human globin (Mellon et al., 1981; Humphries et al., 1982), *E. coli* guanosyl phosphoribosyltransferase (Tsui et al., 1982), and hepatitis B surface antigen (Cattaneo et al., 1983; Crowley et al., 1983; Siddiqui, 1983). In the case of an α-globin RNA, the high level of RNA expression was shown to be directly related to the high DNA copy number (Mellon et al., 1981).

Although these SV40 systems for episomal gene amplification do not involve lytic infection and have been shown to lead to high levels of gene expression, no protein-producing cell lines have yet been established from these cells, perhaps because so much extrachromosomal DNA eventually kills the cells (Rigby, 1983). Most reported gene expression experiments in COS cells have deliberately been terminated in 48–72 hours (Mellon et al., 1981; Gheysen and Fiers, 1982; Cattaneo et al., 1983). Tsui et al. (1982) reported that when COS cells were transfected with a DNA vector expressing *Ecogpt,* only 5–10% of the cells survived after seven days. After three to four weeks, only 10^{-3} to 10^{-4} of the cells survived in selective medium; these surviving cells still contained episomal DNA, but at the reduced level of 5–2,000 copies per cell. Crowley et al. (1983) obtained high levels of secretion of hepatitis B antigen from COS cells over a period of three weeks, but production began to fall off after about two weeks, and the authors did not report attempts to establish producer cell lines.

Since the gene amplification of SV40 vectors in permissive cells leads to increased protein production, attempts may be made to develop vectors that replicate to a moderate level per cell: ones high enough to increase protein production, but low enough to be tolerated by the cells. Recently, Rio et al. (1985) have developed a COS cell line that has a temperature-sensitive T antigen. SV40 origin-based vectors replicate in this cell line at 33°C but not at 44°C. Thus, it may now be possible to regulate the copy number of SV40 vectors by modulating T antigen activity, and possibly allow long-term maintenance of the expression vectors.

However, another issue concerning extrachromosomal SV40 DNA vectors that must be considered is the stability of DNA. Wild-type SV40 DNA frequently suffers deletions in lytically infected cells and sometimes incorporates cellular sequences (Tooze, 1980; Weinberg, 1980), and recombinant DNA SV40 virus stocks give rise to a large number (e.g., 30%) of deleted and rearranged molecules (Hamer and Walling, 1982). This high deletion frequency has also been observed in SV40-derived recombinant DNA plasmids in COS cells. Tsui et al. (1982) examined five cell lines selected after transfection with an SV40-*Ecogpt* expression vector (pSV2-*gpt*). In two lines, the extrachromosomal DNA was the same size as the infecting DNA; in two lines, the DNA had sustained major deletions of 200–1,500 base pairs; and in one cell line, DNA was a mixture of two sizes, one deleted and one the original size. In this case, deletions were in the bacterial pBR322 sequences and not in the *Ecogpt* or SV40 replication sequence being selected. These observations, however, raise the possibility that sequences for a nonselected foreign protein might be lost at a comparatively high rate during extrachromosomal SV40 vector replication. Cattaneo et al. (1983) found that 10–50% of the extrachromosomal SV40 DNA carrying a tandem duplication of the hepatitis B virus (HBV) genome lost 3,200 base pairs of DNA, while a similar vector containing only one HBV genome suffered no deletion. They hypothesized that intramolecular homologous recombination caused the observed deletion. These observations suggest that the high deletion rate of extrachromosomal SV40 vectors may be partially controlled by decreasing sequence homology in the vector and maintaining selective pressure. However, high mutation rates may obviate the use of SV40 extrachromosomal vectors for efficiently establishing a protein-producing cell line.

2.8.5 SV40 Recombinant DNA Vectors Introduced into Nonpermissive Cells

SV40 recombinant DNA vectors have been used to transfect nonpermissive cells and obtain expression of foreign genes after integration into high molecular weight DNA. Genes so expressed include mouse dihydrofolate reductase (DHFR) (Subramani et al., 1981), prokaryotic DHFR (O'Hare et al., 1981), *E. coli* guanosine phosphoribosyltransferase (Mulligan and Berg, 1981), prokaryotic neomycin resistance (Southern and Berg, 1982), human interferon (Scahill et al., 1983), rabbit β-globin (Mulligan et al., 1979), and human hypoxanthine phosphoribosyltransferase (Jolly et al., 1983). Integration of the recombinant DNA allows establishment of cell lines. Stability of expression was studied by Scahill et al. (1983), who cotransfected hamster (CHO) DHFR⁻ cells with two recombinant DNA plasmids, one containing the selectable DHFR gene and one containing the human gene for γ-interferon under the control of SV40 expression sequences. They then selected DHFR-positive cells, screened them for interferon production, and established cell lines from cells that produced high levels of interferon. Once such cell line showed no decrease in cell production after 20 passages (about 12 weeks). However, another cell line decreased production during that time (Scahill et al., 1983). There are not enough data yet available in the literature to ascertain what percentage of integrated SV40-based expression vectors will remain stable producers over a long period of time.

2.8.6 Polyoma Virus

Polyoma virus is closely related to simian virus 40, the major difference being that the host cell for the polyoma lytic cycle is mouse, while that for

SV40 is monkey (Tooze, 1980). Polyoma infection is less efficient than that of SV40, and polyoma vectors are infrequently used. The early gene region and origin of replication of polyoma have been used in vectors to replicate and express foreign genes in mouse cells. The enhancer is unusual in that it consists of two distinct nonoverlapping sequences that have a slightly different tissue specificity (Herbomel et al., 1984).

Deans et al. (1984) have constructed a recombinant vector using the polyoma early-region expression sequences and origin of replication to express immunoglobulin genes in mouse lymphoid cells. They reported very high frequencies of T antigen-producing cells in transient experiments: 35–40% of cells expressed following calcium-phosphate precipitation of the DNA, 60–70% using DEAE-dextran, and 70–80% using protoplast fusion.

2.8.7 Adenovirus and Adeno-Associated Virus

Adenovirus is a human virus with a genome of double-stranded linear DNA, approximately 35 kilobase pairs in length, that encodes at least 30 proteins. Details of its expression and infectious cycle are known (see Tooze, 1980). Adenovirus offers several advantages as a mammalian expression vector (reviewed by Rigby, 1982). Since adenovirus infection inhibits host-cell protein synthesis, genes expressed by adenovirus can account for a greater percentage of total protein synthesis in the cell. A large amount of DNA (up to 7,000 base pairs) can be inserted into the genome without inhibiting viral function (Berkner and Sharp, 1982). Also, the adenovirus major late promoter is a very strong transcriptional promoter. This promoter does not possess an enhancer element, and transcription from this promoter can be further increased by the addition of an enhancer (Kaufman and Sharp, 1982). Adenovirus type 2 is able to replicate in human, simian, and rodent cells.

Among the disadvantages is that adenovirus infection kills the host cell, so that expressing cell lines cannot be established. Also, when adenovirus DNA integrates into the chromosomes of host cells that are nonpermissive for adenovirus replication, only some pieces of the genome integrate, while others are lost (Weinberg, 1980).

The adenovirus major late promoter has been used separately in a number of expression vectors. For instance, it has been used to produce 20- to 40-fold more SV40 large T antigen in monkey cells than is produced by SV40 infection (Thummel et al., 1981); it has been used to express recombinant DHFR gene (Kaufman and Sharp, 1982) and also human erythropoietin (Jacobs et al., 1985).

Adenovirus expresses small transcripts known as VA RNA. This RNA appears to stimulate translation of mRNA species that possess an adenovirus leader sequence. The VA gene has been used in expression vectors to increase the translation efficiency not only of transcripts from the adenovirus major late promoter but also from the SV40 early promoter (Kaufman, 1985).

There is one report of the use of a human parvovirus, adeno-associated virus (AAV), as a mammalian expression vector. Tratschin et al. (1984) transfected the defective AAV genome along with helper adenovirus particles to allow AAV replication and produce infectious AAV particles at high efficiency. A vector was constructed with transcription of the bacterial CAT gene driven by an AAV promoter. After transfection into 293 cells (which express an adenovirus early function) high expression of the CAT gene was obtained without helper virus. In this case, replication did not take place. One advantage of AAV is that it may be possible to control whether the genome integrates into chromosomes or is replicated episomally, depending on whether helper virus is absent or present.

2.8.8 Bovine Papilloma Virus

Bovine papilloma virus (BPV) is a small DNA virus that contains only DNA and protein. Its genome is a double-stranded DNA circle of 7,945 base pairs that has been completely sequenced (Chen et al., 1982). No papilloma virus has yet been cultured in a continuous cell culture system; the complete BPV genome has been cloned into a bacterial plasmid and can therefore be easily propagated and dissected (Danos et al., 1980; Heilman et al., 1980). In fact, BPV cloned into a bacterial plasmid can replicate either in bacteria or in mammalian cells (DiMaio et al., 1982). BPV DNA, either in its entirety or as a subgenomic fragment containing 69% of the original viral DNA, causes morphological transformation of mouse cells in cell culture (Lowy et al., 1980a). Morphological transformation provides a selection for cells that receive BPV DNA.

Cell lines that contain BPV DNA are unusual in that they do not integrate BPV DNA into the cellular chromosomes, but instead carry BPV DNA in an episomal (extrachromosomal) state. Moreover, transformed mouse cells contain 20–100 copies of episomal BPV DNA (Law et al., 1981), providing a natural amplification of the viral vector. Lusky and Botchan (1984) have shown that maintenance of the extrachromosomal state of BPV DNA requires two noncontiguous regions in the BPV DNA as well as an undefined BPV-encoded gene product. When these elements are built into a recombinant DNA molecule, the BPV-recombinant plasmid copy number, once established in a given cell line, is maintained in a stable manner even in the absence of selective pressure.

Sarver et al. (1981) demonstrated that BPV could function as an expression vector by ligating the rat preproinsulin gene to the transforming 69% subgenomic fragment of BPV and establishing cell lines from transformed foci. The cell lines contained the recombinant DNA in an extrachromosomal state at 60–80 copies per cell and secreted proinsulin into the culture medium. Since then, BPV vectors have been used to establish mouse cell lines that produce human β interferon (Zinn et al., 1982; Mitrani-Rosenbaum et al., 1983), hepatitis B surface antigen (Wang et al., 1983), human growth hormone (Pavlakis and Hamer, 1983), and human histocompatibility antigen (DiMaio et al., 1984). An observation important to the possibility of using BPV vectors for manufacturing foreign proteins in stable producer cell lines is the report by Pavlakis and Hamer (1983) that production levels of human growth hormone carried in an episomal BPV vector remained stable through one year of continuous cell passage.

When BPV DNA first enters mammalian cells via transfection of DNA, it may sometimes acquire new DNA or rearrange its sequences (Pavlakis and Hamer, 1983; Mitrani-Rosenbaum et al., 1983). However, once BPV sequences are established in a cell, they then remain identical in sequence and stable in copy number, even after cell passaging for three months (Zinn et al., 1982) or one year (Pavlakis and Hamer, 1983). Therefore, protein-producing stable cell lines can be established after appropriate selection of producer cells. So far, no limit has been observed for the size of foreign DNA that can be inserted into a BPV DNA vector.

Maintenance of expression vectors as extrachromosomal elements may be advantageous since the DNA then resides in a known sequence environment in which expression will not be affected by neighboring host chromosomal regions. Using BPV episomal vectors, foreign protein can be produced at high levels. For example, Fukunaga et al. (1984), using BPV vectors, attained production of human interferon at levels of 4×10^5 international units per ml of culture fluid per day.

In most cases, transcription of heterologous genes in BPV has been controlled by non-BPV promoters. It appears that BPV contains an enhancer type of element (Lusky et al., 1983) and in the future, BPV sequences that regulate gene expression may be defined and employed.

2.8.9 Epstein-Barr Virus

Another virus whose DNA replicates episomally is Epstein-Barr Virus (EBV), a herpes simplex virus that infects human B lymphocytes and transforms them into continuously dividing cells that can be efficiently established as cell lines. The EBV genome of 172,000 DNA base pairs is maintained as a double-stranded circular extrachromosomal DNA molecule (Sugden et al., 1979). Maintenance of EBV DNA as an episome seems to require a fragment of EBV DNA, termed *ori-P*, of about 1,800 base pairs, and the presence of an EBV-encoded protein, Epstein-Barr nuclear antigen (EBNA-1) (Yates et al., 1985). Copy number depends on the cell line used, ranging from 1–8 copies in some cells (DAUDI) to 13–60 copies in other cells (RAJI) (Sugden et al., 1985). An EBV-based vector has been constructed that contains the EBV sequences, *ori-P* and EBNA-1 genes, to allow episomal replication in lymphoblasts, and a dominant selectable marker, the bacterial hygromycin B phosphotransferase gene, placed under eukaryotic transcription control by using promoter sequences from the herpes simplex virus thymidine kinase gene (Sugden et al., 1985).

An EBV vector might offer a few advantages. Episomal replication provides gene amplification. Use of lymphoblasts as host cells means cells can be grown in suspension instead of requiring surfaces for attachment. Since EBV vectors can replicate in human, monkey, or dog cells (Yates et al., 1985), they have a wider host range than the other episomal vectors SV40 and BPV. EBV DNA can infect not only lymphocytes, but also fibroblast and epithelial cells; however, EBV DNA copy number and expression levels vary widely depending on the host cell. A high efficiency of transformation was obtained in one experiment in which hygromycin-resistant cells appeared at a 3% frequency following introduction by electroporation of an EBV DNA vector containing the hygromycin resistance gene (Sugden et al., 1985).

Disadvantages in the use of EBV DNA vectors have also appeared. Work reported so far has introduced EBV DNA into cells only by the methods of electroporation or protoplast fusion. Although transfected cells could be selected using the hygromycin resistance marker, two other dominant selectable markers, *Ecogpt* and G418 resistance, did not function well (Sugden et al., 1985). Future experiments will have to determine the practical utility of EBV vectors.

2.8.10   Retroviruses

Retroviruses (RNA tumor viruses) have an RNA genome but integrate a DNA copy of this RNA into the chromosomes of the cells they infect. They infect a wide range of species and cell types. Most retroviruses do not kill the host cells; instead, virus particles continuously bud from the surface membrane of infected cells. Since infection takes place through the interaction of a host cell receptor protein with the envelope protein of the virus, the envelope protein determines the host range of the retrovirus.

The RNA genome of retroviruses ranges from 5,000–10,000 nucleotides in length and is both capped and polyadenylated. There are two copies of the RNA molecule in each virion. The retrovirus carries an enzyme known as reverse transcriptase that upon infection copies the viral genome RNA into a linear double-stranded DNA molecule. At both ends of this DNA molecule is an identical sequence of 300–1,200 nucleotides called a long terminal repeat (LTR). The DNA molecule is circularized and then integrated into the host-cell DNA. Although the location of integration into the host chromosome is random, the linear sequence of the viral DNA is always rigidly preserved. The integrated viral DNA always joins the host DNA precisely two base pairs from the ends of the linear DNA (Varmus, 1982) and is therefore exactly colinear with its RNA genome with an LTR at either end. The LTR sequences appear to provide the mechanism by which retrovirus DNA precisely integrates into the host-cell genome (Shoemaker et al., 1980). Some trans activity coded by the retrovirus also appears to be required for efficient and accurate integration of the proviral DNA into the host chromosome (Schwartzberg et al., 1984).

The LTR region also provides a transcriptional promoter including an enhancer element, and a polyadenylation sequence for viral transcripts. Thus, transcripts are initiated from a promoter in the LTR upstream of the viral structural genes and are polyadenylated due to the signals in the downstream LTR. Most retroviruses express their two upstream genes, *gag* and *pol,* from a genomic, unspliced RNA molecule. The downstream gene, *env,* is expressed from a spliced mRNA. The splice in this transcript removes the *gag* and *pol* regions and brings the *env* sequence into close proximity to the transcription start site. The unspliced message can be packaged into virions, while the spliced transcript has lost a sequence required for packaging, called ψ, and therefore cannot be packaged. (For a review on retrovirus infection, replication, and expression, see Weiss et al., 1982.)

Retroviruses offer several advantages as eukaryotic expression vectors:

1. Their wide host range allows infection of many cell types.
2. Since retrovirus infection does not kill cells, it is possible to establish infected cell lines after infection by whole viruses.
3. Large pieces of foreign DNA (up to 7,000 bases) can be inserted into the genome, expressed, and packaged (Goff et al., 1982).
4. Insertion of viral DNA into the host-cell genome occurs in a predictable manner that preserves the gene sequence present in the virion. This precision is characteristic of retroviral infection and is not always observed after transfection of retroviral DNA as naked DNA (Doehmer et al., 1982; Varmus, 1982).
5. Retroviral DNA remains very stable in the host genome (Hughes et al., 1979).

Three laboratories have demonstrated that a stock of retrovirus containing a foreign gene can be obtained in high titers; the gene in each case was the herpes simplex thymidine kinase (TK) gene (Shimotohno and Temin, 1981; Wei et al., 1981; Tabin et al., 1982). Recombinant retrovirus DNA containing the *tk* gene was transfected into the appropriate host cells. The transfected cells were then infected with a competent helper virus so that the recombinant retrovirus DNA could be packaged into viral particles. Virus secreted into the culture medium was then assayed for the presence of recombinant virus by infecting TK$^-$ cells and selecting for the TK$^+$ phenotype in HAT medium. Infection of cells by recombinant virus is significantly more efficient than transfection by DNA. The *tk* gene was transferred into mouse cells using Harvey murine sarcoma virus (Wei et al., 1981) or Moloney murine leukemia virus (Tabin et al., 1982) and into chicken and rat cells using spleen necrosis virus (Shimotohno and Temin, 1981). In each case, the recombinant genomes were shown to be inserted into the host-cell DNA in the exact sequence order present in the original cloned DNA, as expected for a normal retrovirus infection.

Vectors can be constructed in which essentially only the LTRs and immediate flanking sequences of the retroviral genome are used. Perkins et al. (1983) used the 5' and 3' LTRs of Moloney murine leukemia virus to flank the *Ecogpt* gene, transfected mouse cells, and selected for cells that expressed *gpt* activity. These cells were then infected with helper Moloney murine leukemia virus to produce a recombinant virus stock. When mouse cells were subsequently infected with the resulting virus, 50% of the cells expressed the *gpt* gene. Miller et al. (1983) produced a virus stock that expressed the human HPRT (hypoxanthine phosphoribosyltransferase) gene in a similar fashion. Thus, all the necessary sequences for expression are present in the LTRs; since the HPRT vector can package 6–7 kilobase pairs of extra DNA, it can be used to carry any nonselectable gene up to 7 kb, with the HPRT gene providing a selectable marker. Gilboa et al. (1982) have shown that two genes, *tk* and *neo*[R], could both be expressed in a Moloney murine leukemia virus vector.

A shortcoming of the preceding experiments is that helper virus was required for the production of recombinant virions. Thus, the viral stock will have a mixture of the two viruses, with the virus titer often composed of approximately 90% helper virus (Miller et al., 1983). In order to circumvent this problem, Mann et al. (1983) have created a mouse cell line that allows the production of recombinant viral stocks free from helper virus. A deletion mutant of Moloney murine leukemia virus was created that lacks the sequence necessary for its RNA to be packaged into a virion (the ψ sequence) but has all the sequences needed to provide, in trans, all other necessary retroviral functions so that defective viruses can be fully complemented by this mutant. They then established a cell line, called ψ2, that contains the mutant viral DNA as part of its genome. Using retroviral DNA containing the *Ecogpt* gene, they demonstrated that these cell lines can act as hosts to package and secrete the recombinant retroviral DNAs as pure retrovirus stocks of approximately 10^4 colony-forming units per ml.

Cepko et al. (1984) have constructed a set of retrovirus vectors known as pZIP-neoSV (shown in Figure 2–4). These vectors are composed of the Moloney murine leukemia virus 5' and 3' LTRs (which contain the transcriptional promoter as well as polyadenylation and integration signals), the packaging site, the primer site for reverse transcription, and the 5' and 3' splice sites for messenger splicing. The vectors have the *neo*[R] gene to confer G418-resistance in mammalian cells and kanamycin resistance when the vector is propagated as a plasmid in *E. coli,* as well as the SV40 and bacterial (plasmid pBR322) origins of replication. Two different clones were constructed that differ in the position of the cDNA insert. If the cDNA is inserted in the upstream position (as shown in Figure 2–4), it is expressed on an unspliced mRNA while the downstream *neo*[R] gene is expressed on a

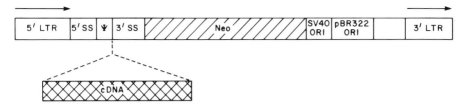

FIGURE 2–4 Map of the retrovirus vector pZIP-neoSV(X)I (redrawn from Cepko *et al.,* 1984). Terminology: LTR, long terminal repeat; 5' SS, 5' splice site or splice donor; ψ, virion packaging site; 3' SS, 3' splice site or splice acceptor; *neo,* bacterial gene encoding G418 resistance; ORI, origin of replication. The cDNA of a gene to be expressed, in this case, is inserted so that it will be expressed on the unspliced RNA.

spliced transcript. The position of the cDNA insert and *neo*^{R} gene can be alternated without effect.

Viral particles are produced by transfecting this recombinant DNA into ψ2 cells. The ψ2 culture fluid is then used to infect 3T3 cells and after selection for G418-resistance, a viral titer of $1-5 \times 10^3$ colony-forming units per ml is reported. Permanent recombinant virus producer lines can be generated by directly selecting for G418-resistance in ψ2 cells. Permanent cell lines yield 10^4 to over 10^6 colony-forming units per ml of culture fluid, making them ideal for long-term recombinant virus production. Spliced and unspliced messages are produced in equal amounts. However, at times, aberrant splicing into the inserted gene can be seen.

It is possible to rescue these vectors from the host cells by a number of means (Cepko et al., 1984). In one protocol, the pZIP-neoSV vectors are transfected into cells that do not allow virus packaging. These cells are then fused with COS cells, a monkey cell line that expresses the SV40 large T antigen. The T antigen induces replication at the SV40 origin of replication and the retroviral vector DNA is generated as episomes, free from the host chromosomes, although sometimes it may carry extra host DNA from the site at which it was integrated.

Another useful property of these and other retrovirus vectors is that genomic DNA-containing introns can be inserted into the vector DNA and the retrovirus finally produced will contain cDNA copies of this genomic clone (Shimotohno and Temin, 1982; Sorge and Hughes, 1982). This occurs because the introns in the genomic DNA are spliced out and the resulting RNA molecules are packaged into virions.

It should be noted that when genes are inserted into retroviral vectors, the genes must not carry their own polyadenylation site. If they did, premature polyA addition would occur and full-length genomic RNA would not be produced (Shimotohno and Temin, 1981). Therefore, polyA addition sequences must be identified and removed from a gene before it can be inserted into a retroviral vector.

Recently, the pZIP-neo vectors of Cepko et al. (1984) have been used to express the human gene for adenine deaminase (Friedman, 1985). Mouse ψ2 cells, transformed to G418-resistance, expressed 20-fold more human adenine deaminase than endogenous mouse adenine deaminase.

Retroviral vectors that carry two genes with different promoters have now been constructed. This is desirable if one wishes to employ a specific inducible promoter to produce a protein. However, an unexpected problem arose when Emerman and Temin (1984) constructed vectors with the neo^R gene transcribed from the LTR and the HSV *tk* gene transcribed from its own promoter. Surprisingly, they found that if only one copy of the vector was present in the host cells, either one of the two genes, but not both, was expressed. This effect is epigenetic and reversible, as rescued viruses can change which gene is expressed after reinfection. This phenomenon is not understood and may be cell-specific, as other laboratories have reported different findings (Miller et al., 1984).

The rat growth hormone with its own inducible promoter was inserted into a murine retrovirus vector downstream of the selectable marker HPRT, which was transcribed from the 5' LTR (Miller et al., 1984). This vector was transfected into HPRT$^-$ cells, and the HPRT$^+$ colonies were selected in HAT medium. The HPRT$^+$ cells were then infected with helper virus and high titers (up to 10^6 per ml) of recombinant virus were obtained and used to infect HPRT$^-$ cells. In the cells infected by the recombinant virus, the growth hormone gene was inducible by both glucocorticoids and thyroid hormone. The growth hormone gene could be expressed and induced when placed in either orientation. The recombinant DNA was found in a single copy per host cell, and in this case, both the growth hormone and HPRT genes were expressed.

The ψ2 cell line, a mouse cell line, produces virions with a host range limited to rodents. Sorge et al. (1984), Cone and Mulligan (1984), and Miller et al. (1985) have now produced helper-free cell lines that package viruses of very wide host range. Recombinant viruses can now be produced that are able to infect avian, rodent, canine, simian, and human cells.

In conclusion, retroviruses offer a number of significant advantages as expression vectors. Once virus is produced, the introduction of the recombinant DNA into cells is very efficient, and the integration into the genome is precise, lacking the rearrangements sometimes seen after transfection of DNA into cells. Also, genes introduced into cells in retroviral vectors as viruses appear to be more efficiently expressed than the same genes transfected as naked DNA (Hwang and Gilboa, 1984). Once integrated, the DNA appears to be very stably maintained. One disadvantage is that the retroviral DNA usually inserts in only one or a few copies. However, if a high gene copy number is desired in order to increase gene expression, the copy number can be increased after infection by use of a retroviral vector that contains a gene, such as DHFR, whose amplification can be selected (Miller et al., 1985). Also, the retrovirus LTRs provide powerful transcriptional promoters that have often been used in nonretrovirus vectors. For instance, Rous sarcoma virus, a chicken retrovirus, has a powerful transcriptional promoter that has been used to enhance gene expression in rat, hamster, monkey, and human cell lines (Gorman et al., 1982; Luciw et al., 1983).

2.9 CONCLUSIONS

The production of useful proteins in mammalian cells in culture has now become technically feasible. Use of this mammalian cell technology will assume major importance in some instances where activity of the protein being produced depends upon posttranslational modifications, which occur only in mammalian cells and not in bacterial host cells. This chapter has attempted to outline what genetic elements are needed for expression in a mammalian system and the protocols used to obtain expression of heterologous proteins. The tools available to the genetic engineer allow for efficient introduction of foreign genes into cells, simple selection of cells expressing the foreign gene, amplification of the specific gene copy number in order to increase expression, and finally, control of gene expression by external signals so that protein production can be induced at an advantageous point in time. While many vectors are now available for use, the vectors and specific elements within them will be constantly refined in the future to provide optimal means for using mammalian cells to manufacture desirable proteins.

REFERENCES

Aaronsen, S.A., and Todaro, G.J. (1969) *Science* 166, 390–391.

Alt, F.W., Kellems, R.E., Bertino, J.R., and Schimke, R.T. (1978) *J. Biol. Chem.* 253, 1357–1370.

Andrulis, I.L., and Siminovitch, L. (1972) in *Gene Amplification* (Schimke, R.T., ed.) pp. 75–80, Cold Spring Harbor Laborataory, N.Y.

Bacchetti, S., and Graham, F.L. (1977) *Proc. Natl. Acad. Sci. USA* 74, 1590–1594.

Banerji, J., Olson, L., and Schaffner, W. (1983) *Cell* 33, 729–740.

Banerji, J., Rusconi, S., and Schaffner, W. (1981) *Cell* 27, 299–308.

Beach, L.R., and Palmiter, R.D. (1981) *Proc. Natl. Acad. Sci. USA* 78, 2110–2114.

Benoist, C., and Chambon, P. (1981) *Nature* 290, 304–310.

Berkner, K.L., and Sharp, P. (1982) in *Eukaryotic Viral Vectors* (Gluzman, Y., ed.) pp. 193–198, Cold Spring Harbor Laboratory, N.Y.

Biedler, J.L., and Spengler, B.A. (1976) *Science* 191, 185–187.

Blochlinger, K., and Diggelmann, H. (1984) *Mol. Cell. Biol.* 4, 2929–2931.

Botchan, M., Topp, W., and Sambrook, J. (1976) *Cell* 9, 269–287.

Breathnach, R., and Chambon, P. (1981) *Ann. Rev. Biochem.* 50, 349–383.

Brennard, J., Chinault, A.C., Konecki, D.S., Melton, D.W., and Caskey, C.T. (1982) *Proc. Natl. Acad. Sci. USA* 79, 1950–1954.

Brown, D.D. (1981) *Science* 211, 667–674.

Byrne, B.J., Davis, M.S., Yamaguchi, J., Bergsma, D.J., and Subramanian, K.N. (1983) *Proc. Natl. Acad. Sci. USA* 80, 721–725.

Canaani, D., and Berg, P. (1982) *Proc. Natl. Acad. Sci. USA* 79, 5166–5170.

Capecchi, M.R. (1980) *Cell* 22, 479–488.

Cattaneo, R., Will, H., Darai, G., Pfaff, E., and Schaller, H. (1983) *EMBO J.* 2, 511–514.

Cepko, C.L., Roberts, B.E., and Mulligan, R.C. (1984) *Cell* 37, 1053–1062.

Chandler, V.L., Maler, B.A., and Yamamoto, K.R. (1983) *Cell* 33, 489–499.

Chang, E.H., Ellis, R.W., Scolnick, E.M., and Lowy, D.R. (1980) *Science* 210, 1249–1251.

Chapman, A.B., Costello, M.A., Lee, F., and Ringold, G.M. (1983) *Mol. Cell. Biol.* 3, 1421–1429.

Chen, E.Y., Howley, P.M., Levinson, A.D., and Seeburg, P.H. (1982) *Nature* 299, 529–534.

Chin, D.J., Luskey, K.L. Anderson, R.J.W., Faust, J.R., Goldstein, J.L., and Brown, M.S. (1982) *Proc. Natl. Acad. Sci. USA* 79, 1185–1189.

Christman, J.K., Gerber, M., Price, P.M., Flordellis, C., Edelman, J., and Acs, G. (1982) *Proc. Natl. Acad. Sci. USA* 79, 1815–1819.

Chu, G., and Sharp, P.A. (1981a) *Nature* 289, 378–382.

Chu, G., and Sharp, P.A. (1981b) *Gene* 13, 197–202.

Colbere-Garapin, F., Chousterman, S., Horodniceanu, F., Kovrilsky, P., and Garapin, A-C. (1979) *Proc. Natl. Acad. Sci. USA* 76, 3755–3759.

Colbere-Garapin, F., Horodniceanu, F., Kovrilsky, P., and Garapin, A.-C. (1981) *J. Mol. Biol.* 150, 1–14.

Cone, R.D., and Mulligan, R.C. (1984) *Proc. Natl. Acad. Sci. USA* 81, 6349–6353.

Conrad, S.E., and Botchan, M.R. (1982) *Mol. Cell. Biol.* 2, 949–965.

Copeland, N.G., Jenkins, N.A., and Cooper, G.M. (1981) *Cell* 23, 51–60.

Corden, J., Wasylyk, B., Buchwalder, A., Sassone-Corsi, P., Kedinger, C., and Chambon, P. (1980) *Science* 209, 1406–1414.

Crawford, B.D., Enger, M.D., Griffith, B.B., Griffith, J.K., Hanners, J.L., Longmire, J.L., Munk, A.C., Stallings, R.L., Tesmer, J.G., Walters, R.A., and Hildebrand, C.E. (1985) *Mol. Cell. Biol.* 5, 320–329.

Crowley, C.W., Liu, C.-C., and Levinson, A.D. (1983) *Mol. Cell. Biol.* 3, 44–55.

Danos, O., Katinka, M., and Yaniv, M. (1980) *Eur. J. Biochem.* 109, 457–461.

Deans, R.J., Denis, K.A., Taylor, A., and Wall, R. (1984) *Proc. Natl. Acad. Sci. USA* 81, 1292–1296.

de Villiers, J., Olson, L., Tyndall, C., and Schaffner, W. (1982) *Nucleic Acids Res.* 10, 7965–7976.

Dierks, P., Van Ooyen, A., Cochran, M.D., Dobkin, C., Reiser, J., and Weissmann, C. (1983) *Cell* 32, 695–706.

DiMaio, D., Corbin, V., Sibley, E., and Maniatis, T. (1984) *Mol. Cell. Biol.* 4, 340–350.

DiMaio, D., Treisman, R., and Maniatis, T. (1982) *Proc. Natl. Acad. Sci. USA* 79, 4030–4034.

Doehmer, J., Barinaga, M., Vale, W., Rosenfeld, M.G., Verma, I.M., and Evans, R.M. (1982) *Proc. Natl. Acad. Sci. USA* 79, 2268–2272.

Dubois, M.-F., Pourcel, C., Rousset, S., Chany, C., and Tiollais, P. (1980) *Proc. Natl. Acad. Sci. USA* 77, 4549–4553.

Efstratiadis, A., Posakony, J.W., Maniatis, T., Lawn, R.M., O'Connell, C., Spritz, R.A., DeRiel, J.K., Forget, B.G., Weissman, S.M., Slightom, J.L., Blechl, A.E., Smithies, O., Barelle, F.E., Shoulders, C.C., and Proudfoot, N.J. (1980) *Cell* 21, 653–668.

Elder, J.T., Spritz, R.A., and Weissman, S.M. (1981) *Annu. Rev. Genet.* 15, 295–340.

Emerman, M., and Temin, H.M. (1984) *Cell* 39, 459–467.

Ephrussi, A., Church, G.M., Tonegawa, S., and Gilbert, W. (1985) *Science* 227, 134–140.

Folger, K.R., Wong, E.A., Wahl, G., and Capecchi, M.R. (1982) *Mol. Cell. Biol.* 2, 1372–1387.

Fraley, R., Subramani, S., Berg, P., and Papahadjopoulos, D. (1980) *J. Biol. Chem.* 255, 10431–10435.

Friedman, R.L. (1985) *Proc. Natl. Acad. Sci. USA* 82, 703–707.

Fromm, M., and Berg, P. (1982) *J. Mol. Appl. Genet.* 1, 457–481.

Fromm, M., and Berg, P. (1983) *Mol. Cell. Biol.* 3, 991–999.

Frost, E., and Williams, J. (1978) *Virology* 91, 39–50.

Fukunaga, R., Sokawa, Y., and Nagata, S. (1984) *Proc. Natl. Acad. Sci. USA* 81, 5086–5090.

Ganem, D., Nussbaum, A., Davoli, D., and Fareed, G.C. (1976) *Cell* 7, 349–359.

Genilloud, O., Garrido, M.C., and Moreno, F. (1984) *Gene* 32, 225–233.

Gheysen, D., and Fiers, W. (1982) *J. Mol. Appl. Genet.* 1, 385–394.

Gilboa, E., Park, J., Kolbe, M., Hwang, S., Kucherlapati, R., Noonan, K., and Freeman, H. (1982) in *Eukaryotic Viral Vectors* (Gluzman, Y., ed.) pp. 145–151, Cold Spring Harbor Laboratory, N.Y.

Gillies, S.D., Morrison, S.L., Oi, V.T., and Tonegawa, S. (1983) *Cell* 33, 717–728.

Gluzman, Y. (1981) *Cell* 23, 175–182.

Gluzman, Y., ed. (1982) *Eukaryotic Viral Vectors,* Cold Spring Harbor Laboratory, N.Y.

Goff, S.P. (1977) Ph.D. Thesis, Stanford University Medical School, Stanford, Calif.

Goff, S.P., and Berg, P. (1976) *Cell* 9, 695–705.

Goff, S.P., and Berg, P. (1979) *J. Mol. Biol.* 133, 359–383.

Goff, S.P., Tabin, C.J., Wang, J.Y.-J., Weinberg, R.A., and Baltimore, D. (1982) *J. Virol.* 41, 271–285.

Gorman, C.M., Moffat, L.F., and Howard, B.H. (1982) *Mol. Cell. Biol.* 2, 1044–1051.

Gorman, C.M., Padmanabhan, R., and Howard, B.H. (1983) *Science* 221, 551–553.

Graessmann, M., and Graessmann, A. (1976) *Proc. Natl. Acad. Sci. USA* 73, 366–370.

Graham, F.L., Abrahams, P.J., Mulder, C., Heijneker, H.L., Warnaar, S.O., de Vries, F.A.J., Fiers, W., and Van der Eb, A.J. (1975) *Cold Spring Harbor Symp. Quant. Biol.* 39, 637–650.

Graham, F.L., and Van der Eb, A.J. (1973) *Virology* 52, 456–467.

Gruss, P., Dhar, R. and Khoury, G. (1981) *Proc. Natl. Acad. Sci. USA* 78, 943–947.

Hakala, M.T., and Taylor, E. (1959) *J. Biol. Chem.* 234, 126–128.

Hall, C.V., Jacob, P.E., Ringold, G.M., and Lee, F. (1983) *J. Mol. Appl. Genet.* 2, 101–109.

Hamer, D.H., Davoli, D., Thomas, Jr., C.A., and Fareed, G.C. (1977) *J. Mol. Biol.* 122, 155–182.

Hamer, D.H., Kaehler, M., and Leder, P. (1980) *Cell* 21, 697–708.

Hamer, D.H., and Leder, P. (1979) *Cell* 17, 737–747.

Hamer, D.H., and Walling, M.J. (1982) *J. Mol. Appl. Genet.* 1, 273–288.

Hardy, S.F., Grabowski, P.J., Padgett, R.A., and Sharp, P.A. (1984) *Nature* 308, 375–377.

Hartman, J.R., Nayak, D.P., and Fareed, G.C. (1982) *Proc. Natl. Acad. Sci. USA* 79, 233–237.

Hearing, P., and Shenk, T. (1983) *Cell* 33, 695–703.

Heilman, C.A., and Law, M.-F., Israel, M.A., and Howley, P.M. (1980) *J. Virol.* 36, 395–407.

Hen, R., Borrelli, E., Sassone-Corsi, P., and Chambon, P. (1983) *Nucleic Acids Res.* 11, 8747–8760.

Herbomel, P., Bourachot, B., and Yaniv, M. (1984) *Cell* 39, 653–662.

Hernandez, N., and Keller, W. (1983) *Cell* 35, 89–99.

Hiscott, J., Murphy, D., and Defendi, V. (1980) *Cell* 22, 535–543.

Hiscott, J., Murphy, D., and Defendi, V. (1981) *Proc. Natl. Acad. Sci. USA* 78, 1736–1740.

Horowitz, M., Cepko, C., and Sharp, P. (1982) in *Eukaryotic Viral Vectors* (Gluzman, Y., ed.) pp. 47–54, Cold Spring Harbor Laboratory, N.Y.

Hughes, S.H., Pavar, F., Spector, D., Schimke, R.T., Robinson, H.L., Payne, G.S., Bishop, J.M., and Varmus, H.E. (1979) *Cell* 18, 347–360.

Humphries, R.K., Ley, T., Turner, P., Moulton, A.D., and Nienhuis, A.W. (1982) *Cell* 30, 173–183.

Hwang, L.-H.S., and Gilboa, E. (1984) *J. Virol.* 50, 417–424.

Hynes, N., Van Ooyen, A.J.J., Kennedy, N., Herrlich, P., Ponta, H., and Groner, B. (1983) *Proc. Natl. Acad. Sci. USA* 80, 3637–3641.

Jacobs, K., Shoemaker, C., Rudersdorf, R., Neill, S.D., Kaufman, R.J., Mufson, A., Seehra, J., Jones, S.S., Hewick, R., Fritsch, E.F., Kawakita, M., Shimizv, T., and Miyaka, T. (1985) *Nature* 313, 806–810.

Jolly, D.J., Okayama, H., Berg, P., Esty, A.C., Filpula, D., Bohlen, P., Johnson, G.G., Shively, J.E., Hunkapillar, T., and Friedmann, T. (1983) *Proc. Natl. Acad. Sci. USA* 80, 477–481.

Kadesch, T.R., and Berg, P. (1983) in *Enhancers and Eukaryotic Gene Expression* (Gluzman, Y. and Shenk, T., eds.) pp. 21–27, Cold Spring Harbor Laboratory, N.Y.

Kanalas, J.J., and Suttle, D.P. (1984) *J. Biol. Chem.* 259, 1848–1853.

Karin, M., Haslinger, A., Holtgreve, H., Richards, R.I., Krauter, P., Westphal, H.M., and Beato, M. (1984) *Nature* 308, 513–519.

Katinka, M., Vasseur, M., Montreau, N., Yaniv, M., and Blangy, D. (1981) *Nature* 290, 720–722.

Kaufman, R.J. (1985) *Proc. Natl. Acad. Sci. USA* 82, 689–693.

Kaufman, R.J., and Sharp, P.A. (1982) *J. Mol. Biol.* 159, 601–621.

Kaufman, R.J., and Sharp, P.A., and Latt, S. (1983) *Mol. Cell. Biol.* 3, 699–711.

Kavathas, P., and Herzenberg, L.A. (1983) *Proc. Natl. Acad. Sci. USA* 80, 524–528.

Klobutcher, L.A., and Ruddle, F.H. (1980) *Nature* 280, 657–660.

Konarska, M.M., Padgett, R.A., and Sharp, P.A. (1984) *Cell* 38, 731–736.

Khoury, G., and Gruss, P. (1983) *Cell* 33, 313–314.

Kramer, A., Keller, W., Appel, B., and Luhrmann, R. (1984) *Cell* 38, 299–307.

Kriegler, M., and Botchan, M. (1983) *Mol. Cell Biol.* 3, 325–329.

Kuhn, L.C., Barbosa, J.A., Kamarck, M.E., and Ruddle, F.H. (1983) *Molec. Biol. Med.* 1, 335–352.

Kuhn, L.C., McClelland, A., and Ruddle, F.H. (1984) *Cell* 37, 95–103.

Kurtz, D.T. (1981) *Nature* 291, 629–631.

Laimins, L.A., Khoury, G., Gorman, C., Howard, B., and Gruss, P. (1982) *Proc. Natl. Acad. Sci. USA* 79, 6453–6457.

Law, M.-F., Lowy, D.R., Dvoretzky, I., and Howley, P.M. (1981) *Proc. Natl. Acad. Sci. USA* 78, 2727–2731.

Lebowitz, P., and Weissman, S.M. (1979) *Curr. Topics Microbiol. Immunol.* 87, 43–172.

Lee, F., Mulligan, R., Berg, P., and Ringold, G. (1981) *Nature* 294, 228–232.

Levinson, B., Khoury, G., Van de Woude, G., and Gruss, P. (1982) *Nature* 295, 568–572.

Lewis, W.H., and Srinivasan, P.R. (1983) *Mol. Cell. Biol.* 3, 1053–1061.

Littlefield, J.W. (1963) *Proc. Natl. Acad. Sci. USA* 50, 568–576.

Lowy, D.R., Dvoretzky, I., Shober, R., Law, M.-F., Engel, L., and Howley, P.M. (1980a) *Nature* 287, 72–74.

Lowy, I., Pellicer, A., Jackson, J.F., Sim, G.-K., Silverstein, S., and Axel, R. (1980b) *Cell* 22, 817–823.

Luciw, P.A., Bishop, J.M., Varmus, H.E., and Capecchi, M.R. (1983) *Cell* 33, 705–716.

Lusky, M., Berg, L., Weiher, H., and Botchan, M. (1983) *Mol. Cell. Biol.* 3, 1108–1122.

Lusky, M., and Botchan, M. (1981) *Nature* 293, 79–81.

Lusky, M., and Botchan, M.R. (1984) *Cell* 36, 391–401.

Maitland, M.J., and McDougall, J.K. (1977) *Cell* 11, 233–241.

Mann, R., Mulligan, R.C., and Baltimore, D. (1983) *Cell* 33, 153–159.

Mantei, N., and Weissmann, C. (1982) *Nature* 297, 128–132.

Mayo, K.E., Warren, R., and Palmiter, R.D. (1982) *Cell* 29, 99–108.

McConologue, L., and Coffino, P. (1983) *J. Biol. Chem.* 258, 12083–12086.

McCormick, F., Trahey, M., Innis, M., Dieckmann, B., and Ringold, G. (1984) *Mol. Cell. Biol.* 4, 166–172.

McCutchan, J.H., and Pagano, J.S. (1968) *J. Natl. Cancer Inst.* 41, 351–357.

Mellon, P., Parker, V., Gluzman, Y., and Maniatis, T. (1981) *Cell* 27, 279–288.

Mercola, M., Goverman, J., Mirell, C., and Calame, K. (1985) *Science* 227, 266–270.

Mercola, M., Wang, X.-F., Olsen, J., and Calame, K. (1983) *Science* 221, 663–665.

Miller, A.D., Jolly, D.J., Friedmann, T., and Verma, I.M. (1983) *Proc. Natl. Acad. Sci. USA* 80, 4709–4713.

Miller, A.D., Law, M.F., and Verma, I.M. (1985) *Mol. Cell. Biol.* 5, 431–437.

Miller, A.D., Ong, E.S., Rosenfeld, M.G., Verma, I.M., and Evans, R.M. (1984) *Science* 225, 993–998.

Mishoe, H., Brady, J.N., Radonovich, M., and Salzman, N.P. (1984) *Mol. Cell. Biol.* 4, 2911–2920.

Mitrani-Rosenbaum, S., Marteaux, L., Mory, Y., Revel, M., and Howley, P.M. (1983) *Mol. Cell. Biol.* 3, 233–240.

Moore, D.D., Marks, A.R., Buckley, D.I., Kapler, G., Payvar, F., and Goodman, H.M. (1985) *Proc. Natl. Acad. Sci. USA* 82, 699–702.

Moreau, P., Hen, R., Wasylyk, B., Everett, R., Gaub, M.P., and Chambon, P. (1981) *Nucleic Acids Res.* 9, 6047–6068.

Moriarty, A.M., Hoyer, B.H., Shih, J.W.-K., Gerin, J.L., and Hamer, D.H. (1981) *Proc. Natl. Acad. Sci. USA* 78, 2606–2610.

Mulligan, R.C., and Berg, P. (1980) *Science* 209, 1422–1429.

Mulligan, R.C., and Berg, P. (1981) *Proc. Natl. Acad. Sci. USA* 78, 2072–2076.

Mulligan, R.C., Howard, B.H., and Berg, P. (1979) *Nature* 227, 108–114.

Muzyczka, N. (1979) *Gene* 6, 107–122.

Myers, R.M., and Tjian, R. (1980) *Proc. Natl. Acad. Sci. USA* 77, 6491–6495.

Nelson, D.L., Weis, J.H., Przyborski, M.J., Mulligan, R.C., Seidman, J.G., and Housman, D.E. (1984) *J. Mol. Appl. Genet.* 2, 563–577.

Nevins, J.R. (1983) *Ann. Rev. Biochem.* 52, 441–466.

Neumann, E., Schaefer-Ridder, M., Wang, Y., and Hofschneider, P.H. (1982) *EMBO J.* 1, 841–845.

Nunberg, J.H., Kaufman, R.J., Chang, A.C.Y., Cohen, S.N., and Schimke (1980) *Cell* 19, 355–364.

O'Hare, K., Benoist, C., and Breathnach, R. (1981) *Proc. Natl. Acad. Sci. USA* 78, 1527–1531.

Okayama, H., and Berg, P. (1983) *Mol. Cell. Biol.* 3, 280–289.

Okayama, H., and Berg, P. (1985) *Mol. Cell. Biol.* 5, 1136–1142.

Ostrowski, M.C., Huang, A.L., Kessel, M., Wolford, R.G., and Hager, G.L. (1984) *EMBO J.* 3, 1891–1899.

Padgett, R.A., Konarska, M.M., Grabowski, P.J., Hardy, S.F., and Sharp, P.A. (1984) *Science* 225, 898–903.

Padgett, R.A., Mount, S.M., Steitz, J.A., and Sharp, P.A. (1983) *Cell* 35, 101–107.

Page, M.J., and Parker, M.G. (1983) *Cell* 32, 495–502.

Pavlakis, G.N., and Hamer, D.H. (1983) *Proc. Natl. Acad. Sci. USA* 80, 397–401.

Pellicer, A., Robins, D., Wold, B., Sweet, R., Jackson, J., Lowy, I., Roberts, J.M., Sim, G.K., Silverstein, S., and Axel, R. (1980) *Science* 209, 1414–1421.

Perkins, A.S., Kirschmeier, P.T., Gattoni-Celli, S., and Weinstein, I.B. (1983) *Mol. Cell. Biol.* 3, 1123–1132.

Perucho, M., Hanahan, D., and Wigler, M. (1980) *Cell* 22, 309–317.

Picard, D., and Schaffner, W. (1984) *Nature* 307, 80–82.

Proudfoot, N.J., and Brownlee, G.G. (1976) *Nature* 263, 211–214.

Queen, C., and Baltimore, D. (1983) *Cell* 33, 741–748.

Rassoulzadegan, M., Binetruy, B., and Cuzin, F. (1982) *Nature* 295, 257–259.

Richards, R.I., Heguy, A., and Karin, M. (1984) *Cell* 37, 263–272.

Rigby, P.W.J. (1982) in *Genetic Engineering 3* (Williamson, R., ed.) pp. 84–141, Academic Press, N.Y.

Rigby, P.W.J. (1983) *J. Gen. Virol.* 64, 255–266.

Ringold, G., Dieckmann, B., and Lee, F. (1981) *J. Mol. Appl. Genet.* 1, 165–175.

Rio, D.C., Clark, S.G., and Tjian, R. (1985) *Science* 227, 23–28.

Roberts, J.M., and Axel, R. (1982) *Cell* 29, 165–175.

Robins, D.M., Axel, R., and Henderson, A.S. (1981a) *J. Mol. Appl. Genet.* 1, 191–203.

Robins, D.M., Paek, I., Seeburg, P.H., and Axel, R. (1982) *Cell* 29, 623–631.

Robins, D.M., Ripley, S., Henderson, A.S., and Axel, R. (1981b) *Cell* 23, 29–39.

Rossana, C., Roa, L.G., and Johnson, L.F. (1982) *Mol. Cell. Biol.* 2, 1118–1125.

Ruskin, B., Krainer, A.R., Maniatis, T., and Green, M.R. (1984) *Cell* 38, 317–331.

Sarver, N., Gruss, P., Law, M.-F., Khoury, G., and Howley, P.M. (1981) *Mol. Cell. Biol.* 1, 486–496.

Sassone-Corsi, P., Dougherty, J.P., Wasylyk, B., and Chambon, P. (1984) *Proc. Natl. Acad. Sci. USA* 81, 308–312.

Sassone-Corsi, P., Wildeman, A., and Chambon, P. (1985) *Nature* 313, 458–463.

Scahill, S.J., Devos, R., Van der Heyden, J., and Fiers, W. (1983) *Proc. Natl. Acad. Sci. USA* 80, 4654–4658.

Scangos, G.A., Huttner, K.M., Juricek, D.K., and Ruddle, F.H. (1981) *Mol. Cell. Biol.* 1, 111–120.

Schaffner, W. (1980) *Proc. Natl. Acad. Sci. USA* 77, 2163–2167.

Schaffner, W., Topp, W., and Botchan, M. (1979) *Experimentia* 35, 977.

Scheidereit, C., Geisse, S., Westphal, H.M., and Beato, M. (1983) *Nature* 304, 749–752.

Schimke, R.T. (1984) *Cell* 37, 705–713.

Schimke, R.T., Brown, P.C., Kaufman, R.J., McGrogan, M., and Slate, D. (1981) *Symp. Quant. Biol.* 45, 785–797.

Schimke, R.T., Kaufman, R.J., Alt, F.W., and Kellems, R.E. (1978) *Science* 202, 1051–1055.

Schwartzberg, P., Colicelli, J., and Goff, S.P. (1984) *Cell* 37, 1043–1052.

Shimotohno, K., and Temin, H.M. (1981) *Cell* 26, 67–77.

Shoemaker, C., Goff, S., Gilboa, E., Paskind, M., Mitra, S.W., and Baltimore, D. (1980) *Proc. Natl. Acad. Sci. USA* 77, 3932–3936.

Siddiqui, A. (1983) *Mol. Cell. Biol.* 3, 143–146.

Simonsen, C.C., and Levinson, A.D. (1983) *Proc. Natl. Acad. Sci. USA* 80, 2495–2499.

Sompayrac, L.M., and Danna, K.J. (1981) *Proc. Natl. Acad. Sci. USA* 78, 7575–7578.

Sorge, J., and Hughes, J.H. (1982) *J. Mol. Appl. Genet.* 1, 547–559.

Sorge, J., Wright, D., Erdman, V.D., and Cutting, A.E. (1984) *Mol. Cell. Biol.* 4, 1730–1737.

Southern, P.J., and Berg, P. (1982) *J. Mol. Appl. Genet.* 1, 327–341.

Southern, P.J., Howard, B.H., and Berg, P. (1981) *J. Mol. Appl. Genet.* 1, 177–199.

Steinberg, B., Pollack, R., Topp, W., and Botchan, M. (1978) *Cell* 13, 19–32.

Stow, N.D., and Wilkie, N.M. (1976) *J. Gen. Virol.* 33, 447–458.

Subramani, S., and Berg, P. (1983) *Mol. Cell. Biol.* 3, 1040–1052.

Subramani, S., Mulligan, R., and Berg, P. (1981) *Mol. Cell. Biol.* 1, 854–864.

Sugden, B., Marsh, K., and Yates, J. (1985) *Mol. Cell. Biol.* 5, 410–413.

Sugden, B., Phelps, M., and Domoradzki, J. (1979) *J. Virol.* 31, 590–595.

Sveda, M.M., and Lai, C.J. (1981) *Proc. Natl. Acad. Sci. USA* 78, 5488–5492.

Tabin, C.J., Hoffmann, J.W., Goff, S.P., and Weinberg, R.A. (1982) *Mol. Cell. Biol.* 2, 426–436.

Thummel, C., Tjian, R., and Grodzicker, T. (1981) *Cell* 23, 825–836.

Tooze, J., ed. (1973) *The Molecular Biology of Tumor Viruses,* Cold Spring Harbor Laboratory, N.Y.

Tooze, J., ed. (1980) *DNA Tumor Viruses,* Cold Spring Harbor Laboratory, N.Y.

Topp, W.C. (1981) *Virology* 113, 408–411.

Tratschin, J.D., West, M.H.P., Sandbank, T., and Carter, B.J. (1984) *Mol. Cell. Biol.* 4, 2072–2081.

Tsui, L.-C., Breitman, M.L., Siminovich, L., and Buchwald, M. (1982) *Cell* 30, 499–508.

Tyndall, C., LaMantia, G., Thacker, C.M., Favaloro, J., and Kamen, R. (1981) *Nucleic Acids Res.* 9, 6231–6250.

Urlaub, G., and Chasin, L.A. (1980) *Proc. Natl. Acad. Sci. USA* 77, 4216–4220.

Vannice, J.L., Taylor, J.M., and Ringold, G.M. (1984) *Proc. Natl. Acad. Sci. USA* 81, 4241–4245.

Varmus, H.E. (1982) *Science* 216, 812–820.

Verma, I.M., Doehmer, J., Barinaga, M., Vale, W., Rosenfeld, M.G., and Evans, R. (1982) in *Eukaryotic Viral Vectors* (Gluzman, Y., ed.) pp. 159–164, Cold Spring Harbor Laboratory, N.Y.

Wahl, G.M., Padgett, R.A., and Stark, G.R. (1979) *J. Biol. Chem.* 254, 8679–8689.

Wallace, J.C., and Edmonds, M. (1983) *Proc. Natl. Acad. Sci. USA* 80, 950–954.

Wang, Y., Stratowa, C., Schaefer-Ridder, M., Doehmer, J., and Hofschneider, P.H. (1983) *Mol. Cell. Biol.* 3, 1032–1039.

Wasylyk, B., Wasylyk, C., Augereau, P., and Chambon, P. (1983a) *Cell* 32, 503–514.

Wasylyk, B., Wasylyk, C., and Chambon, P. (1984) *Nucleic Acids Res.* 12, 5589–5608.

Wasylyk, B., Wasylyk, C., Matthes, H., Wintzerith, M., and Chambon, P. (1983b) *EMBO J.* 2, 1605–1611.

Wei, C.-M., Gibson, M., Spear, P.G., and Scolnick, E.M. (1981) *J. Virol.* 39, 935–944.

Weiher, H., Konig, M., and Gruss, P. (1983) *Science* 219, 626–631.

Weinberg, R.A. (1980) *Annu. Rev. Biochem.* 49, 197–226.

Weiss, R., Teich, N., Varmus, H., and Coffin, H., eds. (1982) *RNA Tumor Viruses,* Cold Spring Harbor Laboratory, N.Y.

Wieringa, B., Hofer, E., and Weissmann, C. (1984) *Cell* 37, 915–925.

Wigler, M., Perucho, M., Kurtz, D., Dana, S., Pellicer, A., Axel, R., and Silverstein, S. (1980) *Proc. Natl. Acad. Sci. USA* 77, 3567–3570.

Wigler, M., Silverstein, S., Lee, L., Pellicer, A., Cheng, Y., and Axel, R. (1977) *Cell* 11, 223–232.

Wigler, M., Sweet, R., Sim, G.K., Wold, B., Pellicer, A., Lacy, E., Maniatis, T., Silverstein, S., and Axel, R. (1979) *Cell* 16, 777–785.

Wildeman, A.G., Sassone-Corsi, P., Grundstrom, T., Zenke, M., and Chambon, P. (1984) *EMBO J.* 3, 3129–3133.

Wold, B., Wigler, M., Lacy, E., Maniatis, T., Silverstein, S., and Axel, R. (1979) *Proc. Natl. Acad. Sci. USA* 76, 5684–5688.

Yamaizumi, M., Horwich, A.L., and Ruddle, F.H. (1983) *Mol. Cell. Biol.* 3, 511–522.

Yaniv, M. (1982) *Nature* 297, 17–18.

Yates, J.L., Warren, N., and Sugden, B. (1985) *Nature* 313, 812–815.

Yeung, C.Y., Ingolia, D.E., Bobonis, C., Dunbar, B.S., Riser, M.E., Siciliano, M.J., and Kellems, R.E. (1983) *J. Biol. Chem.* 258, 8338–8345.

Young, A.P., and Ringold, G.M. (1983) *J. Biol. Chem.* 258, 11260–11266.

Zeitlin, S., and Efstratiadis, A. (1984) *Cell* 39, 589–602.

Zinn, K., Mellon, P., Ptashne, M., and Maniatis, T. (1982) *Proc. Natl. Acad. Sci. USA* 79, 4897–4901.

================= CHAPTER =================
3

Macromolecular Processing
Marsha Rich Rosner

3.1 INTRODUCTION: PROCESSING OF PROTEINS AND THEIR FATES IN MAMMALIAN CELLS

In this chapter, the steps of mRNA translation into protein and the processing of proteins to their final in vivo state are examined. Several issues relating to the introduction of genes into mammalian cells were addressed in Chapter 2, particularly the problem of maximizing the number of mRNA molecules per cell that correspond to a gene of interest. From this perspective, the subsequent steps of protein synthesis, protein processing, and protein secretion were not considered to be rate-limiting. However, if a cell can be engineered to make increasingly larger amounts of mRNA for a specific protein, then a situation may arise in which any of the subsequent processing steps is saturated. Further, it is possible that variations in the response to protein-processing signals by different mammalian cells could alter subsequent expression and secretion of a viable protein from the mRNA introduced. When these problems occur, it becomes necessary to create either genetic or environmental conditions to overcome the processing step that is rate-limiting.

Protein synthesis in mammalian cells occurs in a series of discrete, sequential steps. Initially, a complex is formed between messenger RNA, ribosomes, initiation factors, and the initiator methionyl-tRNA. Subsequent elongation with new aminoacyl tRNAs and termination at a prespecified site lead to the polymerization of amino acids to form a unique protein. In eukaryotic cells, the protein synthetic machinery is compartmentalized on the basis of the function or ultimate destination of the proteins to be synthesized. Thus, cellular cytoplasmic proteins are synthesized on non–membrane-bound ribosomes. These classes of proteins include enzymes such as nucleic acid polymerases and the enzymes of the glycolytic pathway. Secreted proteins, lysosomal proteins, and proteins that are inserted into the plasma membrane are synthesized exclusively on membrane-bound ribosomes (Palade, 1955; Lodish et al., 1981; Sabatini et al., 1982).

During and following this process of translation, newly synthesized proteins may undergo further changes prior to arrival of the protein at its final destination. These modifications, which range from removal of the first amino acid, methionine, to chemical derivatization and alteration of the entire three-dimensional structure, are termed processing. Many of these changes require transport to a particular compartment containing the relevant processing enzymes. Interference with an early processing step may prevent all subsequent processing steps and dramatically alter either the native state or the final location of the protein.

Proteins that require membrane association during synthesis undergo the most extensive degree of macromolecular processing and thus pose the most challenges for genetic engineers. In the following sections, we discuss the different stages of protein synthesis and related modifications that proteins can undergo, with emphasis upon membrane-bound systems. Although little is known about the recognition signals involved in determining discrete processing steps or directing protein transport, it is clear that the process is highly controlled and well coordinated. The limited information available indicates that amino acid sequence, three-dimensional structure, and the nature of the particular cell type all contribute to the type of processing that occurs. To illustrate these points, we focus on selected examples with particular emphasis on the processing of glycosylated polypeptides, which comprise one of the most abundant classes of derivatized proteins.

3.2 PROTEIN PROCESSING: GENERAL FEATURES AND SPECIFIC EXAMPLES

3.2.1 General Features

During and following protein translation, polypeptides can undergo a number of different modification or compartmentalization steps. At least four different types of protein processing have been identified. Amino acids, peptides, and proteins can all undergo chemical derivatization of their accessible functional groups (reviewed in Wold, 1981). These sites include free amino termini, free carboxyl termini, and the side chains of individual amino acids. Another major form of processing involves proteolytic cleavage of either the nascent polypeptide or the complete protein following synthesis. A third processing step is the assembly of the three-dimensional structure of proteins via chain or subunit association. The factors that govern protein folding have been extensively reviewed and will not be discussed here (see Jaenicke, 1980; Ghelis and Yon, 1982; Kim and Baldwin, 1982). Finally, the transportation of a protein to a site for further modification or to the final destination may be considered a fourth type of cellular processing.

Protein processing can occur at several stages during protein synthesis. Translation of both cytoplasmic and membrane proteins is initiated on mRNA in the cytoplasm. Subsequent association of the synthetic machinery of secretory and membrane proteins with the membrane of the endoplasmic reticulum takes place via an interaction with specific amino acids of the nascent polypeptide chain. Following translocation of the nascent chain across the membrane, processing such as proteolytic cleavage and glycosylation can occur. Upon completion of polypeptide synthesis, the proteins are then transported to the Golgi apparatus for further processing and packaging prior to arrival at the final destination.

3.2.2 Chemical Derivatization

Although there are a wide variety of different chemical derivatives of proteins or amino acids, most of the enzymatically catalyzed modifications fall into a few general categories (see Wold, 1981). Oligosaccharides linked to the amino acids serine, threonine, or asparagine comprise the largest group of protein derivatives. Phosphorylation, which plays an important role in cellular regulatory processes, can occur through a number of linkages: monoesters of serine, threonine, or tyrosine residues; phosphoramides of arginine, histidine, or lysine residues; or phosphodiesters of serine and threonine residues. Stable N-methylated derivatives of arginine, histidine, lysine, glutamine, and free alpha-amino groups have been noted as well as putative O-methyl esters of serine and threonine. Proteins can also be acylated through alpha and epsilon amino groups or serine and threonine esters. Other chemical modifications, in addition to derivatized amino acids such as hydroxyproline, include ADP-ribosylations, halogenations, and a number of nonenzymatic reactions. Glycosylation and acylation, two modifications characteristic of proteins synthesized on membrane-bound ribosomes, are discussed in more detail in the following sections.

3.2.2.1 Glycosylation. Glycosylation, one of the major modifications that polypeptides can undergo following synthesis, involves the attachment of sugars or oligosaccharide chains to the protein. There are two basic types of oligosaccharide linkages to proteins: O-glycosidic and N-glycosidic linkages.

The O-linked oligosaccharides are attached to polypeptide chains via glycosidic linkages to the hydroxyl groups of serine, threonine, hydroxylysine, or hydroxyproline. Many glycoproteins, such as the submaxillary mucins (Carlson, 1968; Baig and Aminoff, 1972; Lombard and Winzler, 1974; Oates et al., 1974) contain a serine and/or threonine linkage to N-acetylgalactosamine. Other examples of glycoproteins with this linkage include the blood group substances (Feizi et al., 1971; Watkins, 1972), fetuin (Baenziger and Kornfeld, 1974) and human IgA (Spiro and Bhoyroo, 1974). Oligosaccharides with linkages between serine and mannose are found commonly in yeasts and fungi (Nakajima and Ballou, 1974; Raizada et al., 1975); other sugars linked to serine or threonine, such as fucose (Hallgren et al., 1975), have also been detected in various species. O-glycosidic linkages between galactose and hydroxylysine are characteristic of collagens and basement-membrane glycopeptides (Butler and Cunningham, 1966; Spiro, 1967). Plants have an analogous set of structural proteins that contain arabinose-hydroxyproline linkages. Finally, the proteoglycans, which are connective tissue polysaccharides linked to a small protein core, contain a unique O-glycosidic linkage between D-xylose and serine as well as the more common N-acetylgalactosamine bond to serine or threonine. The proteoglycans, which include heparin, chondroitin-sulfate, and dermatan sulfate, are differentiated from glycoproteins by the presence of repeating disaccharide units containing a hexosamine residue as well as uronic acid and ester sulfate groups (reviewed in Roden, 1980; Hascall, 1981). In general, the O-glycosidic oligosaccharides are more antigenic than the N-glycosidic sugars and not as highly conserved.

Biosynthesis of the O-glycosidic oligosaccharides in both glycoproteins and proteoglycans occurs via single sugar addition onto a protein core from a nucleotide sugar precursor. Nucleotide sugars are the source of all mammalian complex carbohydrates. The actual chain elongation process and termination process appear to be governed by a number of factors, including the substrate specificities of the glycosyltransferases involved (Schachter and Roseman, 1980) as well as the effective compartmentalization of the synthetic apparatus.

The N-linked oligosaccharides are linked to polypeptide chains through an N-glycosidic bond between an N-acetylglucosamine residue and the amido nitrogen of an asparagine residue on the protein (reviewed in Kornfeld and Kornfeld, 1980; Hubbard and Ivatt, 1981). Many different types of glycoproteins, including lysosomal enzymes, membrane proteins, viral-envelope proteins, nonenzymatic secretory proteins, and immunoglobulins, contain N-linked oligosaccharides. Keratin sulfate proteoglycans are also similarly derivatized (reviewed in Hascall, 1981).

The asparagine-linked oligosaccharide chains in mammals fall broadly into two classes, high-mannose and complex types. With a few exceptions, both carbohydrate chains are composed of a pentasaccharide core consisting of three branched mannose residues sequentially linked to two N-acetylglucosamine residues that are attached to protein through an amide linkage to asparagine. The high-mannose types contain up to an additional six mannose residues; the complex types are further derivatized with a number of sugars, including N-acetylglucosamine, galactose, sialic acid, and fucose (Kornfeld and Kornfeld, 1980). Yeast glycoproteins have a similar mannose-chitobiose core, but may contain over 100 additional alpha-mannose residues (Nakajima and Ballou, 1974).

3.2.2.2 Fatty acylation. A number of membrane proteins are derivatized with long-chain fatty acids, including the acetylcholine and transferrin receptors, the Ca^{2+}-dependent ATPase of the sarcoplasmic reticulum, viral-envelope glycoproteins, viral oncogene products, and numerous other proteolipids that have been detected in the membranes of tissue culture cells (reviewed in Omary and Trowbridge, 1981; Schlesinger, 1981; Olson et al., 1984). Acylated viral glycoproteins were first detected in studies on the two glycoproteins E1 and E2 from the small-enveloped Sindbis virus (Schmidt et al., 1979). Analytical studies based upon chemical and radioactive detection revealed that palmitic acid was attached to a serine residue in that portion of the glycoprotein embedded within the membrane bilayer. In E1, the fatty acids were present at 1–2 moles per mole of protein; E2 contained approximately one-third of that amount. Thus, the proportion of protein-bound fatty acids in the membrane of virally infected cells due to viral glycoproteins can be 3–6%, a significant fraction. Similar fatty acid derivatives have been found in a number of other viral-envelope glycoproteins, including G protein of VSV, HA of influenza and Newcastle disease viruses, p15E of murine leukemia virus, and the glycoprotein of Coronavirus (Schlesinger, 1981). The attachment of the palmitic acid residues appears to be via alkali-labile bonds at internal amino acids such as cysteine and serine within the lipid bilayer (*c.f.* Willumsen et al., 1984).

Several proteins that contain a myristic acid residue at or near the amino terminus have also been identified. These include the viral transforming protein pp60[src] (Buss and Sefton, 1984; Cross et al., 1984), the inner core structural protein p15[gag] of mammalian retroviruses (Henderson et al., 1983), the protein phosphatase calcineurin B (Aitken et al., 1982), and the catalytic subunit of cAMP-dependent ATPase of bovine cardiac muscle (Carr et al., 1982). A number of gag-onc fusion proteins of transforming viruses that have been identified as oncogene products are also myristylated (Schultz and Oroszlan, 1984). In contrast to palmitic acid, the myristic acid residue appears to be attached to the NH_2-terminal glycine residue, presumably after cleavage of the initial methionine group.

The actual time and location of addition of these fatty acids vary with the type of fatty acid added. For several viral glycoproteins such as VSV G protein, palmitic acid addition has been shown to occur at a discrete step during posttranslational processing in the Golgi apparatus, about 15 minutes after completion of the polypeptide chain synthesis (*c.f.* Schmidt and Schlessinger, 1980). Furthermore, palmitylation appears to be an unstable modification subject to removal and replacement prior to degradation of the protein (Omary and Trowbridge, 1981). In contrast, myristylation occurs more rapidly, possibly during protein synthesis, and is metabolically stable (Buss et al., 1984).

The precise signals that specify fatty acid addition remain to be determined. Fusion of the DNA sequence coding for the N-terminal 14 amino acids of p60[src] to the *fps* gene of the F36 Fujinami sarcoma virus resulted in both myristylation and membrane localization of the fused gene product in contrast to the nonfused fps proteins (Pellman et al., 1985). Thus, a small recognition sequence is sufficient for myristylation.

3.2.3 Proteolytic Cleavage

Processing of proteins by proteolytic cleavage occurs as a series of distinct steps either during nascent protein synthesis or at a later stage prior to final protein assembly (reviewed in Wold, 1981). Initially, soon after protein synthesis has begun, the amino terminal methionine is removed in many proteins. Following translocation of nascent chains across the endoplasmic reticulum membrane, proteins such as those that will be secreted from the cell lose their amino terminal residues or "signal sequences" responsible for the translocating process. Many proteins are synthesized in an inactive or precursor form and require proteolytic cleavage after release of the completed polypeptide chain from the ribosome to become active. Examples include the conversion of many prohormones to hormones, complement activation, blood coagulation, and the assembly of macromolecular structures such as viruses (reviewed in Hershko and Fry, 1975; Krieger and Ganong, 1977; Jackson and Nemerson, 1980; Reid and Porter, 1981). Certain proteins, such as adrenocorticotropic hormone (ACTH), are derived by selective proteolytic cleavages of precursor proteins that actually encode more than one protein. Multiple products can be generated by simultaneous cleavages, or unique single products can be generated by cleavages at different sites.

A good illustration of the role of proteolytic cleavage in the processing of proteins is the biosynthesis of insulin, a secreted peptide hormone (Chan et al., 1979). Soon after the initiation of protein synthesis, the polysomes become membrane-associated and the amino terminal methionine of the nascent polypeptide chain is removed. Following translocation of the nascent chain across the endoplasmic reticulum membrane, the signal sequence is cleaved, converting the preproinsulin molecule into the proinsulin precursor form. Once the completed proinsulin molecule has been released from the protein-synthesizing machinery, the protein is transported from the endoplasmic reticulum to the Golgi apparatus where protein folding occurs and stabilizing disulfide bridges are formed. As a final step in the pancreatic cell, the proinsulin molecule is packaged in secretory granules and transported to the plasma membrane for release into the exterior of the cell. During this time, an inactive propeptide of 35 amino acids is removed from the interior of the molecule, yielding the fully processed insulin composed of two distinct polypeptide subunits.

Proteolytic processing of proteins largely depends upon the cell type. For instance, insulin is normally synthesized in a specialized secretory cell. Processing of the insulin gene to yield proinsulin, but not insulin, as a final product has been demonstrated in several nonsecretory cell types such as mouse fibroblasts (Lomedico, 1982; Laub and Rutter, 1983). However, Kelly and co-workers were able to demonstrate selective proteolytic cleavage of the proinsulin precursor to a protein the size of insulin in a secretory adrenal cell type that normally synthesizes fully processed adrenocorticotropin hormone (Moore et al., 1983). Thus, by the judicious choice of appropriate cell types, it should be possible for the genetic engineer to utilize the full spectrum of proteolytic enzymes required for the complete processing of complex proteins.

3.3 PROCESSING DURING NASCENT PROTEIN SYNTHESIS

3.3.1 Membrane Association of Polypeptides during Protein Synthesis

Early studies by Palade and co-workers pointed out that the ribosomes in eukaryotic cells were present in both a free cytoplasmic and a membrane-bound form (Palade, 1955). Later investigations suggested that cytoplasmic proteins were synthesized predominantly on cytoplasmic ribosomes, whereas secretory proteins were synthesized in the rough endoplasmic reticulum (Siekevitz and Palade, 1960; Hicks et al., 1969). These observations led to the idea that secretory proteins cross the endoplasmic reticulum membrane before completion of protein synthesis—"cotranslational" translocation of nascent polypeptide chains across the membrane (Redman and Sabatini, 1966). This process has now been demonstrated for secretory proteins as well as a number of other cellular proteins, including proteins localized in the endoplasmic reticulum or Golgi apparatus, lysosomal enzymes, and integral membrane proteins.

Numerous biochemical studies of membrane and secretory proteins have outlined the basic steps of processing involved in synthesis and transport of these proteins to the membrane (reviewed in Sabatini et al., 1982; Walter et al., 1984). Localized initially on the rough endoplasmic reticulum during de novo synthesis, proteins such as the G protein of vesicular stomatitis virus (VSV) are inserted into the membrane as nascent chains (Morrison and Lodish, 1975; Rothman and Lodish, 1977; Toneguzzo and Ghosh, 1978). For most of the proteins studied to date, the process of membrane association and subsequent translocation is mediated via specific protein-encoded sequences (the signal sequence) and signal recognition particles, which act as "adapters" between the cytoplasmic and membrane-bound protein-synthesizing machinery (Stoffel et al., 1981; Walter et al., 1981; Meyer et al., 1982a, 1982b; Walter and Blobel, 1983).

Signal recognition particles, composed of six different polypeptides and a small 7S RNA from the cytoplasm, recognize specific amino acid sequences on the nascent chains of secretory, lysosomal, and certain integral membrane proteins, resulting in a tight association with the ribosomes of the protein-translating complex in the cytoplasm (Anderson et al., 1982; Walter and Blobel, 1983). This interaction causes site-specific arrest of the protein elongation process. Elongation and synthesis are resumed following displacement of the signal recognition particles by a receptor that is integrally located within the endoplasmic reticulum membrane (Gilmore et al., 1982a, 1982b; Meyer et al., 1982a, 1982b; Gilmore and Blobel, 1983). Upon resumption of synthesis, the nascent chain is now translocated across the membrane into the lumen of the endoplasmic reticulum (Blobel and Dobberstein, 1975a, 1975b). Subsequently, the hydrophobic signal sequence may be cleaved off from the amino terminus of the elongating polypeptide chain (Rose, 1977; Lingappa et al., 1978; Irving et al., 1979). For integral membrane proteins that span the membrane, a specific stop sequence blocks further translocation of the nascent peptide across the membrane (Sabatini et al., 1982). These halt signals usually consist of a hydrophobic region adjacent to highly charged amino acids near the carboxy-terminal end.

To date, a large number of secretory and membrane proteins containing a signal sequence have been identified. These include serum proteins such as mouse immunoglobulin and serum albumin, hormones such as human proinsulin and growth hormone, egg proteins such as lysozyme, and other proteins such as interferon (reviewed in Kreil, 1981). Analyses of the actual amino acid sequences of these different polypeptide signals reveal little evolutionary relationship or regions of great conservation beyond a stretch of nine hydrophobic amino acids in the middle of the sequence. Most signal sequences have a positively charged residue close to the N-terminus as well as near the beginning of the hydrophobic core (von Heijne, 1984). Further, the amino acid residue just before the signal peptidase cleavage site, which usually has a small side chain, also appears to be highly conserved. The signal sequences differ in size, ranging from about 15 amino acids to over 60 amino acids in length. However, many signal peptides are composed of approximately 40 amino acids, a length just sufficient for the nascent chain to span the ribosome (Scheele et al., 1980). Studies with chimeric signal recognition particles derived from mammalian, amphibian, and insect sources have demonstrated that these particles as well as the actual translocation process have been highly conserved during evolution (Walter and Blobel, 1983).

There are a number of exceptions to this scenario. Membrane proteins with multiple domains such as the calcium-dependent ATPase have been reported to utilize the signal recognition particle but not to undergo elongation arrest (Anderson et al., 1983). Further, there are proteins that contain an internal signal sequence rather than the more common N-terminal amino acid signal (Braell and Lodish, 1982). Finally, proteins such as cytochrome b5 that are synthesized on free ribosomes become membrane-associated posttranslationally through a mechanism that does not depend upon the signal recognition particle (Anderson et al., 1983). In the latter case specific hydrophobic amino acid residues near the carboxy terminus of the protein may initiate transfer. Thus, certain proteins presumably contain an "insertion" sequence that mediates membrane transfer through a receptor-independent mechanism that may be nonselective.

3.3.2 Glycosylation following Peptide Translocation

3.3.2.1 Oligosaccharide transfer. During synthesis on membrane-bound ribosomes, the nascent chain can be glycosylated at N-asparagine residues via lipid-linked precursors on the lumen (noncytoplasmic) side of the endoplasmic reticulum membrane (Katz et al., 1977; Hanover and Lennarz, 1980; Snider and Robbins, 1982). Biosynthesis of N-linked oligosaccharides to glycoproteins in mammals occurs through a discrete series of steps. Initially, the complete high-mannose chain is assembled from nucleotide sugar precursors onto a lipid carrier, dolichyl phosphate, to form the Glc3Man9GlcNAc2-pyrophosphoryldolichol precursor. This oligosaccharide precursor has been identified in a number of cell types from different species, including Chinese hamster ovary cells (Li et al., 1978), chick embryo and hamster fibroblasts (Hubbard and Robbins, 1979, 1980), and yeast (Lehle et al., 1980; Trimble et al., 1980a, 1980b). Recent studies by Hsieh and Robbins (1984) have suggested that a similar precursor is also present in insect cells. The only presently known exception to this precursor structure in eukaryotes is in *Trypannosome cruzi*, which synthesize and transfer the nonglucosylated analogue (Parodi and Quesada-Allue, 1982). Both in vivo and in vitro evidence from a variety of vertebrate systems indicates that transfer of the oligosaccharide precursor occurs by en bloc addition of Glc3Man9GlcNAc2 to asparagine residues (reviewed in Hubbard and Ivatt, 1981). As noted, glycosylation generally occurs cotranslationally during synthesis of the polypeptide chain, although some evidence for posttranslational glycosylation has been obtained (Marshall, 1974, Jamieson, 1977; Bergman and Kuehl, 1978).

3.3.2.2 Determinants of glycosylation: amino acid sequence and three-dimensional protein structure. Although the precise signals that specify whether a particular protein site gets N-glycosylated and the manner in which it is processed are not presently known, several of the critical factors have been identified. Proteins are always glycosylated at asparagine residues embedded within a asp-X-ser/thr sequence, where X can be any of the 20 amino acids with the possible exception of proline and asparagine (Eylar, 1966; Marshall, 1974). Only about one-third of the known tripeptides with this particular sequence get glycosylated, however (Struck and Lennarz, 1980). For example, some protein sites containing this sequence have never been glycosylated; other sites, such as one sequence in bovine pancreatic ribonuclease, exist in both a glycosylated (RNase B) and unglycosylated (RNase A) form. Thus, the fidelity of glycosylation is not 100% at sites that are normally glycosylated. These rules apply to other forms of chemical derivatization as well; although only certain amino acid residues can be modified, not all such residues are modified in a single protein.

The factors that regulate initial glycosylation at a molecular level are not known; however, many parameters such as rate of translation, glycosyl transfer, and posttranslational folding all may play a role. For some proteins disruption of tertiary structure may be sufficient to allow glycosylation. In vitro studies on 13 reduced and derivatized proteins including ovalbumin, DNase, and elastase, showed that six of the proteins could be glycosylated after denaturation whereas none of the 13 proteins in its native state was an effective acceptor. The remaining seven proteins could not be glycosylated regardless of the extent of denaturation (Kronquist and Lennarz, 1978). However, further peptide fragmentation of at least three of these seven proteins allowed subsequent glycosylation to occur, suggesting that the acceptor tripeptide sequence is not only necessary but also is sufficient for glycosylation; neighboring sequences appear to inhibit the process when the protein is in its native state. Further evidence for the ability of the tripeptide sequence to act as substrate comes from studies of smaller peptide fragments (Struck et al., 1978) and synthetic peptides, indicating that the tripeptide is sufficient if the amino terminus of the asparagine residue is blocked by an acetyl group and the carboxy terminus blocked by formation of an amide (Hart et al., 1979). These studies suggest that accessibility of the sequence is a major, if not the primary, factor in determining whether a site becomes glycosylated. It has been proposed on the basis of predicted amino acid structures that the glycosylation sites are located preferentially at beta-turns or loops within the protein (Beeley, 1977; Aubert et al., 1976). According to this model, secondary and tertiary structures would ultimately be the main factors in determining whether a potential glycosylation site specified by the primary sequence in fact becomes glycosylated.

3.4 TRANSPORT TO AND PROCESSING IN THE GOLGI APPARATUS

3.4.1 Transport to the Golgi

Following synthesis in the endoplasmic reticulum, the polypeptide chains are transported to the Golgi apparatus where further processing and sorting for different intracellular compartments such as the plasma membrane, lysosomes, and secretion granules occurs (Bergmann et al., 1981). Certain lines of evidence suggest that the translocation to the plasma membrane may be mediated via clathrin-coated vesicles that bud from one membrane and fuse to another (Rothman and Fine, 1980). The Golgi apparatus is a complicated array of submembranous vesicles that appear to have a clear directionality in terms of site of protein entry, location of discrete processing enzymes, and site of packaging or targeting for secretion, lysosomal entry, or membrane insertion (Rothman, 1981). Membrane and secretory proteins transported from the endoplasmic reticulum enter the cis face of the Golgi stack and exit from the trans side (Farquhar and Palade, 1981; Bergmann and Singer, 1983; Saraste and Hedman, 1983).

3.4.2 Compartmentation and Processing in the Golgi

At least three distinct Golgi compartments with discrete functions have been identified on the basis of histochemical and biochemical studies: cis, medial (central), and trans cisternae (Smith, 1980; Griffiths et al., 1983; Tartakoff and Vassalli, 1983). The locations of different glycosylation-processing enzymes have been used to differentiate between the three compartments of the Golgi apparatus. During passage through the Golgi, the neutral "high-mannose" oligosaccharide structures at asparagine sites (N-linked) are often modified to the more branched, often acidic "complex" oligosaccharide chains; further oligosaccharide addition at serine or threonine residues (O-linked) may take place as well at this point. Other processing steps such as polypeptide cleavage, sulfation, phosphorylation, and addition of fatty acids (Rothman, 1981) can also occur between passage through the Golgi and subsequent arrival at the final destination. The elaborate cisternae of the Golgi seem particularly appropriate for accomplishing at least part of the formidable task of modifying and sorting the multitudinous proteins in the cell.

3.4.3 Processing of Glycosylated Proteins

3.4.3.1 Oligosaccharide processing steps. Oligosaccharide processing begins very rapidly following transfer of the polysaccharide precursor to protein. The half-time for removal of the first glucose residue is approximately two minutes in chick embryo fibroblasts (Hubbard and Robbins, 1979), that for the second glucose is about five minutes, and removal of the third glucose is even slower. Similar studies have shown rapid removal of the glucose residues in a variety of cultured cells (Kornfeld et al., 1978; Hunt, 1979, 1980) and yeast (Parodi, 1979). At least two enzymes are responsible for removal of the glucose residues (reviewed in Hubbard and Ivatt, 1981), presumably in the endoplasmic reticulum. Until ten minutes after transfer in chick embryo fibroblasts, the predominant species is the Man9-containing oligosaccharide, which may be left intact or processed further. Removal of one to four mannose residues by the early mannosidases IA and IB is the next step in processing, presumed to occur in the Golgi apparatus and thus accounting for the time lag. After addition of an N-acetylglucosamine residue by the Golgi enzyme N-acetylglucosaminyl transferase I (Narasimhan et al., 1977; Tabas and Kornfeld, 1978; Harpaz and Schachter, 1980), the remaining two alpha-linked mannose residues may be cleaved by a third Golgi enzyme, alpha-mannosidase II. Although the oligosaccharide products of these enzymes generally do not accumulate due to the rapidity of the hydrolytic steps, these intermediates are the major oligosaccharide species in certain glycoproteins such as rhodopsin (Fukuda et al., 1979; Liang et al., 1979).

In the final Golgi processing step, the core pentasaccharide unit may be extended by the sequential addition of N-acetylglucosamine, galactose, and sialic acid by at least three glycosyl transferases (reviewed in Schachter and Roseman, 1980). Fucose is probably added in an alpha-1,6 linkage to the N-acetlyglucosamine residues proximal to the asparagine residue at this stage as well (Wilson et al., 1976). The resultant oligosaccharides, depending upon the extent of processing, may contain both high-mannose and complex-type branches (hybrid structures), two complex-type branches (biantennary), or three complex-type branches (triantennary) as an extension of the basic trimannose core. Recent studies suggest that the addition of N-acetylglucosamine occurs in the medial cisternae, thus determining the branching pattern of the complex-type oligosaccharides, whereas final capping of the branched oligosaccharides with galactose and sialic acid would take place in the trans region (Roth and Berger, 1982; Dunphy et al., 1985).

3.4.3.2 Determinants of oligosaccharide processing. The nature of the processing steps following oligosaccharide transfer to protein, although largely dependent upon the particular processing enzymes within a given cell type, also reflects the local sequence and structure at a particular glycosylation site. Studies of strain-related viral glycoproteins glycosylated within the same host cells indicate that primary amino acid sequence is an important factor in the final processing regimen (Rosner et al., 1980a; Schwarz and Klenk, 1981; Hunt et al., 1983). The incorporation of amino acid analogues into plasmacytoma kappa light chain results in altered oligosaccharide composition (Green, 1982). Evidence based upon HPLC analysis of glycopeptides at individual glycosylation sites in Sindbis viral glycoproteins (Rosner and Robbins, 1982; Hsieh et al., 1983a) suggests that certain glycosylation sites are preferentially either high-mannose or complex-type independent of the particular host cell, whereas other sites exhibit host-cell dependence. Studies involving degradation of viral, lysosomal, and yeast glycoproteins by glycosidases suggest that high-mannose sites may be less processed because of lack of accessibility to the processing enzymes (Howard et al., 1982; Natowicz et al., 1982; Hsieh et al., 1983b; Trimble et al., 1983). Crystallographic studies of both viral-envelope glycoproteins and immunoglobulins generally support this interpretation (Wilson et al., 1981).

Other factors beside local steric accessibility presumably also play a role. In particular, specific structure recognition by certain processing enzymes such as the lysosomal enzyme GlcNAc-1-PO4 transferase (Reitman and Kornfeld, 1981) acts as a mechanism for specific intracellular targeting. Atkinson and co-workers have proposed that the length of exposure of oligosaccharide chains to enzymes decreases as the carboxy terminus is approached (Pollack and Atkinson, 1983). However, other mechanisms could explain the observation that complex sites appear to be preferentially clustered at the amino terminus of glycoproteins and the high mannose at the carboxy terminus (Pollack and Atkinson, 1983).

Finally, the nature of the host cell plays an important role in processing due to differences in enzyme levels, specific activity, substrate specificities, and rates of intracellular transport. Host-dependent variations in oligosaccharide structure have been observed for a number of glycoproteins from viruses grown in different host cells, among them VSV G protein (Etchison and Holland, 1974), influenza virus hemagglutinin (Klenk et al., 1978; Nakamura and Compans, 1979), and E1 and E2 from Sindbis (Burke and Keegstra, 1976; 1979). The increase in sialic acid content characteristic of glycoproteins from transformed cells (reviewed in Atkinson and Hakimi, 1980), and the unusual sulfated oligosaccharides found primarily in embryonic tissues (Heifetz and Lennarz, 1979) suggest that the developmental or growth state of the cell may also regulate the nature and extent of oligosaccharide processing. Although the actual steps involved in oligosaccharide processing in eukaryotes and yeast are well established, much remains to be learned about the factors that actually regulate these processes.

3.5 SEGREGATION OF PROTEINS AND RATE OF TRANSPORT TO FINAL DESTINATION

One of the major problems in protein biosynthesis is deciphering the signals that direct proteins to different compartments within and outside the cell. With the exception of certain mitochondrial and chloroplast proteins, translation of protein mRNA occurs in the cytoplasm of the cell. Thus, the cell must devise regulatory signals for targeting newly synthesized proteins to their final destinations. At present, such signals have been classified into groups based on the nature of the macromolecular processing that will take place, since there appear to be multiple pathways for targeting proteins to a particular compartment.

A large variety of cellular proteins, including secretory, integral membrane, mitochondrial, nuclear, and lysosomal proteins, contain cellular targeting signals (reviewed in Kreil, 1981). Perhaps the best characterized of the peptide signal sequences are those that direct the vectorial transport of nascent polypeptide chains across the endoplasmic reticulum membrane (see section 2.3). Synthesis of intracellular proteins on cytoplasmic ribosomes and posttranslational translocation across the membranes of organelles such as chloroplasts and mitochondria have also been described. For example, a transit peptide of 5–6,000 M^r from the small subunit of ribulose 1,5-bis-phosphate carboxylase was fused to a cytoplasmic bacterial protein and shown to direct the foreign protein to chloroplasts posttranslationally (Van den Broeck et al., 1985). Short peptide targeting sequences have also been identified that can direct mitochondrial and nuclear proteins to subcellular locations (Schatz and Butow, 1983; Hall et al., 1984; Kalderon et al., 1984).

The assumption that there is only one signal region on the protein directing recognition is too simplistic in most cases. For instance, oligomer formation and protein-ligand interactions can also regulate the intracellular transport of many secretory and integral membrane proteins in mammalian cells (*c.f.* Mains and Sibley, 1983). Studies with bacterial fusion proteins have revealed more than one region that regulates the process of secretion. Many of these processes have been extensively reviewed (e.g., Kreil, 1981). The purpose of this section is to provide a few presently known examples of the various pathways and recognition signals in order to impart a feeling for the complexity of the processing and targeting systems within the cell.

3.5.1 Segregation of Proteins

Biosynthesis of secretory and lysosomal proteins appears to diverge from other membrane-bound ribosomal proteins after cotranslational insertion into the lumen of the rough endoplasmic reticulum. The amino terminal signal peptide that directs secretory and lysosomal proteins across the membrane is cleaved immediately following transfer. This type of proteolytic processing may precede the cotranslational glycosylation step, as shown by in vitro studies on the biosynthesis of amylase in germinating rice seed (Miyata and Akazawa, 1982). Disulfide bond formation, such as on Ig light chain, also occurs around this time (Bergman and Kuehl, 1979).

Several divergent pathways for packaging and secretion also presumably exist. Gumbiner and Kelly (1982) were able to physically separate secretory granules containing mature ACTH (adrenocorticotropic hormone) from viral glycoprotein (gp70) and precursor ACTH, which were cosynthesized and transported within the same cell. The half-time for appearance of the viral membrane glycoprotein, gp70, from MuLV in pituitary cells was 40 minutes, whereas that for secretion of mature ACTH was three to four hours. The former pathway for secreted hormone is sensitive to regulation by cAMP and is probably characteristic only of specialized secretory cells, whereas the latter pathway appears to be constitutive and more general.

Another segregation problem is how proteins get targeted to intracellular locations such as the rough endoplasmic reticulum (RER) or the Golgi, in contrast to membrane and secretory proteins that pass through the RER and Golgi on their way to the plasma membrane. Studies of the biosynthesis of the Golgi processing enzyme galactosyltransferase suggest that the protein follows the same pathway as membrane and secreted proteins, except that it is delayed in the distal Golgi cisternae prior to release at the cell surface into the medium (Strous and Berger, 1982). Thus, galactosyltransferase has a 19-hour intracellular half-life compared to less than one to four hours for other membrane and secretory proteins. Lysosomal enzymes also share the same initial steps of synthesis but differ at the point of oligosaccharide processing, leading to altered intracellular localization (see the following).

3.5.2 Processing Rates

The rates of processing and transport for a number of membrane and secreted proteins have been determined. In general, membrane glycoproteins are synthesized and transported to the cell surface in about 25–50 minutes. Measurements of the half-time for transport of VSV G protein to the plasma membrane following synthesis in at least two different cell types range around thirty minutes (Knipe et al., 1977; Strous and Lodish, 1980; Bergmann et al., 1981). Many secretory proteins such as albumin and fibronectin display similar kinetics, although the actual transport pathway must differ to some extent. Certain membrane-bound and secretory proteins that utilize the constitutive pathway within the same cell type cannot be differentiated either by kinetics of appearance outside the cell after synthesis (e.g., acetylcholine receptor and acetylcholinesterase; Rotundo and Fambrough, 1980) or by localization studies (e.g., transferrin and VSV G protein in hepatocytes; Strous and Lodish, 1980).

Differences in the rates of transport between membrane and secretory proteins within the same cell type have been detected, however. Secreted forms of VSV G protein, generated by deleting the COOH terminal regions of the protein through recombinant DNA manipulations, have a half-time of two to four hours for secretion, a significant increase over the normal transport rate (Rose and Bergmann, 1982). Such differences in rates between membrane and secretory proteins have been noted in other systems, suggesting that there may be different processing pathways, depending upon the ultimate destination of the protein (Strous and Lodish, 1980; Gumbiner and Kelly, 1982). Extensive studies by several groups of different secretory proteins such as albumin, transferrin, and retinol-binding protein indicate that each protein is transported from the endoplasmic reticulum to the Golgi apparatus at a discrete rate ranging from about 14 minutes to over 137 minutes (Ledford and Davis, 1983; Lodish et al., 1983; Fries et al., 1984). In contrast, the kinetics of transport of proteins from the Golgi complex to the cell surface is essentially the same for a variety of membrane and secretory proteins (Fitting and Kabat, 1982; Lodish et al., 1983; Fries et al., 1984). These results suggest that the rate-limiting steps for transport to the cell surface are between the endoplasmic reticulum and the Golgi.

To explain the different transport rates, Lodish and co-workers (1983) postulated that a specific recognition protein(s) in the Golgi determines the rate of association of secretory proteins. Such receptor molecules, which could be localized to sites where transport vesicles form, might regulate the selective packaging of proteins into transport vesicles on route to the Golgi. Specific differences in intracellular rates of transport of membrane proteins have also been noted, leading other investigators to postulate a similar new class of transport signals and membrane-bound receptors to mediate the transport of newly synthesized proteins from the endoplasmic reticulum to the Golgi apparatus (Fitting and Kabat, 1982; Madoff and Lenard, 1982). Although the mechanism for determining rate and directionality of transport within the cell following protein synthesis is not known yet, specific information encoded within the protein is clearly one factor in the decision; the particular recognition components within different cell types also add another level of selectivity. All of these aspects must be considered when production of proteins via genetic engineering techniques is contemplated.

3.5.3 Transport Signals: Lysosomal Enzyme Targeting

One of the few intracellular processing systems that is well understood is the phosphomannosyl recognition signal used for transport of lysosomal enzymes within and between cells (reviewed in Sly and Fischer, 1982). For the purposes of this review, we will focus on the intracellular transport, although it should be kept in mind that phosphomannosyl receptors are also present on cell surfaces, facilitating recapture of secreted acid hydrolases.

Studies have identified a number of structural features required for acid hydrolase recognition and binding. A critical factor is the presence of mannose-6-phosphate on high-uptake lysosomal enzymes (von Figura and Klein, 1979; Natowicz et al., 1979). Optimal recognition occurs when the phosphomonoester group is not blocked by other sugar residues. Other structural features in the lysosomal enzymes, either multiple mannose-6-phosphate sites or other factors, must also be involved in recognition since the affinity of the free mannose-6-phosphate sugar is lower by several orders of magnitude than that of the receptor for the intact enzymes (Kaplan et al., 1977; Sando and Neufeld, 1977). In particular, two features may be important. Structural studies have demonstrated that multivalent interactions arising from multiple phosphomannose groups are present and appear to confer enhanced affinity. Thus, individual oligosaccharide chains can be derivatized with up to three phosphate residues at any one of five mannose sites (Varki and Kornfeld, 1980); overall, up to 4.4 moles of 6-phosphomannose per mole of enzyme have been demonstrated (Natowicz et al., 1979). Alternatively, the multiple derivatization of the oligosaccharide chains may serve only to enhance affinity of a single ligand-receptor interaction.

The actual point in the cell where phosphorylation and processing of the phosphomannosyl signal occurs is not clear, since the enzymes catalyzing these steps have been localized in both the endoplasmic reticulum and the Golgi apparatus. Isolation of newly synthesized, nonglucosylated acid hydrolases containing phosphorylated sugars suggests that phosphorylation occurs after the action of the glucosidases in the endoplasmic reticulum but before alpha-mannosidase cleavage in the Golgi apparatus (Goldberg and Kornfeld, 1981). Rothman and colleagues (Dunphy et al., 1985) recently proposed that the enzymes that generate the mannose-6-phosphate recognition marker reside in the cis-most cisternae of the Golgi, where the mannose-6-phosphate receptor for lysosomal enzymes has been localized (Brown and Farquhar, 1984). Thus, targeting of lysosomal enzymes appears to be a very early processing event.

The presence of the mannose-phosphate recognition marker clearly influences the nature of the processing of the oligosaccharide chains as well as their compartmentation and final destination. The oligosaccharide chains containing these markers do not get processed further to complex-type chains, although in mutant cells unable to phosphorylate the sugars, processing to complex-type chains can occur (Vladutiu and Rattazzi, 1975). The actual signals that determine whether an oligosaccharide is phosphorylated are not known yet. In vitro studies have shown that nonlysosomal glycopeptides can also serve as acceptors for the glycoprotein N-acetylglucosaminyl phosphotransferase, indicating that the enzyme specificity is not limited to acid hydrolase substrates (Reitman and Kornfeld, 1981). Since newly synthesized lysosomal enzymes are in a precursor form that is cleaved proteolytically over a period of hours or days (Hasilik and Neufeld, 1980a, 1980b), it is possible that specific protein sequences or other structural features of these proteins direct the recognition process for phosphoryl transfer either directly or through compartmentation into regions containing the processing enzymes.

The current model depicting posttranslational modification of lysosomal enzymes may be summarized as follows: After transfer of the N-acetylglucosamine-1-phosphate moiety to the 6-position of up to three mannose residues on the high-mannose oligosaccharide chains, the N-acetylglucosamine-blocking groups are removed by phosphodiesterase treatment (Varki and Kornfeld, 1980; Hasilik et al., 1981; Reitman and Kornfeld, 1981; Waheed et al., 1981a, 1981b). The monophosphate-containing enzymes, which now exhibit high receptor binding and uptake, presumably bind to intracellular phosphomannosyl receptors that are then sequestered into vesicles budding from the Golgi apparatus. Cell fractionation studies have demonstrated the partial inaccessibility of bound enzyme-receptor complexes to mannose-6-phosphate in the Golgi and endoplasmic reticulum (Fischer et al., 1980). At this point, different channeling pathways may occur. Enzymes directed to primary lysosomes would dissociate from their receptors once exposed to low-pH conditions, leaving the receptors free for reuse. Acid phosphatases and proteases would then inactivate the recognition signal by removing the phosphate residue and trimming the excess polypeptide. Transport of some receptor-bound enzyme to the cell surface may occur. Alternatively, in cells that lack the recognition marker or for enzymes not bound to the receptor, secretion of the enzymes from the cell will occur. In certain cell types, secreted "high-uptake" enzymes may reenter the cell through pinocytosis. Thus, the lysosomal recognition signal clearly influences the intracellular transport of these enzymes, but alternative pathways may also be utilized.

3.6   APPLICATION TO GENETIC ENGINEERING: IMPORTANCE OF PROCESSING

To evaluate the importance of processing to a final product of genetic engineering, one must first determine the function of the various processing options. In the following section we discuss the role of glycosylation and other types of processing in stabilizing or altering proteins.

3.6.1   Role of Glycosylation

Glycoproteins serve a variety of functions in cells as lysosomal enzymes, cell surface proteins, and secreted proteins. Cell surface glycoproteins have been implicated in differentiation, pinocytosis, tumor formation, viral and hormone receptors, and are involved in immunological specificity (reviewed in Hughes, 1976). Among the secreted proteins are hormones, immuno-globulins, enzymes, and serum transfer factors (cited in Olden et al., 1982). Suggested roles for the oligosaccharide moieties of glycoproteins have included metabolite transport across cell membranes, proper insertion and orientation into membranes, secretion, and protection against proteolytic degradation.

Although glycoproteins comprise a major fraction of eukaryotic cellular proteins, the precise role of the particular oligosaccharide moieties largely remains to be determined. However, with the recent proliferation of studies based on the use of oligosaccharide inhibitors and glycosylation mutants, much more information is now available (reviewed in Olden et al., 1982). While there is no absolute requirement for oligosaccharides for membrane protein insertion or secretion, oligosaccharides play a clear role in targeting of proteins to intracellular compartments through specific receptor recognition. A brief description of some of these studies and conclusions follows.

Although the contribution of N-linked oligosaccharides to the biological properties of glycoproteins has not been established in all cases, a variety of effects have been identified, particularly in relation to processing and protein turnover. Glycosylation of fibronectin, surface acetylcholine receptor, and other proteins appears to protect the protein from proteolytic degradation (Olden et al., 1978; Prives and Bar-Sagi, 1983). Since proteolytic turnover of proteins with abnormal conformations seems to be a general feature of bacterial and eukaryotic systems, this result is not surprising. However, the actual mechanism by which this enhancement in metabolic instability occurs, either by exposing new proteolytic sites, activating certain enzyme systems within the cell, or increasing exposure to lysosomal enzymes through altered packaging, remains to be determined. There also may be a connection to the ubiquitin-activated proteolytic system through binding to exposed asparagine residues or lysine residues.

In addition to stabilizing proteins against external agents, oligosaccharides also appear to stabilize the three-dimensional structure of proteins such as RNase (Plummer and Hirs, 1964). In this case, the enzymatic activity is unaffected by glycosylation. X-ray crystallographic studies of immunoglobulin fragments demonstrate that oligosaccharides can modulate the interactions between the fab and fc segments (Koide et al., 1977; Silverton et al., 1977). Similarly, the proper folding of the subunits of lutropin and thyrotropin pituitary hormones and the association of the alpha and beta subunits of these hormones appear to be oligosaccharide-dependent (Weintraub et al., 1980; Strickland and Pierce, 1983).

In many instances protein secretion or appearance at the cell surface appears to be impaired upon loss of glycosylation (reviewed in Olden et al., 1982). These cases include IgG of MOPC 21 cells, K-light chain K-46 of plasmacytoma-46B, IgA of MOPC 315, IgE of IR 162 plasma cells, yeast invertase and acid phosphatase, and viral proteins such as SFV. For other proteins such as chick embryo fibroblast fibronectin, muscle cell acetylcholine receptor, and T25 glycoprotein of plasmacytoma, apparent inhibition has been shown to be due to enhanced degradation and protein turnover. Loss of glycosylation during protein synthesis can also lead to defects in intracellular processing or protein degradation. Among these cases are a number of viral glycoproteins that, when synthesized in the absence of oligosaccharide transfer, lose their normal association with the intracellular transport machinery due to aggregation or instability and fail to appear on the cell surface (Schwarz et al., 1976; Leavitt et al., 1977; Gibson et al., 1979).

In other systems, such as synthesis of pro-opiomelanocortin in mammalian pituitary cells, glycosylation does not appear to be required for proper proteolytic cleavage or secretion of the various hormone species (Budarf and Herbert, 1982). No effect of loss of glycosylation on the biological activity of a number of glycoproteins could be observed, including colony stimulating factor, bungarotoxin binding to the acetylcholine receptor, and leukocyte interferon. The factors that determine why some glycoproteins are so dependent upon oligosaccharides for structural stability or biological activity are not known, although it is clear that carbohydrates do influence the final physical properties of these proteins.

In several cases, a specific processed form of the oligosaccharide is required for proper protein function. For example, the stability of the multimeric forms of VIII/von Willebrand factor relies on the presence of the penultimate galactose residues (Gralnick et al., 1983). Treatment of Sindbis virus-infected cells with bromoconduritol, an inhibitor that blocks the alpha-glucosidase leading to accumulation of the GlcMan9-7GlcNac2 protein intermediate, results in loss of proteolytic cleavage of the envelope glycoprotein E2 (Datema et al., 1984) and inhibition of infectious viral particle release. Removal of glucose and some mannose residues may also be required for release of infectious fowl plague particles (Datema et al., 1982; Elbein et al., 1982).

As a consequence of effects on protein folding and other interactions, glycosylation may also influence the resultant antigenicity of a protein. Thus, variation in glycosylation patterns may lead to altered recognition by the immunological system (Rosner et al., 1980b) or other receptor-ligand interactive systems such as that for acetylcholine (Prives and Bar-Sagi, 1983). Further, if the fidelity of glycosylation at one of these sites is not 100%, then one glycoprotein might theoretically be present on the cell surface in a variety of different antigenic forms.

Finally, glycosylation may play a major role in the intracellular transport of glycoproteins, a complicated process subject to a variety of regulatory events. While the initial vectorial insertion of nascent polypeptides into the lumen of the endoplasmic reticulum appears to be independent of carbohydrate, the oligosaccharide moiety may play a role in subsequent routing of membrane and secretory glycoproteins (Blobel and Dobberstein, 1975a, 1975b; Wickner, 1980). As noted previously, mannose-6-phosphate appears to be a unique targeting residue on lysosomal enzymes, and the complementary lectin receptor for this residue has been identified in vertebrate cells. Olden and co-workers have expanded this idea and suggested that all glycoprotein pathways within the cell are mediated by similar lectin-specific sugar interactions, which would act to sequester particular proteins into discrete membrane areas that could bud off into vesicles for transport to specific organelles. The recent observation that the carbohydrate moiety of glycoproteins is degraded 3–7 times faster than the protein (Kriesel et al., 1980) suggests a possible role for covalent modification of carbohydrates in membrane recycling. Although the specific carbohydrate signals have only begun to be deciphered, these subtle regulatory controls could clearly be a major factor in determining the successful production of membrane, secretory, and lysosomal proteins in mammalian cells.

3.6.2 Fatty Acylation

The functions of the added fatty acid residues, aside from membrane anchoring, are not known at present. It has been suggested that the additional hydrophobic groups are important for targeting proteins within the cell, either for association of certain proteins such as those involved in virus assembly, or for peripheral attachment of certain transforming proteins within the membrane. However, recent studies suggest that fatty acylation may not be a general requirement for either the maturation or budding of viruses (Kotwal and Ghosh, 1984). Further, fatty acids may be necessary but are certainly not sufficient for targeting of transforming proteins such as pp60src (Buss et al., 1984). Alternatively, the insertion of new fatty acids within the membrane may induce perturbations in the membrane resulting in changes in local membrane properties.

3.6.3 Other Modifications

Protein processing performs a wide variety of functions (reviewed in Wold, 1981). One of the most important roles is to provide reversible regulatory switches in the cell. Chemical derivatives such as phosphate groups, N-acetates, methyl esters of glutamine, adenylyl- and uridylyl-O-tyrosine, as well as poly(ADP)ribosyl derivates of nuclear proteins have been implicated in such forms of cellular regulation. A broad range of chemical derivatives act to link coenzymes or prosthetic groups to the appropriate enzyme. These include amides, aldimides, ethers, thioethers, phosphate diesters, and N-alkyl derivatives. Cross-linking agents such as phosphate diesters, disulfides, allysine (in collagen and elastin), lanthionine (in keratins), and bis- and tertyrosine act to stabilize three-dimensional structure as well as to impart an appropriate degree of elasticity or rigidity to proteins. Other derivatives perform one specific function, such as the binding of calcium.

3.7 CONCLUSION

Clearly, protein processing is a vital component of the protein synthetic apparatus in mammalian cells. When contemplating genetic engineering of complex proteins, one must take into account a number of factors important to the processing pathway. These include cell type and associated processing enzymes and compartments as well as the specific structural features of the protein such as amino acid sequence and three-dimensional folding. Finally, the genetic engineer must be aware that many of these processing options, such as the N-asparagine-linked glycosylation discussed extensively here, are limited to eukaryotic cells.

REFERENCES

Aitken, A., Cohen, P., Santikarn, S., Williams, D.H., Calder, A.G., Smith, A., and Klee, C.B. (1982) *FEBS Lett.* 150, 314–318.

Anderson, D.J., Moster, K.E., and Blobel, G. (1983) *Proc. Natl. Acad. Sci. USA* 86, 7249–7253.

Anderson, D.J., Walter, P., and Blobel, G. (1982) *J. Cell. Biol.* 93, 501–506.

Atkinson, P.H., and Hakimi, J. (1980) in *The Biochemistry of Glycoproteins and Proteoglycans* (Lennarz, W., ed.) pp. 191–239, Plenum Press, New York.

Aubert, J.-P., Biserte, G., and Loucheux-LeFebvre, M.-H. (1976) *Arch. Biochem. Biophys.* 175, 410–418.

Baenziger, J., and Kornfeld, S. (1974) *J. Biol. Chem.* 149, 7270–7281.

Baig, M.M., and Aminoff, D. (1972) *J. Biol. Chem.* 247, 6111–6118.

Beeley, J.G. (1977) *Biochem. Biophys. Res. Commun.* 76, 1051–1055.

Bergman, L.W., and Kuehl, W.M. (1978) *Biochemistry* 17, 5174–5180.

Bergman, L.W., and Kuehl, W.M. (1979) *J. Biol. Chem.* 254, 8869–8876.

Bergmann, J.E., and Singer, S.J. (1983) *J. Cell. Biol.* 97, 1777–1787.

Bergmann, J.E., Tokuyasu, K.T., and Singer, S.J. (1981) *Proc. Natl. Acad. Sci. USA* 78, 1746–1750.

Blobel, G., and Dobberstein, B. (1975a) *J. Cell. Biol.* 67, 835–851.

Blobel, G., and Dobberstein, B. (1975b) *J. Cell. Biol.* 67, 852–862.

Braell, W.A., and Lodish, H.F. (1982) *Cell* 28, 23–31.

Brown, W.J., and Farquhar, M.G. (1984) *Cell* 36, 295–307.

Budarf, M.L., and Herbert, E. (1982) *J. Biol. Chem.* 257, 10128–10135.

Buss, J.E., Kamps, M.P., and Sefton, B. (1984) *Mol. Cell. Biol.* 4, 2697–2704.

Buss, J.E., and Sefton, B. (1984) *J. Virol.* 53, 7–12.

Burke, D.J., and Keegstra, K. (1976) *J. Virol.* 20, 676–686.

Burke, D.J., and Keegstra, K. (1979) *J. Virol.* 29, 546–554.

Butler, W.T., and Cunningham, L.W. (1966) *J. Biol. Chem.* 241, 3882–3888.

Carlson, D. (1968) *J. Biol. Chem.* 243, 616–626.

Carr, S.A., Biemann, K., Shoji, S., Parmalee, D.C., and Titani, K. (1982) *Proc. Natl. Acad. Sci. USA* 79, 6128–6131.

Chan, S.J., Patzelt, C., Duguid, J.R., Quinn, P., Labrecque, A., Noyes, B., Keim, P., Heinrikson, R.L., and Steiner, D.F. (1979) in *From Gene to Protein: Information Transfer in Normal and Abnormal Cells* (T.R. Russell, K. Brew, H. Faber, and J. Schultz, eds.) pp. 361–377, Academic Press, New York.

Cross, F.R., Garber, E.A., Pellman, D., and Hanafusa, H. (1984) *Mol. Cell Biol.* 4, 1834–1842.

Datema, R., Romero, P.A., Legler, G., and Schwarz, R.T. (1982) *Proc. Natl. Acad. Sci. USA* 79, 6787–6791.

Datema, R., Romero, P.A., Rott, R., and Schwarz, R.T. (1984) *Arch. Virol.* 81, 25–39.

Dunphy, W.G., Brands, R., and Rothman, J.E. (1985) *Cell* 40, 463–472.

Elbein, A.D., Dorling, P.R., Vosbeck, K., and Horrisberger, M. (1982) *J. Biol. Chem.* 257, 1573–1576.

Etchison, J.R., and Holland, J.J. (1974) *Proc. Natl. Acad. Sci. USA* 71, 4011–4014.

Eylar, E.H. (1966) *J. Theor. Biol.* 10, 89–113.

Farquhar, M.G., and Palade, G.E. (1981) *J. Cell. Biol.* 91, 77s–103s.

Feizi, T., Kabat, E.A., Vicari, G., Anderson, B., and Marsh, W.L. (1971) *J. Immunol.* 106, 1578–1592.

Fischer, H.D., Gonzalez-Noriega, A., Sly, W.S., and Morre, D.J. (1980) *J. Biol. Chem.* 255, 9608.

Fitting, T., and Kabat, D. (1982) *J. Biol. Chem.* 257, 14011–14017.

Fries, E., Gustafsson, L., and Peterson, P.A. (1984) *EMBO J* 3, 147–152.

Fukuda, M.N., Papermaster, D.S., and Hargrave, P.A. (1979) *J. Biol. Chem.* 254, 8201–8207.

Ghelis, C., and Yon, J., eds. (1982) *Protein Folding,* Academic Press, New York.

Gibson, R., Schlesinger, S., and Kornfeld, S. (1979) *J. Biol. Chem.* 254, 3600–3607.

Gilmore, R., and Blobel, G. (1983) *Cell* 35, 677–685.

Gilmore, R., Blobel, G., and Walter, P. (1982a) *J. Cell. Biol.* 95, 463–469.

Gilmore, R., Walter, P., and Blobel, G. (1982b) *J. Cell. Biol.* 95, 470–477.

Goldberg, D.E., and Kornfeld, S. (1981) *Fed. Proc.* 40, 1861.

Gralnick, H.R., Williams, S.B., and Rick, M.E. (1983) *Proc. Natl. Acad. Sci. USA* 80, 2771–2774.

Green, M. (1982) *J. Biol. Chem.* 257, 9039–9042.

Griffiths, G., Quinn, P., and Warren, G. (1983) *J. Cell. Biol.* 96, 835–850.

Gumbiner, B., and Kelly, R.B. (1982) *Cell* 28, 51–59.

Hall, M.N., Hereford, L., and Herskowitz, I. (1984) *Cell* 36, 1057–1065.

Hallgren, P., Lundblad, A., and Svensson, S. (1975) *J. Biol. Chem.* 250, 5312–5314.

Hanover, J.A., and Lennarz, W.J. (1980) *J. Biol. Chem.* 255, 3600–3604.

Harpaz, N., and Schachter, J. (1980) *J. Biol. Chem.* 255, 4884–4893.

Hart, G.W., Brew, K., Grant, G.A., Bradshaw, R.A., and Lennarz, W.J. (1979) *J. Biol. Chem.* 254, 9747.

Hascall, V.C. (1981) in *Biology of Carbohydrates,* vol. 1, (Ginsburg, V., and Robbins, P.W., eds.) pp. 1–49, John Wiley and Sons, New York.

Hasilik, A., and Neufeld, E.F. (1980a) *J. Biol. Chem.* 255, 4937–4945.

Hasilik, A., and Neufeld, E.F. (1980b) *J. Biol. Chem.* 255, 4946–4950.

Hasilik, A., Waheed, A., and von Figura, K. (1981) *Biochem. Biophys. Res. Commun.* 98, 761–767.

Heifetz, A., and Lennarz, W.J. (1979) *J. Biol. Chem.* 254, 6119–6127.

Henderson, L.E., Krutzsch, H.C., and Oroszlan, S. (1983) *Proc. Natl. Acad. Sci. USA* 80, 339–343.

Hershko, A., and Fry, M. (1975) *Annu. Rev. Biochem.* 44, 775–797.

Hicks, S.J., Drysdale, J.W., and Munro, H.N. (1969) *Science* 164, 584–585.

Hsieh, P., and Robbins, P.W. (1984) *J. Biol. Chem.* 259, 2375–2382.

Hsieh, P., Rosner, M.R., and Robbins, P.W. (1983a) *J. Biol. Chem.* 258, 2548–2554.

Hsieh, P., Rosner, M.R., and Robbins, P.W. (1983b) *J. Biol. Chem.* 258, 2555–2561.

Howard. D., Natowicz, M., and Baenziger, J.U. (1982) *J. Biol. Chem.* 257, 10861–10868.

Hubbard, S.C., and Ivatt, R.I. (1981) *Annu. Rev. Biochem.* 50, 555–583.

Hubbard, S.C., and Robbins, P.W. (1979) *J. Biol. Chem.* 254, 4566–4576.

Hubbard, S.C., and Robbins, P.W. (1980) *J. Biol. Chem.* 255, 11782–11793.

Hughes, R.C. (1976) *Membrane Glycoproteins,* Butterworth, London, pp. 269–284.

Hunt, L.A. (1979) *J. Supramol. Struct.* 12, 209–226.

Hunt, L.A. (1980) *J. Virol.* 35, 362–370.

Hunt, L.A., Davidson, S.K., and Golemboski, D.B. (1983) *Arch. Biochem. Biophys.,* 347–356.

Irving, R.A., Toneguzzo, F., Rhee, S.H., Hofmann, T., and Ghosh, H.P. (1979) *Proc. Natl. Acad. Sci. USA* 76, 570–574.

Jackson, C.M., and Nemerson, Y. (1980) *Annu. Rev. Biochem.* 49, 765–811.

Jaenicke, R., ed. (1980) *Protein Folding,* Elsevier/North-Holland Biomedical Press, Amsterdam.

Jamieson, J.C. (1977) *Can. J. Biochem.* 55, 408–414.

Kalderon, D., Richardson, W.D., Markham, A.F., and Smith, A.E. (1984) *Nature* 311, 33–38.

Kaplan, A., Achord, D.T., and Sly, W.S. (1977) *Proc. Natl. Acad. Sci. USA* 74, 2026–2030.

Katz, F.N., Rothman, J.R., Lingappa, V.R., Blobel, G., and Lodish, H.F. (1977) *Proc. Natl. Acad. Sci. USA* 74, 3278–3282.

Kim, P.S., and Baldwin, R.L. (1982) *Annu. Rev. Biochem.* 51, 459–489.

Klenk, H.-D., Schwarz, R.T., Schmidt, M.F.G., and Wollert, W. (1978) in *Topics in Infectious Diseases,* vol. 3 (Laver, W.G., Bachmayer, H., and Weil, R., eds) pp. 83–99, Springer-Verlag, Vienna.

Knipe, D.M., Lodish, H.F., and Baltimore, D. (1977) *J. Virol.* 21, 1121–1127.

Koide, N., Nose, M., and Muramatsu, T. (1977) *Biochem. Biophys. Res. Commun.* 75, 838–844.

Kornfeld, R., and Kornfeld, S. (1980) in *The Biochemistry of Glycoproteins and Proteoglycans* (Lennarz, W., ed.) pp. 1–34, Plenum Press, New York.

Kornfeld, S., Li, E., and Tabas, I. (1978) *J. Biol. Chem.* 253, 7771–7778.

Kotwal, G.J., and Ghosh, H.P. (1984) *J. Biol. Chem.* 259, 4699–4701.

Kreil, G. (1981) *Annu. Rev. Biochem.* 50, 317–348.

Kreisel, W., Volk, B.A., Büchsel, R., and Reutter, W. (1980) *Proc. Natl. Acad. Sci. USA* 77, 1828–1831.

Krieger, D.T., and Ganong, W.F., eds. (1977) *Ann. NY Acad. Sci.* 297, 664.

Kronquist, K.E., and Lennarz, W.J. (1978) *J. Supramol. Struct.* 8, 51–65.

Laub, O., and Rutter, W.J. (1983) *J. Biol. Chem.* 258, 6043–6050.

Leavitt, R., Schlesinger, S., and Kornfeld, S. (1977) *J. Biol. Chem.* 252, 9018–9020.

Ledford, B.E., and Davis, D.F. (1983) *J. Biol. Chem.* 258, 3304–3308.

Lehle, L., Schulz, I., and Tanner, W. (1980) *Arch. Microbiol.* 127, 231–237.

Li, E., Tabas, I., and Kornfeld, S. (1978) *J. Biol. Chem.* 253, 7762–7770.

Liang, C.-J., Yamashita, K., Muellenberg, C.G., Shichi, H., and Kobata, A. (1979) *J. Biol. Chem.* 254, 4554–4559.

Lingappa, V.R., Katz, F.N., Lodish, H.F., and Blobel, G. (1978) *J. Biol. Chem.* 253, 8667–8670.

Lodish, H.F., Braell, W.A., Schwartz, A.L., Strous, G.J.A.M., and Zilberstein, A. (1981) *Int. Rev. Cytol. (Suppl.)* 12, 247–307.

Lodish, H.F., Kong, N., Snider, M., and Strous, G.J.A.M. (1983) *Nature* 304, 80–83.

Lombard, C.G., and Winzler, R.J. (1974) *Eur. J. Biochem.* 49, 77–86.

Lomedico, P.T. (1982) *Proc. Natl. Acad. Sci. USA* 79, 5798–5803.

Madoff, D.H., and Lenard, J. (1982) *Cell* 28, 821–829.

Mains, P.E., and Sibley, C.H. (1983) *J. Biol. Chem.* 258, 5027–5033.

Marshall, R.D. (1974) *Biochem. Soc. Symp.* 40, 17–26.

Meyer, D.I., Krause, E., and Dobberstein, B. (1982a) *Nature* 297, 647–650.

Meyer, D.I., Louvard, D., and Dobberstein, B. (1982b) *J. Cell. Biol.* 92, 579–583.

Miyata, S., and Akazawa, T. (1982) *Proc. Natl. Acad. Sci. USA* 79, 6566–6568.

Moore, H.-P.H., Walker, M.D., Lee, F., and Kelly, R.B. (1983) *Cell* 35, 531–538.

Morrison, T.G., and Lodish, H.F. (1975) *J. Biol. Chem.* 250, 6955–6962.

Nakajima, T., and Ballou, C.E. (1974) *J. Biol. Chem.* 249, 7679–7684.

Nakamura, K., and Compans, R.W. (1979) *Virology* 95, 8–23.

Narasimhan, S., Stanley, P., and Schachter, H. (1977) *J. Biol. Chem.* 252, 3926–3933.

Natowicz, M.R., Chi, M.M.-Y., Lowry, O.H., and Sly, W.S. (1979) *Proc. Natl. Acad. Sci. USA* 76, 4322–4326.

Natowicz, M., Baenziger, J.U., and Sly, W.S. (1982) *J. Biol. Chem.* 257, 4412–4420.

Oates, M.D., Rosbottom, A.C., and Schrager, J. (1974) *Carbohydr. Res.* 34, 115–137.

Olden, K., Parent, J.B., and White, S.L. (1982) *Biochim. Biophys. Acta* 650, 209–232.

Olden, K., Pratt, R.M., and Yamada, K.M. (1978) *Cell* 13, 461–473.

Olson, E.N., Glaser, L., and Merlie, J.B. (1984) *J. Biol. Chem.* 259, 5364–5367.

Omary, M.B., and Trowbridge, I.S. (1981) *J. Biol. Chem.* 256, 4715–4718.

Palade, G. (1955) *J. Biophys. Biochem. Cytol.* 1, 59–68.

Parodi, A.J. (1979) *J. Biol. Chem.* 254, 10051–10061.

Parodi, A.J., and Quesada-Allue, L.A. (1982) *J. Biol. Chem.* 257, 7637–7640.

Pellman, D., Garber, E.A., Cross, F.R., and Hanafusa, H. (1985) *Nature* 314, 374–377.

Plummer, T.H., Jr., and Hirs, W.H.W. (1964) *J. Biol. Chem.* 239, 2530.

Pollack, L., and Atkinson, P. (1983) *J. Cell. Biol.* 97, 293–300.

Prives, J., and Bar-Sagi, D. (1983) *J. Cell. Biol.* 97, 1375–1380.

Raizada, M.K., Schutzbach, J.S., and Ankel, H. (1975) *J. Biol. Chem.* 250, 3310–3315.

Redman, C.M., and Sabatini, D.D. (1966) *Proc. Natl. Acad. Sci. USA* 56, 608–615.

Reid, K.B.M., and Porter, R.R. (1981) *Annu. Rev. Biochem.* 50, 433–464.

Reitman, M.C., and Kornfeld, S. (1981) *J. Biol. Chem.* 246, 11977–11980.

Roden, L. (1980) in *The Biochemistry of Glycoproteins and Proteoglycans* (Lennarz, W., ed.) pp. 267–371, Plenum Press, New York.

Rose, J.K. (1977) *Proc. Natl. Acad. Sci. USA* 74, 3672–3676.

Rose, J.K., and Bergmann, J.E. (1982) *Cell* 30, 753–762.

Rosner, M.R., Grinna, L.S., and Robbins, P.W. (1980a) *Proc. Natl. Acad. Sci. USA* 77, 67–71.

Rosner, M.R., and Robbins, P.W. (1982) *J. Cell. Biochem.* 18, 37–86.

Rosner, M.R., Tang, J.-S., Hopkins, N., and Robbins, P.W. (1980b) *Proc. Natl. Acad. Sci. USA* 77, 6420–6424.

Roth, J., and Berger, E.G. (1982) *J. Cell. Biol.* 93, 223–229.

Rothman, J.E. (1981) *Science* 213, 1212–1219.

Rothman, J.E., and Fine, R.E. (1980) *Proc. Natl. Acad. Sci. USA* 77, 780–784.

Rothman, J.E., and Lodish, H.F. (1977) *Nature* 269, 775–780.

Rotundo, R.L., and Fambrough, D.M. (1980) *Cell* 22, 595–602.

Sabatini, D.D., Kreibich, G., Morimoto, T., and Adesnik, M. (1982) *J. Cell. Biol.* 92, 1–22.

Sando, G.N., and Neufeld, R.F. (1977) *Cell* 12, 619–627.

Saraste, J., and Hedman, K. (1983) *EMBO J.* 2, 2001–2006.

Schachter, H., and Roseman, S. (1980) in *The Biochemistry of Glycoproteins and Proteoglycans* (Lennarz, W., ed.) pp. 85–160, Plenum Press, New York.

Schatz, G., and Butow, R.A. (1983) *Cell* 32, 316–318.

Schlesinger, M.J. (1981) *Annu. Rev. Biochem.* 50, 193–206.

Scheele, G., Jacoby, R., and Carne, T. (1980) *J. Cell. Biol.* 87, 611–628.

Schmidt, M.F.G., Bracha, M., and Schlesinger, M.J. (1979) *Proc. Natl. Acad. Sci. USA* 76, 1687–1691.

Schmidt, M.F.G., and Schlesinger, M.J. (1980) *J. Biol. Chem.* 255, 3334–3339.

Schultz, A., and Oroszlan, S. (1984) *Virology* 133, 431–437.

Schwarz, R.T., Rohrschneider, J.M., and Schmidt, M.F.G. (1976) *J. Virol.* 19, 782–792.

Schwarz, R.T., and Klenk, H.-D. (1981) *Virology* 113, 584–593.

Siekevitz, P., and Palade, G.E. (1960) *J. Biophys. Biochem. Cytol.* 7, 619–631.

Silverton, E.W., Manuel, A.N., and Davies, D.R. (1977) *Proc. Natl. Acad. Sci. USA* 74, 5140–5144.

Sly, W.S., and Fischer, H.D. (1982) *J. Cell. Biochem.* 18, 67–98.

Smith, C.E. (1980) *J. Histochem. Cytochem.* 28, 16–26.

Snider, M.D., and Robbins, P.W. (1982) *J. Biol. Chem.* 257, 6796–6801.

Spiro, R.G. (1967) *J. Biol. Chem.* 242, 4813–4823.

Spiro, R.G., and Bhoyroo, V.C. (1974) *J. Biol. Chem.* 249, 5704–5714.

Stoffel, W., Blobel, G., and Walter, P. (1981) *Eur. J. Biochem.* 120, 519–522.

Strickland, T.W., and Pierce, J.G. (1983) *J. Biol. Chem.* 258, 5927–5932.

Strous, G.J.A.M., and Berger, E.C. (1982) *J. Biol. Chem.* 257, 7623–7628.

Strous, G.J.A.M., and Lodish, H.F. (1980) *Cell* 22, 709–717.

Struck, D.K., Lennarz, W.J., and Brew, K. (1978) *J. Biol. Chem.* 253, 5786–5795.

Struck, D.K., and Lennarz, W.J. (1980) in *The Biochemistry of Glycoproteins and Proteoglycans* (Lennarz, W., ed.) pp. 35–83, Plenum Press, New York.

Tabas, I., and Kornfeld, S. (1978) *J. Biol. Chem.* 253, 7779–7786.

Tartakoff, A.M., and Vassalli, P. (1983) *J. Cell. Biol.* 97, 1243–1248.

Toneguzzo, F., and Ghosh, H.P. (1978) *Proc. Natl. Acad. Sci. USA* 75, 715–719.

Trimble, R.B., Byrd, J.D., and Maley, F. (1980a) *J. Biol. Chem.* 255, 11892–11895.

Trimble, R.B., Maley, F., and Tarentino, A.C. (1980b) *J. Biol. Chem.* 255, 10232–10238.

Trimble, R.B., Maley, F., and Chu, F.K. (1983) *J. Biol. Chem.* 258, 2562–2567.

Van den Broeck, G., Timko, M.P., Kausch, A.P., Cashmore, A.R., Montagu, M.V., and Herrera-Estrella, L. (1985) *Nature* 313, 358–363.

Varki, A., and Kornfeld, S. (1980) *J. Biol. Chem.* 255, 10847–10858.

Vladutiu, G.D., and Rattazzi, M. (1975) *Biochem. Biophys. Res. Commun.* 67, 956–964.

von Figura, K., and Klein, U. (1979) *Eur. J. Biochem.* 94, 347–354.

von Heijne, G. (1984) *EMBO J.* 3, 2315–2318.

Waheed, A., Hasilik, A., and von Figura, K. (1981a) *J. Biol. Chem.* 256, 5717–5721.

Waheed, A., Pohlmann, R., Hasilik, A., and von Figura, K. (1981b) *J. Biol. Chem.* 256, 4150–4152.

Walter, P., and Blobel, G. (1983) *Cell,* 34, 525–533.

Walter, P., Gilmore, R., and Blobel, G. (1984) *Cell* 38, 5–8.

Walter, P., Ibrahimi, I., and Blobel, G. (1981) *J. Cell. Biol.* 91, 545–550.

Watkins, W.M. (1972) in *Glycoproteins,* 2nd ed. (Gottschalk, A., ed.) pp. 830–891, Elsevier, Amsterdam.

Weintraub, B.D., Stannard, B.S., Linnekin, D., and Marshall, M. (1980) *J. Biol. Chem.* 255, 5715–5723.

Wickner, W. (1980) *Science* 210, 861–868.

Willumsen, B.M., Christensen, A., Hubbert, N.L., Papageorge, A.G., and Lowy, D.R. (1984) *Nature* 310, 583–586.

Wilson, J.R., Williams, D., and Schachter, H. (1976) *Biochem. Biophys. Res. Commun.* 72, 909–916.

Wilson, I.A., Skehel, J.J., and Wiley, D.C. (1981) *Nature* 289, 366–373.

Wold, F. (1981) *Annu. Rev. Biochem.* 50, 783–814.

Serum-Free Media

Michael Butler

4.1 INTRODUCTION

The first studies by Harrison and Burrows in 1907 of cell growth and division in vitro utilized blood plasma as growth medium for pieces of tissue taken from frog embryos. In their hanging drop technique, the clotted plasma was suspended below a coverslip held over a microscope slide. The fibrin matrix of the clot served as an anchor for cell growth, while the nutrient requirements of the cell were provided by the remaining supernatant.

Cockerel plasma was widely used in subsequent developments of these techniques. This plasma was easily obtainable and preferred to hen plasma because of the high calcium content of the latter. Extracts from chick embryos were frequently used in these pioneering days, and a cocktail of embryo extract and donor plasma became the natural medium for studying the growth of cells on a small scale.

It was not until the 1950s that detailed studies on the nutritional requirements of animal cells were initiated, chiefly in response to the need for large-scale cell culturing to satisfy demands for mass vaccination programs. In 1959, Eagle introduced his minimal essential medium for the growth of mammalian cells. This consisted of a defined medium containing glucose, amino acids, and vitamins in a balanced salt solution. However, the cellular requirements for growth were not found to be satisfied until a 5% to 10% addition of blood serum was made.

Blood serum, which is produced by taking the supernatant of clotted blood, seemed to contain undefined materials essential for cell proliferation. Serum from young or unborn animals was found to be particularly efficacious, and fetal calf serum became valued for its excellent growth-promoting qualities.

However, blood serum is of undefined composition and varies between batches. This leads to many difficulties in reproducing experiments on a small scale and in maintaining consistent yields of cells or their products on the large scale. Consequently, over the last 15 years numerous attempts have been made to develop media suitable for the growth of cells in vitro in the absence of serum (Higuchi, 1976).

4.2 DEVELOPMENT AND DESIGN OF SERUM-FREE MEDIUM

The design of serum-free media has tended to follow an empirical pattern in which cell growth is measured in the presence of putative growth stimulators. Difficulties of isolating the growth factors and the variation in requirements between cell lines have not helped in this work.

The experimental design for testing stimulation of these factors has generally followed the logic of gradually lowering the serum content of the medium and attempting to maintain growth levels by addition of specific supplements. At each stage when the serum is lowered, the medium should become limiting in one particular component which if replaced can reestablish normal cell growth (Barnes and Sato, 1980a). Experiments are designed so that the growth rate of cells in serum-containing medium (positive control) is compared with the growth rate of cells in the absence of serum but in the presence of all likely factors (Barnes and Sato, 1979; Taub and Livingston, 1981). Measurement of growth in the absence of growth factors or serum serves as a negative control. However, it is also possible that an added factor might stimulate growth by a means independent of the serum growth support limited by dilution.

Variation in the concentrations of individual growth factors establishes their optimal concentrations for cell growth. In most cases these have been found to approximate the physiological concentrations. However, some factors (e.g., insulin) have been found stimulatory at much higher levels. Although serum-supplemented medium is used to establish a positive control for cell growth, there is no reason to suppose that even higher growth levels may not be achieved with the appropriate growth factor supplementation. The natural physiological environment of each cell type is quite different with respect to exposure to these growth factors and may show considerable variation from that of blood serum. In fact 100% serum is toxic to many cells and may contain growth inhibitors as well as growth stimulators.

The response of cell types to growth stimulation is specific, and thus studies for optimal growth media formulations must be made independently for each cell line. This point has been admirably taken up in the recently published series of volumes dealing with the preparation of serum-free media and formulations found suitable for cells derived from the endocrine system, epithelial and fibroblast cells, and neuronal and lymphoid cells (Barnes et al., 1984a; 1984b; 1984c; 1984d).

4.3 NATURE OF THE GROWTH FACTORS

The macromolecular growth factors required for supplementation in serum-free media are distinguished from cellular nutrients required in the growth medium. The nutrients are used by the cells as metabolic substrates, whereas the growth factors are not normally metabolized to any great extent and are active at much lower concentrations. It is thought that the cell growth-promoting properties of serum lie in the provision of such growth factors. The characteristic properties of these growth factors include the stimulation of DNA synthesis and the induction of one or several cycles of division of quiescent cells.

The growth factors can be divided into two main categories related to the degree to which they can be characterized: those of defined molecular structure and known physiological function (e.g., insulin, transferrin, steroids), and those substances of unknown physiological function that can be extracted from biological sources. In some cases extraction can be made from the conditioned medium of cultures of growing cells that secrete the growth factor. These growth factors are characterized by their ability to promote the growth of specific cells and are generally named from their experimentally determined growth properties. They can be used at various degrees of purity and homogeneity.

4.4 EXTRACTION OF GROWTH FACTORS

The growth-promoting effects of serum added to chemically defined media are associated with its protein content (Brooks, 1975). These have been implicated as regulators of membrane permeability, as passive carriers of essential micronutrients, or as participants in cell-substratum binding. Therefore, it would seem logical to fractionate the serum proteins in order to isolate the growth-promoting properties of individual proteins.

Attempts have been made to define the roles of individual serum proteins. Electrophoresis of serum taken from the medium before and after cell growth shows some selective depletion (Figure 4–1). A marked lower content in the α-2 and β fractions after growth indicates that proteins from these fractions are absorbed into the cells (Kent and Gey, 1960). In radioactive labeling experiments, 3–6% of rabbit serum protein entered HeLa cells during culture (Eagle and Piez, 1960). Undoubtedly, other proteins

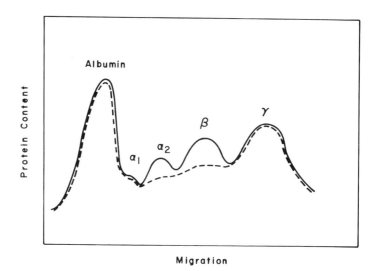

FIGURE 4–1   Electrophoresis of serum proteins taken from culture medium before (——) and after (-----) the culture of rat tumor cells (Kent and Gey, 1960).

may be utilized in the growth process without being depleted from the medium.

Although considerations have been given to these techniques in attempting to analyze and characterize the essential individual serum proteins, there are fundamental difficulties in this approach. Serum is a complex mixture of proteins, many of which are at low concentrations. At a serum content of 10–20%, the medium protein content would be 6–12 mg/ml. Within this mixture of proteins an individual mitogen would be active at 10^{-10}–10^{-8} M and would normally have a molecular weight of between 5,000 and 100,000. This would then account for between 2×10^{-2}–$5 \times 10^{-6}\%$ of the serum protein and is an unreasonably low fraction from which to expect a successful extraction. Analyzing the situation is made even more difficult because some of these proteins are synergistic in their activity, and so bioassays for individual proteins are not the most logical experimental approach (Gospodarowicz and Moran, 1976).

A far more rewarding approach to the identification and isolation of these growth factors has resulted from extractions of secretory glands such as the pituitary and submaxillary, which have proved to be a much richer source of the growth factors than circulating blood plasma. From such sources as these secretory glands, chemically defined substances such as insulin or undefined protein fractions in varying degrees of purity can be isolated. An alternative approach that has met with some success is the isolation of factors that accumulate in the culture medium of growing cells. Such conditioned medium has been a source of extraction of growth factors used for culturing various cell lines.

Looking to the future, the development of systems that permit separation of complex proteins while maintaining biological activity offers new opportunities. It now seems feasible to pass whole or albumin-depleted serum through such separation systems, reconstitute all fractions save one, and test the mixture for growth-supporting activity. By performing a series of such studies it should be possible to focus attention on serum fractions the *absence* of which removes growth support, rather than to continue the search for factors that alone or in simple combinations support cell growth. In effect, the emphasis is to find the combinations of serum factors that do in fact support growth rather than to discover factors that, at concentrations *higher* than found in serum, independently support cell proliferation.

4.5 THE ROLE OF INDIVIDUAL GROWTH FACTORS

Individual growth factors required as supplements in serum-free media can be divided into two main categories: (1) substances whose structure and physiological role have been established and well-characterized; and (2) substances of unknown physiological function, and in some cases of unknown structure, that are known to promote cell growth.

The following section describes some substances that have been observed to promote the growth of animal cells in culture. However, this section should not be considered an exhaustive list; many other isolates from biological sources will undoubtedly promote cell growth.

Table 4–1 lists examples of the concentrations of the factors used in serum-free formulations. It is of particular interest to note the relatively higher quantities of growth factors required for growth of the two primary human cell lines cited.

4.5.1 Growth Factors of Known Effects on Cell Physiology

4.5.1.1 Insulin. Insulin is a relatively small polypeptide (molecular weight: 5,700) that is known to have multiple effects on cell metabolism. In particular, cell membrane substrate transport, glucose metabolism, and biosynthesis of nucleic acids and fatty acids have all been stimulated by the presence of insulin (Komolov, 1978).

Whereas many growth stimulators are required specifically for certain cell lines, insulin appears to be a universal requirement for the in vitro growth of cells and is included in most serum-free media formulations. It is, of course, possible that the insulin requirement is linked to cell survival in the presence of the high glucose concentrations found in most media or to other nonphysiological conditions of cell culture. It is notable that the insulin concentration optimal for in vitro cell growth is considerably higher than

TABLE 4–1   **Macromolecular Supplements of Serum-free Media**[a]

Cell Type	Cells	Ins µg/ml	Trn µg/ml	EGF ng/ml	FGF ng/ml	HC µM
Established/ transformed	MRC-5/Vero[b]	1	25	10	—	—
	MDCK[c]	5	5	5	100	0.05
Tumorigenic	human carcinoma[d]	5	100	—	—	0.01
	HeLa[e]	5	5	10	50	0.05
Primary	embryonic lung (hn)[f]	10^3	10^4	10^4	—	—
	keratino- cytes (hn)[g]	10	10	10	—	50

[a] Abbreviations: Ins, insulin; Trn, transferrin; EGF, epidermal growth factor; FGF, fibroblast growth factor; HC, hydrocortisone; hn, human.

[b] Clark et al., 1982.

[c] Taub and Livingstone, 1981.

[d] Simms et al., 1980.

[e] Sato, 1980.

[f] Kan and Yamane, 1982; Hashi et al., 1982.

[g] Maciag et al., 1981.

that found in serum. The concentration level of insulin chosen for most serum-free media formulations is 5 µg/ml. This is approximately a thousand times greater than the concentration found in blood serum (Florini and Roberts, 1979), but serves to produce maximum growth stimulation for many cell lines including hybridoma cells (Chang et al., 1980) (Figure 4–2), muscle fibroblasts (Florini and Roberts, 1979), and lung carcinoma cells (Simms et al., 1980). In the case of lung carcinoma cells, some growth inhibition is observed at concentrations above 100 µg/ml (Simms et al., 1980).

Mather and Sato (1979a) relate the need for such high concentrations to the inactivation of free insulin in serum-free growth medium. By radioimmunoassay, 90% of the insulin content of F-12 medium is destroyed in one hour at 37°C (Hayashi et al., 1978). This is likely to be due to the reduction of the disulfide bridges in insulin by agents such as cysteine in the medium. Replacement of cysteine by cystine in F-12 medium reduces the insulin concentration, producing maximal stimulation in GH3 cells from 5 µg/ml to 0.5 µg/ml (Hayashi et al., 1978). The presence of serum in the medium reduces this inactivation process, and much lower insulin concentrations can be used to stimulate growth.

It has also been suggested that under physiological conditions insulin may not act as a mitogen; rather, under the relatively lower concentrations

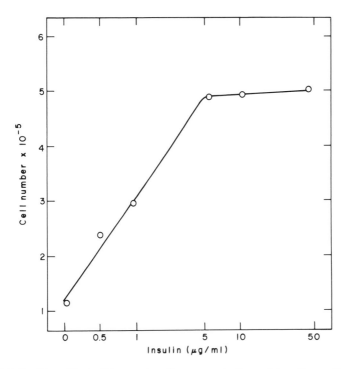

FIGURE 4–2   The effect of increasing the concentration of insulin on the growth of hybridoma cells (Chang et al., 1980).

in vitro it may be important as an anabolic agent maintaining the responsiveness of cells to other mitogenic stimuli (Gospodarowicz and Moran, 1976).

The stimulation of DNA synthesis by insulin is particularly important for in vitro cell growth. In mouse fibroblasts, Komolov (1978) showed that insulin can stimulate the uptake of tritiated thymidine into the nuclei and also increase the transformation of cells from the gap G_1 phase into the synthetic S phase during the mitotic cycle. However, in human lung carcinoma cells, Simms et al. (1980) showed that whereas deletion of insulin from a serum-free medium delayed the entry of cells into logarithmic growth, normal growth rates were eventually reestablished at the same doubling time observed in the presence of insulin.

4.5.1.2 Transferrin.   Transferrin is a protein constituent (molecular weight: 86,000) of the β-globulin fraction of blood serum and is well-characterized as being important in the transport of iron under normal physiological conditions. Virtually every cell line investigated shows positive growth response to transferrin in vitro, and consequently it has been included in most serum-free formulations.

The role of transferrin in growth stimulation is thought to be related to its ability to transport iron into the cell. To test this supposed function, Mather and Sato (1979a) determined the growth of mouse melanoma cells in serum-free medium containing varying concentrations of transferrin (Figure 4–3). They found that the observed growth stimulatory effects were dependent on the presence or absence of $FeSO_4$ in the medium. In the absence of iron there was a 15-fold increase in the cell growth at a transferrin concentration of 1 μg/ml. However, at this same transferrin concentration in the presence of iron only a 2-fold stimulation was observed.

These experiments indicate the close relationship between transferrin and iron in growth stimulation. Even though these results were obtained with iron-free transferrin, it is thought that enhanced stimulation in the absence of iron is related to the ability of transferrin to transport low contaminant levels of iron present in the medium. Mather and Sato (1979a) concluded that the role of iron transport may not be the sole effect of transferrin in cell growth stimulation. Barnes and Sato (1980b) maintained

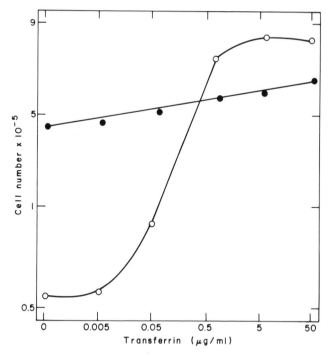

FIGURE 4–3 The effect of transferrin on the growth of mouse melanoma cells in the presence (●——●) and absence (○——○) of $FeSO_4$ (3 μM) in Hams F-12 medium (Mather and Sato, 1979a).

that transferrin can act by detoxifying trace amounts of toxic metals from the medium.

The growth-responsive concentration range for transferrin is 0.5 to 100 µg/ml (Barnes and Sato, 1980b). One report (Florini and Roberts, 1979) stated that a cell type—rat myoblasts—was unresponsive to transferrin.

4.5.1.3 Steroid hormones. A wide range of steroid hormones have been shown to be stimulatory to cell growth in culture. In a study of growth stimulation in mouse melanoma cells, Mather and Sato (1979a) showed that testosterone, progesterone, and dexamethasone are individually stimulatory in serum-free medium. This stimulation can be provided by each of these steroids, but is not additive when optimal concentrations of other hormones are provided in the medium. It is suggested that in these cells the activity of the steroids is elicited by a common metabolic product.

The specificity of growth stimulation is confined to the glucocorticoid steroids, which show only small variations in their stimulatory activity within the range $\sim 10^{-8}$ M, the concentration normally found circulating in the bloodstream under physiological conditions (Florini and Roberts, 1979).

In a study of the mode of growth stimulation of steroids, Baker et al. (1978) (Figure 4–4) showed that the synthetic glucocorticoid dexamethasone increases the binding capacity of cell membrane receptors for insulin and epidermal growth factor. This increased binding enhances the mitogenic action of these components.

Similar action is shown by hydrocortisone, which also promotes spreading of diploid fibroblasts on a substratum (Hoshi et al., 1982). However Wu et al. (1981) distinguished the growth stimulation capacity of hydrocortisone that occurs at physiological levels (5×10^{-9} M) from the capacity to affect binding and growth stimulation by hydrocortisone at higher concentrations ($> 5 \times 10^{-8}$ M).

4.5.1.4 Fibronectin. Fibronectin is a high molecular weight, multimeric glycoprotein found on the surface membrane of cells. It is associated with a host of biological functions including cell adhesion, cell aggregation, and changes in cell surface morphology (Yamada and Olden, 1978).

There are two commercially available forms that differ in source of origin but are biochemically and immunologically similar. Plasma fibronectin is isolated from blood plasma by salt fractionation and ion exchange chromatography (Grinnell and Feld, 1980) and is also known as cold-insoluble globin (CIg). This is a dimeric glycoprotein of subunit size of 200,000 to 220,000 daltons. Cellular fibronectin is isolated from the surface of fibroblast cells on which it forms a matrix of subunit size 200,000 to 250,000 daltons. This is also known as large-external-transformation-sensitive (LETS) protein or cell-surface protein (CSP).

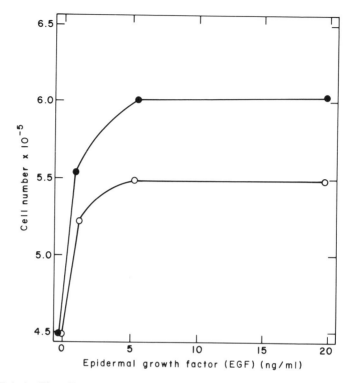

FIGURE 4–4   The effect of epidermal growth factor (EGF) on the growth of human diploid fibroblasts in the presence (●——●) or absence (○——○) of dexamethasone (Baker et al., 1978).

In cultures fibronectin is important in cell-substratum adhesion of anchorage-dependent cells. Grinnell and Feld (1980) inhibited cellular synthesis of fibronectin in human fibroblasts by dithiothreitol. This adversely affects the initial cell spreading onto culture dish surfaces in serum-free medium. However, the addition of plasma fibronectin to these inhibited cultures restores the ability of cells to adhere to their substratum.

The need for a brief preincubation with serum-containing medium before growth of rat follicular cells was recognized by Orly and Sato (1979) to be a requirement for cell-substratum adhesion. They discovered that either a preincubation of culture flasks with fibronectin or the addition of fibronectin to the serum-free medium enables cell adhesion and proliferation.

In the absence of either serum or fibronectin, these cells do not attach well to the surface of culture dishes and 60% of cells become binucleated after 24 hours (Figure 4–5). This indicates a role for fibronectin in the organization of the cytoskeleton during cytokinesis, which involves the separation of cells following DNA replication. It would appear that this role of fibronectin is specific and dose dependent.

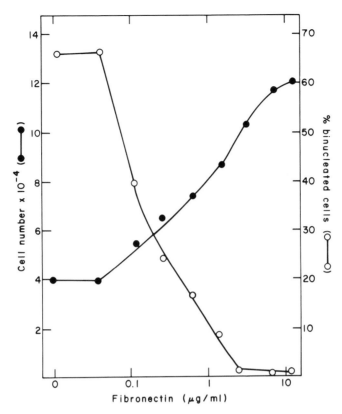

FIGURE 4–5   The growth and extent of binucleation of rat follicular cells grown on surfaces preincubated with various concentrations of fibronectin (Orly and Sato, 1979).

A fibronectin concentration of 8 μg/ml in the medium or in the preincubation solution is sufficient for the growth of some cells (Orly and Sato, 1979). This is a lower concentration compared to the 200 μg/ml measured in human serum (Mosesson and Umfleet, 1970).

As cells can synthesize fibronectin, the need for fibronectin supplementation in culture medium varies among cell types. Some transformed cells have apparently lost the ability to produce fibronectin, and this may be related to their loss of anchorage dependence.

Fibronectin is purported to be important to cell growth under conditions where cell-substratum attachment may be problematic. This has been reported to be necessary for some cell attachment on microcarriers (Clark et al., 1982), but under other circumstances cells may synthesize quantities themselves without the necessity for medium supplementation (Grinnell and Feld, 1979). In our experience with a wide variety of cell lines grown on

DEAE-dextran microcarriers, addition of fibronectin has not improved cell attachment or growth.

4.5.2   Growth Factors of Unknown Effects on Cell Physiology

4.5.2.1   Epidermal growth factor.   This is a low molecular weight (6,100) acidic protein originally isolated from the submaxillary gland of adult male mice (Cohen, 1962). Although the protein is present in many other tissues, this gland has been found to be the richest source of this factor. The concentration of the factor increases in the submaxillary gland of the male mouse during puberty. However, its physiological function is uncertain. It has been found to be a mitogen for many cell lines, although its original bioassay was the induction of precocious eyelid opening and acceleration of incisor eruption in newborn mice (Cohen, 1962; Taylor et al., 1972).

Its mitogenic property is related to the large number of receptor sites present on the cell membrane, which can be determined by ^{125}I-EGF binding (Baker et al., 1978; Johnson et al., 1980). The response range for growth of cell lines in vitro is 1–100 ng/ml (Barnes and Sato, 1980a). However, cells that are transformed and show a lower serum requirement lose their requirement for EGF in serum-free media. Cherington et al. (1979) found that baby hamster kidney (BHK) and Chinese hamster embryo fibroblast (CHEF) cells lost their EGF requirement on transformation. An EGF concentration of 1 μg/ml in the presence of insulin enables normal chicken heart mesenchymal cells to proliferate at the same rate as their Rous sarcoma virus-infected counterparts (Balk et al., 1982).

EGF from mouse submaxillary gland, readily available commercially, is used in the formulation of most serum-free media. However, Carpenter and Cohen (1976) used a protein extract from human urine. This human EGF (hEGF) gives a $4\times$ increase in the cell density and a $20\times$ increase in the incorporation of tritiated thymidine when added to cultures of human foreskin fibroblasts.

Steroids can enhance the mitogenic activity of EGF. Increased binding of EGF to the cellular membrane of human fibroblasts is found in the presence of the synthetic glucocorticoid steroid dexamethasone (Figure 4–4) (Baker et al., 1978). The addition of the steroid alone has no effect on these cells. However, 100 ng/ml dexamethasone increases the dose-dependent growth response by 50%. These studies show that the steroid increases the ability of ^{125}I-EGF to bind by between 50% and 100%. This enhancement in binding, which is EGF concentration-dependent, is shown to be a result of an increased affinity of binding by the available receptors rather than an increase in the number of receptors. The increased receptor binding is specific for the glucocorticoid steroids dexamethasone, cortisol, estrogen, and cholesterol. Other reports confirm this synergistic effect of steroids and EGF on the growth of various cells (Hoshi et al., 1982).

In some cases EGF can inhibit cell growth even in the presence of a high number of membrane receptors. Barnes (1982) showed that 10 ng/ml EGF completely inhibits the growth of human carcinoma cells. This effect is not due to its toxicity and is reversible on removal of EGF from the medium or on addition of neutralizing antibodies to EGF.

EGF can elicit major effects on phenotypic expression of particularly sensitive differentiated cell lines such as those from rat pituitary (Johnson et al., 1980; Schonbrunn et al., 1980). In these cells EGF changes the pattern of hormonal control. It acts as a regulator in increasing prolactin synthesis, decreasing growth hormone synthesis, and changing the cells' response to other hormones. The cell morphology is also changed from a spherical to an elongated appearance.

4.5.2.2 Fibroblast growth factor. Fibroblast growth factor is a class of polypeptides first isolated from bovine pituitary gland and subsequently from bovine brain (Gospodarowicz et al., 1978). Isolates from both sources stimulate growth and division of the same range of fibroblastic connective tissue cells in culture.

Brain fibroblast growth factor has been separated into three fractions of molecular weights 11,000 to 13,000, but unexpectedly shows little structural resemblance to the pituitary gland isolate (Gospodarowicz et al., 1978). However, it is suggested (Westall et al., 1978; Thomas et al., 1980) that the biological activity is associated with an acid-insoluble component present in low concentrations in the brain isolates.

4.5.2.3 Nerve growth factor. One of the first growth factors to be described, nerve growth factor stimulates the growth and differentiation of the cells of the peripheral nervous system (Bradshaw, 1978). Its biological assay is based upon its ability to promote neurite outgrowth in pheochromocytoma cells (Andres et al., 1977). In addition to its ability to stimulate innervation of transplanted sarcomas, its other stimulatory activities include neurotubule polymerization (Angeletti et al., 1965), anabolic metabolism, and sensitivity of neural cells to electrical or acetylcholine stimuli (Dichter and Tischler, 1977).

Nerve growth factor was first extracted from the submaxillary gland of the male mouse as a high molecular weight complex classified as 7S. Further purification (100×) reveals biological activity in a 2.5S complex extracted from the mouse submaxillary gland (Bocchini and Angeletti, 1969). This consists of a dimer of two identical polypeptide chains of molecular weight 13,000 linked noncovalently. Investigations into its site of action reveal the presence of two distinct receptor sites in embryonic dorsal root neurons (Andres et al., 1977). One group of sites is associated with the plasma membrane while the other group is located in the nucleus. This suggests a biphasic mechanism of action in which interaction with plasma membrane receptors is followed by internalization and complexation with the secondary receptors in the nuclei of the target cells.

Structural and functional relationships have been found between nerve growth factor and the hormones insulin and relaxin. The sequence homologies and similar three-dimensional structure suggest a common ancestral molecular origin (Bradshaw, 1978).

4.5.2.4 Gimmel factor. McClure et al. (1981) have isolated an extract of rat submaxillary gland that stimulates the growth of glioma cells in vitro. Crude extracts of this factor show that it is heat-labile, acid-stable, and partially inactivated by protease or mercaptoethanol. Activity of the extract is shown in molecular weight fractions 20,000 and 40,000 and is distinct from either fibroblast or epidermal growth factors, also extracted from the submaxillary gland. The range of mitogenic activities of Gimmel factor is distinct from FGF or EGF, and antibodies to the latter factors do not inhibit the activity of Gimmel.

4.5.2.5 Human T-cell growth factor. Human T-cell growth factor or interleukin-2 is a mitogenic protein released into the medium by T-lymphocytes that have been exposed to the lectin phytohemagglutinin (PHA) in culture. It can be purified $800\times$ as a 13,000 molecular weight protein from conditioned serum-free medium of such cells (Mier and Gallo, 1982). Its target cells in terms of mitogenic activity include the T-lymphocytes from which it is extracted. Its assay is based on its ability to induce the uptake of tritiated thymidine into these cells.

4.5.2.6 Multiplication-stimulating activity. Multiplication-stimulating activity (MSA) is isolated from conditioned medium of cultures of rat liver cells. Its mitogenic activity includes growth stimulation and DNA-synthesis stimulation in chick fibroblasts (Dulak and Temin, 1973a). It consists of four biologically active polypeptides of molecular weights around 10,000 (Dulak and Temin, 1973b).

Its mitogenic action has been compared to that of insulin. At 100 ng/ ml it can replace the insulin requirement in serum-free medium for the growth of embryonic carcinoma cells, although the mitogenic activity is not mediated through the same membrane receptors (Nagarajan et al., 1982).

4.6 ADVANTAGES OF SERUM-FREE MEDIUM

4.6.1 Endocrine Regulation of Cells

The response of cells to hormones and growth factors in vitro is of interest in order to attain an understanding of their interactions in vivo under normal physiological conditions. However, the varied hormonal composition of serum renders the results of these types of experiments difficult to assess unless the cells are grown in a completely chemically defined medium.

Examples of this type of study include the use of primary kidney cells for examining renal transport functions (Taub and Livingston, 1981). Steroid synthesis of a primary culture of ovarian cells can be studied in response to the addition of stimulators to the serum-free medium (Schreiber et al., 1980). Human keratinocytes can be isolated from newborns or adults (Maciag et al., 1981). The response of these and other cells to endocrine stimulation is of particular interest in understanding hormonal control during normal physiological development (McEvery and Leung, 1982).

These types of study, requiring the extrapolation of the results of the response of cells in vitro to their normal physiological response, are particularly relevant when primary cells are involved. Although it has been found much easier to promote the growth of transformed cells in serum-free medium, the more fastidious growth requirements of primary cells are being established.

The growth of tumor cells in cultures of serum-free media has been studied extensively. This has been possible because the limited requirement of these cells for hormones and growth factors means that the formulation of the serum-free media of these cells is relatively simple compared to the fastidious growth requirements of other cells. A plausible explanation for this behavior is the production of growth factors (autocrine factors) by the tumor cells themselves. By careful control of the medium composition of cells taken from biopsies, the tumor cells can be selected from a mixture of cell types (Sato, 1980; Carney et al., 1981). Such cultures could be used to study the sensitivity of the cells to therapeutic drugs and represent a process that may find important clinical application.

4.6.2 Large-scale Cultures

In assessing the feasibility of using animal cell cultures for the production of biologicals on a large scale (> 10 liters), overall operational costs must be assessed along with the reliability of the process. In nearly all cases, the apparent cost of a serum-supplemented medium is lower than a medium supplemented with hormones and growth factors (Kromer et al., 1982). However, the dangers of contamination of blood serum batches as well as variability in composition among batches could result in a cost accounting that strongly favors serum-free formulations.

The financial argument in favor of the use of serum-free medium on a large scale becomes stronger when it is considered that the major cost of such operations is the work force labor cost. Thus, a higher failure rate of large batches of serum-supplemented cultures could prove very wasteful financially.

In assessing the production of biologicals in a pure form, the ease of purification is a crucial factor. In most cases the extraction of extracellularly released products from a defined medium can be much easier than from the mass of unknown proteins associated with a serum-supplemented medium. The extraction and purification of human lymphoblastoid interferon from the medium of growing Namalva cells can be accomplished easily using the serum-free medium developed for this system (Lazar et al., 1982; Zoon et al., 1979). Also, the purification of monoclonal antibodies is eased by the development of a serum-free medium for hybridomas whose antibody production is no different in such a medium from that supplemented with 10% fetal calf serum (Chang et al., 1980).

4.7 CONCLUSION

In the development of serum-free media for cell growth over the last ten years, numerous formulations can be cited for transformed and tumorigenic cells. Compared with primary and normal diploid cells they have a lowered serum requirement, and this seems to translate into a less fastidious requirement for hormones and growth factors in the absence of serum.

However, good progress is now being made to induce the growth in culture of those primary cell types that have hitherto proved difficult; in particular, formulations now available enable desired cell types to proliferate from primary sources (Mather and Sato, 1979b). Cultures of these primary cells are important in enabling studies of physiological interactions that sometimes prove difficult and time-consuming in whole animal studies.

Development of low-cost, serum-free media formulations offers the twin advantages of reproducibility and relative freedom from undesired biological contamination.

REFERENCES

Andres, R.Y., Jeng, I., and Bradshaw, R.A. (1977) *Proc. Natl. Acad. Sci. USA* 74, 2785–2789.

Angeletti, P.U., Gandini-Attardi, D., Toschi, G., Salvi, M.L., and Levi-Montalcini, R. (1965) *Biochim. Biophys. Acta* 95, 111–120.

Baker, J.B., Barsh, G.S., Carney, D.H., and Cunningham, D.D. (1978) *Proc. Natl. Acad. Sci. USA* 75, 1882–1886.

Balk, S.D., Shiu, R.P.C., Lafleur, M.M., and Young, L.L. (1982) *Proc. Natl. Acad. Sci. USA* 79, 1154–1157.

Barnes, D., and Sato, G. (1979) *Nature* 281, 388–389.

Barnes, D., and Sato, G. (1980a) *Anal. Biochem.* 102, 255–320.

Barnes, D., and Sato, G. (1980b) *Cell* 22, 649–655.

Barnes, D.W. (1982) *J. Cell Biol.* 93, 1–4.

Barnes, D.W., Sirbasku, D.A., and Sato, G.H., eds. (1984a) *Methods for Preparation of Media, Supplements, and Substrata for Serum-Free Animal Cell Culture*, 355 pp., Alan R. Liss, Inc., New York.

Barnes, D.W., Sirbasku, D.A., and Sato, G.H., eds. (1984b) *Methods for Serum-Free Culture of Cells of the Endocrine System*, 255 pp., Alan R. Liss, Inc., New York.

Barnes, D.W., Sirbasku, D.A., and Sato, G.H., eds. (1984c) *Methods for Serum-Free Culture of Epithelial and Fibroblastic Cells*, 291 pp., Alan R. Liss, Inc., New York.

Barnes, D.W., Sirbasku, D.A., and Sato, G.H., eds. (1984d) *Methods for Serum-Free Culture of Neuronal and Lymphoid Cells*, 263 pp., Alan R. Liss, Inc., New York.

Bocchini, V., and Angeletti, P.U. (1969) *Proc. Natl. Acad. Sci. USA* 64, 787–794.

Bradshaw, R.A. (1978) *Annu. Rev. Biochem.* 47, 191–216.

Brooks, R.F. (1975) in *Structure and Function of Plasma Proteins* (Allison, A.C., ed.) pp. 1–112, Plenum Press, New York.

Carney, D.N., Bunn, P.A., Gazdar, A.F., Pagan, J.A., and Minna, J.D. (1981) *Proc. Natl. Acad. Sci. USA* 78, 3185–3189.

Carpenter, G., and Cohen, S. (1976) *J. Cell Physiol.* 88, 227–237.

Chang, T.H., Steplewski, Z., and Koprowski, H. (1980) *J. Immunol. Meth.* 39, 369–375.

Cherington, P.V., Smith, B.L., and Pardee, A.B. (1979) *Proc. Natl. Acad. Sci. USA* 76, 3937–3941.

Clark, J.M., Gebb, C., and Hirtenstein, M.D. (1982) *Develop. Biol. Stand.* 50, 81–91.

Cohen, S. (1962) *J. Biol. Chem.* 237, 1555–1562.

Dichter, M.A., and Tischler, A.S. (1977) *Nature* 268, 501–504.

Dulak, N.C., and Temin, H.M. (1973a) *J. Cell Physiol.* 81, 153–160.

Dulak, N.C., and Temin, H.M. (1973b) *J. Cell Physiol.* 81, 161–170.

Eagle, H., and Piez, K.A. (1960) *J. Biol. Chem.* 235, 1095–1097.

Florini, J.R., and Roberts, S.B. (1979) *In Vitro* 15, 983–992.

Gospodarowicz, D., and Moran, J.S. (1976) *Annu. Rev. Biochem.* 45, 531–558.

Gospodarowicz, D., Bialecki, H., and Greenburg, G. (1978) *J. Biol. Chem.* 253, 3736–3743.

Grinnell, F., and Feld, M.K. (1979) *Cell* 17, 117–129.

Grinnell, F., and Feld, M.K. (1980) *J. Cell Physiol.* 104, 321–334.

Hayashi, I., Larner, J., and Sato, G. (1978) *In Vitro* 14, 24.

Higuchi, K. (1976) *Meth. Cell Biol.* 14, 131–143.

Hoshi, H., Kan, M., Yamane, I., and Minamoto, Y. (1982) *Biomed. Res.* 3, 546–552.

Johnson, L.K., Baxter, J.D., Vlodavsky, I., and Gospodarowicz, D. (1980) *Proc. Natl. Acad. Sci. USA* 77, 394–398.

Kan, M., and Yamane, I. (1982) *J. Cell Physiol.* 111, 155–162.

Kent, H.N., and Gey, G.O. (1960) *Science* 131, 666–668.

Komolov, I.S. (1978) *Endocrinol. Exp.* 12, 43–48.

Kromer, E., Scheirer, W., and Katinger, H.W.D. (1982) *Develop. Biol. Stand.* 50, 355–359.

Lazar, A., Reuveny, S., Traub, A., Minai, M., Grosfield, H., Feinstein, S., Gez, M., and Mizrahi, A. (1982) *Develop. Biol. Stand.* 50, 167–171.

Maciag, T., Nemore, R.E., Weinstein, R., and Gilchrest, B.A. (1981) *Science* 211, 1452–1454.

Mather, J.P., and Sato, G.H. (1979a) *Exp. Cell Res.* 120, 191–200.

Mather, J.P., and Sato, G.H. (1979b) *Exp. Cell Res.* 124, 215–221.

McClure, D.B., Ohasa, S., and Sato, G.H. (1981) *J. Cell Physiol.* 107, 195–208.

McEvery, R., and Leung, P.E. (1982) *Endocrinology* 111, 1568–1575.

Mier, J.W., and Gallo, R.C. (1982) *J. Immunol.* 128, 1122–1127.

Mosesson, M.W., and Umfleet, R.A. (1970) *J. Biol. Chem.* 245, 5728–5736.

Nagarajan, L., Nissley, S.P., Rechler, M.M., and Anderson, W. B. (1982) *Endocrinology* 110, 1231–1237.

Orly, J., and Sato, G. (1979) *Cell* 17, 295–306.

Sato, G.H. (1980) *Progress Cancer Res. Ther.* 14, 281–286.

Schonbrunn, A., Krasnoff, M., Westendorf, J.M., and Tashjian, A.H. (1980) *J. Cell Biol.* 85, 786–797.

Schreiber, J.R., Hsuh, A.J.W., Weinstein, D.B., and Erickson, G.F. (1980) *J. Steroid Biochem.* 13, 1009–1014.

Simms, E., Gazilar, A.F., Abrams, P.G., and Minna, J.D. (1980) *Cancer Res.* 40, 4356–4363.

Taub, M., and Livingston, D. (1981) *Ann. N.Y. Acad. Sci.* 372, 406–421.

Taylor, J.M., Mitchell, W.M., and Cohen, S. (1972) *J. Biol. Chem.* 247, 5928–5934.

Thomas, K.A., Riley, M.C., Lemmon, S.K., Baglan, N.C., and Bradshaw, R.A. (1980) *J. Biol. Chem.* 255, 5517–5520.

Westall, F.C., Lennon, V.A., and Gospodarowicz, D. (1978) *Proc. Natl. Acad. Sci. USA* 75, 4675–4678.

Wu, R., Wolfe, R.A., and Sato, G.H. (1981) *J. Cell Physiol.* 108, 83–90.

Yamada, K.M., and Olden, K. (1978) *Nature* 275, 179–184.

Zoon, K.C., Bridgen, P.J., and Smith, M.E. (1979) *J. Gen. Virol.* 44, 227–229.

Nutrients, Oxygen, and pH

James N. Thomas

5.1 INTRODUCTION

Since it is becoming increasingly important to produce biologically active proteins in mammalian cells, it is also important to focus attention on providing an optimum in vitro growth environment for cultured cells. An adequate discussion of all the components that make up the cellular environment would be beyond the scope of this chapter; therefore, I address in detail three important and controllable factors: nutrients, oxygen, and pH. This chapter is not intended to be an exhaustive review of the literature in these areas, but rather to give the reader a better perspective of the problems facing cell culturists as they try to optimize these parameters for their specific cell culture systems. The final section of the chapter discusses how some of these parameters, and others, affect medium design.

5.2 NUTRIENTS

The nutritional requirements of cells in vitro differ considerably from the nutritional requirements of intact animals. This is not surprising, since we ask cultured cells to survive without normal interaction with other cells and tissues in the body. Requirements also differ from cell line to cell line because of differences in tissue or species origin or level of adaptation and/

or transformation. Despite the many differences in the nutritional requirements of cell lines, some trends are apparent.

In this section, I deal with nutrients from a utilization perspective, where applicable. I also discuss how some nutrients are metabolized. The nutrients that seem to disappear from the medium at the fastest rate, namely the amino acids and carbohydrates, are covered in more detail than the other nutritional components.

5.2.1 Amino Acids

Eagle (1955) found that 12 amino acids were required for proliferation of strain L mouse fibroblasts in a medium containing 0.25 to 2% dialyzed horse serum. If any of the 12 amino acids was omitted from the medium, cells died within one to three days. Later, Eagle (1959) found glutamine to be the most heavily consumed of all the amino acids, bringing the list of essential amino acids for mouse L cells to 13. These 13 amino acids in Eagle's popular culture medium MEM (minimum Eagle's medium) are arginine, cyst(e)ine, glutamine, histidine, isoleucine, leucine, lysine, methionine, phenylalanine, threonine, tryptophan, tyrosine, and valine. With some exceptions, these amino acids are considered essential for both normal and established cell lines. Their rates of utilization by cells in culture vary drastically and, as discussed later, are affected by a number of culture conditions.

Table 5–1 provides data on the disappearance and production of amino acids in several cell lines, including both normal and transformed cells.

The amino acid utilized to the greatest extent in each of these cultures is glutamine, although its rate of utilization varies considerably. From Table 5–1 we can see that human epithelioma cells (McCarty, 1962) consume around 72×10^{-9} µM of glutamine/cell/hour, whereas BHK-21 clone 13 cells consume only 6.9×10^{-9} µM of glutamine/cell/hour (Arathoon and Telling, 1982). Several researchers have found that glutamine disappearance from cell culture media is 5 or 10 times the rate of other amino acids (Mohberg and Johnson, 1963; Griffiths and Pirt, 1967; Blaker et al., 1971; Lambert and Pirt, 1975; Butler and Thilly, 1982; Butler et al., 1983). Griffiths and Pirt (1967) suggested that glutamate could be substituted for most of the glutamine in mouse LS cell suspension cultures, and Blaker et al. (1971) made the same suggestion for HeLa cells. This observation did not hold true for MDCK cells (Imamura et al., 1982), which indicates that substitution of glutamate for glutamine in the culture environment may be a function of cell type.

The reason for this high rate of utilization is still not completely understood, but may be related to the use of glutamine as an energy source. A large portion of the carbon skeleton of glutamine seems to be oxidized in the tricarboxylic acid (TCA) cycle (Pardridge et al., 1978). Carbon dioxide has been shown to be the major end product of glutamine metabolism in cultured cells by several workers (Kovacevic and Morris, 1972; Stoner and

TABLE 5-1 Disappearance or Production of Amino Acids in Different Cell Lines ($\times 10^{-9}$ μM/cell h)

Cell Type	Jensen Sarcoma[a]	MOPC-31 C/R Mouse Plasma-cytoma[b]	L-M Mouse Fibroblast[c]	Normal Human Embryo Intestine[c]	Normal Human Pituitary[d]	HeLa Gey-Cervical Carcinoma[d]	KB, Eagle-Squamous Cell Carci-noma of the Lip[d]	H.Ep.No.2 Fjelde Human Epithelioma of Larynx[d]	BHK-21 Clone 13 (Suspen-sion)[e]
1. Glutamine	−59.45	−26.20	−57.60	−62.0	−25.6	−51.2	−58.0	−71.7	−6.9
2. Leucine	−7.15	−10.10	−3.7	−14.9	−19.4	−11.7	−10.2	−13.6	−2.3
3. Isoleucine	−6.68	−15.10	−3.6	−10.4	−14.2	−9.9	−9.0	−12.1	−2.3
4. Lysine	−7.65	−8.70	−1.5	−9.8	−10.5	−9.9	−10.2	−9.8	−1.8
5. Threonine	−2.65	nc	−1.8	−17.5	−3.4	−1.3	−3.1	−3.5	−1.2
6. Valine	−3.93	−1.6	−3.0	−4.3	−19.3	−8.8	−0.5	−9.7	−2.3
7. Tyrosine	−1.53	−7.0	−1.1	−0.3	−5.0	−5.8	−2.4	−4.6	−1.5
8. Phenylalanine	−2.45	−1.30	−1.1	−0.3	−5.0	−5.1	−2.4	−1.5	−0.30
9. Asparagine	−14.22	nc	nc	nm	nm	nm	nm	nm	2.6
10. Arginine	−2.73	nc	−1.7	−28.3	−23.5	−20.3	−17.1	−4.0	−1.9
11. Methionine	−2.6	−1.9	−1.0	−5.0	−13.4	−0.3	−0.3	−3.1	−1.1
12. Histidine	−2.4	nc	−0.5	−6.7	−5.3	−5.6	−5.6	−2.9	nm
13. Alanine	+3.25	nc	+0.4	+9.5	+11.1	+1.4	+15.8	+9.0	+5.8

TABLE 5-1 (Continued)

Cell Type	Jensen Sarcoma[a]	MOPC-31 C/R Mouse Plasma-cytoma[b]	L-M Mouse Fibroblast[c]	Normal Human Embryo Intestine[d]	Normal Human Pituitary[d]	HeLa Gey-Cervical Carcinoma[d]	KB, Eagle-Squamous Cell Carcinoma of the Lip[d]	H.Ep.No.2 Fjelde Human Epithelioma of Larynx[d]	BHK-21 Clone 13 (Suspension)[c]
14. Serine	-7.63	+2.6	+0.3	nc	-2.6	+0.4	nc	nc	-3.4
15. Glycine	-0.4	+1.9	+6.9	+1.6	-10.5	+5.0	+1.5	+0.3	+2.9
16. Tryptophan	nm	nm	nm	-0.3	-1.3	-2.0	-3.1	-0.5	-0.30
17. Cystine	-1.68	nm	-0.8	+0.1	-1.3	+0.5	-5.4	-3.8	-0.30
18. Proline	-4.5	+1.5	+2.9	+1.1	-5.4	+1.5	+2.6	+1.4	+0.30
19. Aspartic Acid	+6.6	+0.80	+2.0	nc	nc	+3.1	+1.1	nc	-1.71
20. Glutamic Acid	+14.1	+3.1	+5.0	+4.4	+3.2	+16.4	+7.8	+15.2	-5.4

nc = no change

nm = not measured

[a] Kruse et al. (1967)

[b] Roberts et al. (1976)

[c] Stoner and Merchant (1972)

[d] McCarty (1962)

[e] Arathoon and Telling (1982)

Merchant, 1972; Lavietes et al., 1974; Zielke et al., 1978). Approximately 40% of the energy requirement of Chinese hamster fibroblasts (Donnelly and Scheffler, 1976) and 30% of the energy requirement of human diploid fibroblasts (Zielke et al., 1978) were found to be met by glutamine in a 5.5-mM glucose medium. Lower glucose concentrations resulted in higher rates of glutamine utilization.

Glutamine also serves in the biosynthesis of aspartic acid, proline (Levintow et al., 1957), and asparagine (Levintow, 1957) in some cells and may also be critical for DNA replication as measured by autoradiographic determinations of ^{3}H-thymidine incorporation (Zetterberg and Engstrom, 1981). Reed et al. (1981) have suggested that some of the carbon atoms of glutamine might also function as precursors for the synthesis of lipids.

The branched-chain amino acids, namely, leucine, isoleucine, and valine, also disappear from the culture medium at relatively high rates, but at much slower rates than glutamine. These amino acids are of course incorporated into cellular protein, but may also function, like glutamine, as energy sources in cells. In support of this, Pardridge et al. (1981) found the utilization of branched-chain amino acids to increase more than 4-fold in primary myoblasts incubated in a medium depleted of glucose.

Some cells have an unusually high requirement for one amino acid or another. Examples of this behavior, listed in Table 5–1, are the elevated consumption of arginine in normal human intestine, normal human pituitary, HeLa, KB, and H. Ep. No. 2 cells. Whether the high level of arginine disappearance was due to high levels of arginase in the serum, mycoplasma (PPLO) contamination, or to a true metabolic need of the cells is not clear. However, it is now known that PPLO contamination was widespread at the time McCarty's work was published, and this contamination causes a higher rate of arginine disappearance from the medium (Kruse et al., 1967). Other unusual amino acid requirements are Jensen Sarcoma cells' requirement for asparagine, serine, glycine, and proline; normal human pituitary cells' requirement for serine, glycine, and proline; and BHK-21 clone 13 cells' requirement for glutamic acid, aspartic acid, and serine.

The specific amino acids provided in the medium and their quantity may also affect utilization rates, and might account for some of the differences in utilization pattern seen in Table 5–1. Nevertheless, some general statements can be made about amino acid utilization. Glutamine is almost always highly utilized; and leucine, isoleucine, lysine, threonine, valine, tyrosine, methionine, histidine, and phenylalanine are also utilized, but to a much lesser extent than glutamine. Alanine, glutamic acid, serine, glycine, proline, and aspartic acid concentration in culture media generally remain unchanged or increase. The changes in concentrations of the other amino acids tend to be much less predictable. In order to effectively meet the amino acid requirements of a particular cell line, an analysis of the disappearance and appearance of individual amino acids should be done using medium intended for the production of the desired product.

5.2.2 Carbohydrates

For several years, it has been known that cells cultured in vitro survive and grow in media containing a variety of carbohydrates other than glucose. Eagle (1958) used nine cell lines, both normal and transformed, to study the effect of a variety of carbohydrates on cell growth. He found that the compounds that promoted growth in a similar fashion to glucose were two disaccharides (trehalose and turanose), three hexoses (D-fructose, D-galactose, and D-mannose), and two phosphate esters (D-glucose-1-phosphate and D-glucose-6-phosphate). The concentrations of some of these compounds had to be increased for this effect, and 1 mM pyruvate was essential to produce consistent growth when D-galactose was tested. Burns et al. (1976) examined 93 carbohydrates in five cell lines and found that 15 supported cell proliferation in one or more of the cell lines, and 42 were toxic or growth-inhibitory. In addition to the compounds found by Eagle (1959) to support growth, D-xylose, sorbitol, maltose, maltotriose, dextrine, glycogen, amylose, and D-galacturonate were found to support growth to some extent. Most of these additional compounds also required pyruvate to support growth. The most effective compounds are the di-, tri-, and polysaccharides that are composed of glucose monomers. The ability of cells to utilize some of these carbohydrates probably depends on the type and concentration of enzymes present in the serum used.

Cristofalo and Kritchevsky (1965) cultured WI-38 cells on media containing glucose, mannose, fructose, or galactose and found that these carbohydrates would substitute for glucose in this cell line. As seen in Table 5–2, the other carbohydrates are utilized at a slower rate than glucose, but fructose utilization is especially slow. In addition, less lactate was produced per mole of fructose and galactose than per mole of glucose and mannose.

Imamura et al. (1982) found that when MDCK cells were grown in media containing either 20 mM glucose, 20 mM fructose, or 5 mM maltose,

TABLE 5–2 Sugar Utilization and Lactate Production in WI-38

Sugar, 5.5 mM	Sugar Utilized, μmoles/ml	%	% of Control*	Lactate Produced, μmoles/ml	Lactate: Hexose
Glucose	3.61	66	100	8.33	2.3
Mannose	3.14	57	87	6.37	2.03
Fructose	1.58	29	44	2.36	1.49
Galactose	2.78	50	77	2.50	1.11

* Control value, glucose = 100%

Reprinted with permission from Cristofalo, V.J., and Kritchevsky, D. (1965) *Proc. Soc. Exp. Biol. Med.* 118, 1109–1112.

a maximum cell density of 2.0×10^6 cells per ml was obtained for each carbon source (Figure 5–1). The amount of lactate produced was considerably less in the fructose- and maltose-containing cultures (Figure 5–2), although the low values in the maltose cultures may be due to the lower initial concentration of maltose compared to the other carbohydrates and to the concentration of maltase in the serum.

The rate of utilization of carbohydrates, especially glucose, can vary tremendously between cell types, although culture conditions probably affect this rate considerably. Table 5–3 shows the rate of utilization of glucose, maltose, and fructose in MDCK cells and of glucose in a number of other cell lines.

The concentration of glucose in the culture medium seems to be critical in determining its rate of utilization. For most cell lines, the higher the concentration, the faster the disappearance from the medium. This may not be the case for other hexoses such as fructose. Imamura et al. (1982) compared the utilization rates of fructose and glucose at different concentrations in the culture medium. They found at higher concentrations that

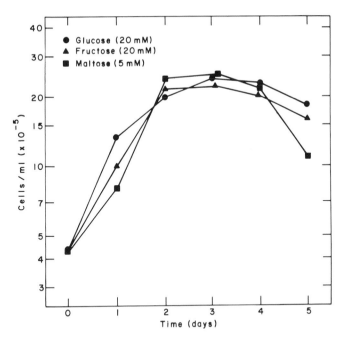

FIGURE 5–1 Growth curves of MDCK cells in medium containing glucose (20 mM), fructose (20 mM), or maltose (5 mM). Reprinted with permission from Imamura, T., Crespi, C.L., Thilly, W.G., and Brunengraber, H. (1982) *Anal. Biochem.* 124, 353–358.

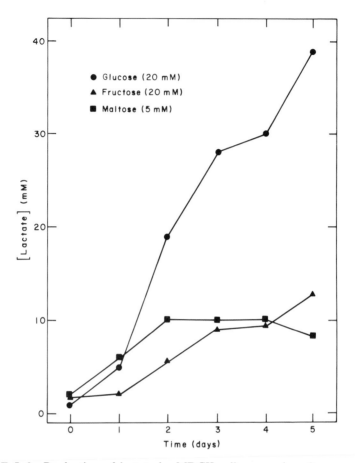

FIGURE 5–2 Production of lactate by MDCK cells grown in cultures containing glucose (20 mM), fructose (20 mM), or maltose (5 mM). Reprinted with permission from Imamura, T., Crespi, C.L., Thilly, W.G., and Brunengraber, H. (1982) *Anal. Biochem.* 124, 353–358.

glucose was removed more rapidly, but fructose removal from the medium did not appear to be concentration-dependent. This information is summarized in Figure 5–3.

Reitzer et al. (1979) grew HeLa cells on either glucose, galactose, or fructose and found growth to be similar on each carbon source. However, they found that the metabolic pathways used by the cells were much different for each compound. When glucose was present at > 1 mM concentration, 80% of it was converted to lactic acid and only 4–5% entered the TCA cycle for production of energy via oxidative phosphorylation. On the other hand, when fructose was present as the carbohydrate source, the glycolytic

TABLE 5–3   **Carbohydrate Utilization in Different Cell Lines** ($\times 10^{-9}$ μmoles/cell/h)

Cell line	Glucose	Maltose	Fructose
MDCK, Canine kidney epithelium[a]	116.6	81.8	28.5
Jensen rat sarcoma[b]	258.0	—	—
Walker rat carcinosarcoma 256[b]	467.0	—	—
WISH human amnion[b]	116.0	—	—
H. Ep.-2 human carcinoma[b]	195	—	—
WI-38 human lung (diploid)[b]	324	—	—
BHK-21 Clone 13[c]	90	—	—
HeLa[d]	136	—	—

[a] Imamura et al., 1982

[b] Kruse and Miedema, 1965

[c] Arathoon and Telling, 1982

[d] Blaker et al., 1971

pathway was almost inactive, and most of the carbon from fructose entered the pentose phosphate pathway. Galactose seemed to be somewhere between glucose and fructose in its effect on energy metabolism. The significance of this observation is that when the carbohydrate is switched from glucose to galactose to fructose, HeLa cells must radically change their energy metabolism and increasingly derive their energy from oxidative phosphorylation. This is supported by work done by Fleischaker (1982) on the oxygen uptake rate of FS-4 (normal human diploid fibroblast) cells grown on different carbohydrates. FS-4 cells grown on galactose consumed more oxygen than those grown on glucose, suggesting a higher rate of oxidative phosphorylation in the galactose-containing cultures. (See Table 9–1 in Chapter 9 for an example.)

The question that naturally occurs at this point is: What compound is being oxidized to provide needed energy for the cells? The answer is probably glutamine. Reitzer et al. (1979) have suggested that as much as 98% of the energy requirement of HeLa cells is met by glutamine when these cells are grown on galactose or fructose. The uptake of glutamine plus glutamate has been shown to be higher in MDCK cells grown on fructose than in those grown on glucose, and the rate of ammonia production is higher in the fructose-containing cultures (Imamura et al., 1982). The choice of carbohydrate will therefore affect other components in the medium.

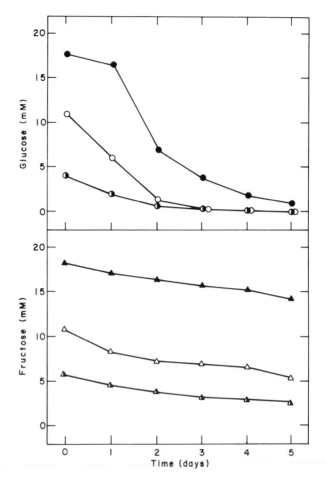

FIGURE 5–3 Disappearance of glucose and fructose from cultures of MDCK cells as a function of initial carbohydrate concentration. The initial concentrations of glucose and fructose were 20 mM (●, ▲), 10 mM (○, △), and 5 mM (◑, ▲), respectively. Reprinted with permission from Imamura, T., Crespi, C.L., Thilly, W.G., and Brunengraber, H. (1982) *Anal. Biochem.* 124, 353–358.

5.2.3 Other Nutrients

5.2.3.1 Lipids. Some controversy exists as to the essentialness of lipids for cells cultured in vitro. It has been known for years that intact animals require the ω6 fatty acid series, in particular, linoleic acid, for optimum growth and health. Cells in culture generally do not seem to have this requirement, even though they are unable to synthesize linoleic acid or any of the ω6 series (Bailey and Menter, 1967; Bailey and Dunbar, 1973). Serum is a rich source of lipids, and cultured cells have been shown to preferentially incorporate these lipids into their own cellular lipid pool (Bailey, 1966;

Spector, 1972; Bailey et al., 1972). In the absence of lipids, approximately 90% of cellular lipids are synthesized from glucose and another 8% from acetate. When cells are exposed to serum lipids, only 8% of the total cellular lipids originate from glucose and less than 1% from acetate (Bailey et al., 1972).

Several lipids, including cholesterol, linoleic acid, oleic acid, and certain phospholipids, have been shown to stimulate the growth of a variety of cell lines (Holmes et al., 1969; King and Spector, 1981; Spector, 1972; McKeehan and Ham, 1978; Chen and Kandutsch, 1981). Liposomes containing a mixture of lipids have also been used in a serum-free environment to stimulate the clonal growth of human lung and foreskin fibroblasts, rabbit chondrocytes, mouse 3T3 cells, and human keratinocytes (Bettger and Ham, 1982). These findings demonstrate that the importance of lipids in the growth environment of cells should not be underestimated. The necessity of adding additional lipids to the culture environment will depend on the individual needs of the cell line being grown, and the concentration of serum being used.

5.2.3.2 Water-soluble vitamins. Almost 30 years ago, Eagle (1955) reported that mouse L cells and HeLa cells had a strict requirement for seven vitamins (choline, folic acid, nicotinamide, pantothenate, pyridoxal, riboflavin, and thiamine). If only one of these vitamins was omitted from the culture environment, the cells would undergo degenerative changes within five to 15 days, resulting in eventual culture death. Most modern culture media contain at least one or more forms of these vitamins today. In some media, biotin, vitamin B_{12}, ascorbate, or inositol are added. This is especially true when cells have specific requirements for these nutrients, when the serum content is greatly reduced or eliminated, or when clonal growth is necessary. Lockart and Eagle (1959) showed that various requirements, such as that for inositol, became apparent when cells were cultured at very low densities. This group was the first to recognize differences in the nutritional requirements of cells undergoing clonal growth at very low densities and those of cells in higher-density culture. Biotin becomes increasingly important when serum is reduced or eliminated because of its function in lipid biosynthesis as the prosthetic group of acetyl CoA carboxylase. Chalifour and Dakshinamurti (1982) have demonstrated that biotin-deficient human fibroblasts have a decreased viability even in the presence of lipids. They also found that the uptake of biotin by cells was enhanced when biotin was incubated in the presence of avidin, presumably because of pinocytosis of the avidin-biotin complex.

5.2.3.3 Lipid-soluble vitamins. Vitamins A, E, D, and K are rarely found in culture media, even though requirements for these fat-soluble vitamins are well established for higher animal species. Vitamin A has been shown to increase DNA synthesis in guinea pig epidermal cells (Christophers, 1974), and Sporn et al. (1975) have demonstrated a stimulation of macromolecular synthesis in mouse epidermal cultures exposed to retinoic acid and retinoic acid analogues. Vitamin E has been shown to be an inhibitor of lipid peroxidation in vitro, although this has not been correlated directly to the extension of the lifespan of cultured cells (Balin et al., 1974; Smith, 1981). As yet, no requirement has been found for vitamins D and K, although few studies have focused on this question. Perhaps, as Bettger and Ham (1982) suggest, it is time to begin incorporating these vitamins into culture media, "at least until it can be demonstrated unequivocally that they are not beneficial." The levels they suggest are "well above the levels of apparent minimal requirements but always below the level of toxicity."

5.2.3.4   Trace elements.   Defining the type and concentration of trace elements needed for optimum cell growth may be one of the most difficult challenges facing those involved in cellular nutrition in the future. Currently, up to 15 trace elements may be essential or at least beneficial for the growth of some vertebrate cells (Nielsen, 1981). This list of essential or potentially beneficial trace elements includes: cobalt, copper, iodine, iron, manganese, molybdenum, zinc, selenium, chromium, nickel, vanadium, arsenic, silicon, fluorine, and tin. In addition, work by Barnes and Sato (1980) showed that cadmium caused a favorable growth response in some cell lines. Iron, zinc, and selenium have produced a strong stimulation of growth in several cell types, and should definitely be included in modern culture media (Ham, 1981). Establishing essential trace-element requirements will be difficult because of the contamination of these elements in the other nutritional components of culture media, and knowledge of requirements will become more and more critical as cells are grown in serum-free conditions. The addition of trace metals in serum and as contaminants of other nutrients may be masking their real importance in cellular nutrition. If serum is eliminated and purification of nutritional components improved, real deficiencies of these compounds may develop.

5.2.3.5   Major ions.   Eagle (1955) found sodium, potassium, calcium, magnesium, chloride, and phosphate to be essential for cell growth in HeLa and mouse L cells. This list of major ions still holds true today, with only the addition of organically bound sulfate to bring it up to date. Mixtures of these ions can be found in various balanced salt solutions, which include Ringer's, Locke's, and Tyrode's physiological salt solutions, or in Gey's, Earle's, Hank's, Puck's, and other salt solutions designed for use with specific media (Waymouth, 1981). These salt solutions are either approximations of physiological concentrations, or they have been designed for specific cells. It is now known that changes in the extracellular concentrations of the major ions can affect growth and differentiation of many cultured cells. This is not due just to osmotic changes, but seems to be due to specific functions of some of the ions (Kuchler, 1967; Whitfield et al., 1976; Rubin and Sanui, 1977; Sanui and Rubin, 1977; Ham, 1981; Waymouth, 1981; Bettger and Ham, 1982). The relative concentrations of the major ions should be customized for the cell being used because of their significant effect on cell division (Leffert and Koch, 1980).

5.3 pH

There is little doubt that the pH of the culture environment is important for optimal growth of cells, but the optimum pH range may vary considerably from cell line to cell line. In experiments conducted by Eagle (1973) it was shown that, in general, virus-transformed or human cancer cells tended to have a more acid pH optimum than normal fibroblasts, and monkey and rat strains had a broader pH range than human or mouse cells. These experiments are summarized in Table 5–4.

Rubin (1971) found that sparse cultures of chick embryo cells were able to grow equally well at pH 6.6 and 7.6, although dense cultures of the cells had lower rates of multiplication and lower rates of ^{3}H-thymidine incorporation when the pH was lowest. These rates gradually increased as the pH of the medium increased, up to pH 7.6. When chick embryo cells were transformed with Rous sarcoma virus and grown to high density, they were less sensitive to pH than normal chick embryo cells at similar density. In another study, the final cell density of HeLa cells was similar, in the pH range of 6.8 to 7.5, but the time required to reach this density was less when the cells were cultured above pH 7.2 (Barton, 1971). Vero cells grown in microcarrier culture in pH-adjusted L-15 media have also been observed to have a wide pH optimum (Thomas, unpublished data).

5.4 OXYGEN

Oxygen can be considered an essential nutrient in both whole animals and individual cultured cells. It functions as the terminal electron acceptor in the electron transport chain and, as such, serves as a driving force for energy production via oxidative phosphorylation. A major concern of those that grow cells in culture is the optimum level of oxygen that should be provided in the culture environment.

Kilburn et al. (1969) grew mouse LS cells under different dissolved oxygen partial pressures (pO_2) and found the optimum range to be between 40 and 100 mm Hg. At this pO_2 the final cell population was constant between replicate cultures, which reached a final concentration of around 1.2×10^6 cells per ml. Growth was limited in cultures grown under low and

TABLE 5-4 pH Optima for Growth of Mammalian Cells as Determined by Cell Protein in 6-11 Days

Species	Cell Type	Specific Strain	Optimum pH for Growth[a]
Human	Normal		
	embryonic lung fibroblast	WI 38	7.65; 7.7; 7.7
	embryonic skin fibroblast	KL	7.5–7.7; 7.5; 7.5–7.8
	skin fibroblasts (normal)	MS2	7.7; 7.6
	(homocystinuria)	Penny	7.7
	(homocystinuria)	Renee	7.6–7.9; 7.45–7.95
	Cancer	HeLa	6.9–7.4; 7.0–7.9; 6.9–7.6
		KB	7.0; 7.0
	Virus (SV40)-transformed	WI 18VA	7.3
	fibroblasts	WI 26VA	7.3–7.6; 7.3–7.5
Hamster	Normal		
	whole embryo fibroblast	NIL 2[b]	7.2; 7.1–7.6
	baby kidney	BHK[b]	7.4; 6.8–7.6
Monkey	Normal		
	green monkey kidney	Primary culture	6.65–7.5
		CV 1[b]	6.5–7.5; 6.7–7.7; 6.6–7.65
	Virus (adeno)-transformed	AGMK-adeno	6.6–7.4; 6.8–7.1
Mouse	Normal		
	total embryo	Primary culture	7.15–7.5
	skin fibroblast	929[b]	7.1–7.3; 6.9–7.9(!)
	skin fibroblast	3T3[b]	7.4–7.7; 7.4–7.65; 7.6
	skin fibroblast	Cl 1-D	7.35; 7.35

				pH
	Cancer	renal adenocarcinoma	RAG	6.4–7.4; 7.1–7.3; 7.15; 7.35
		myeloma	425	7.35; 6.9–7.5
	Virus (SV40)-transformed		SV 3T3	7.1–7.3; 6.8–7.5
Rabbit	Normal		Lens epithelium[b]	6.85
Rat	Normal	lung fibroblast	BL	7.35
		liver epithelium	E3	7.7; 7.8
			G1	7.55–7.85
			B1	7.5–7.9; 7.45–7.9
	Cancer	hepatoma	HTC	7.5
		glial tumor	C6	7.1; 7.15; 7.15–7.85
Hybrids	Mouse-human		C1 1D × 18VA Clone 1	7.0–7.65; 7.3
			Clone 2	7.05–7.8; 7.3
	Mouse-human		RAG × WI 38	7.2

[a] Results in individual experiments. The ranges (e.g., pH 6.7–7.7) indicate experiments in which there was a broad optimal range, rather than a well-defined peak.

[b] Isolated from normal tissue but subsequently underwent "spontaneous" transformation in culture.

Reprinted with permission from Eagle, H. (1973) *J. Cell. Physiol.* 82, 1–8.

high pO_2 conditions (1.6 mm Hg and 320 mm Hg). Kilburn and Webb (1968) grew mouse LS cells under controlled dissolved pO_2 conditions and found that these cells grew best in the range of 40–100 mm Hg. Rueckert and Mueller (1960) cultured HeLa cells in several concentrations of oxygen and found that about 20% (or approximately 150 mm Hg) was optimum for their growth and survival. High levels of oxygen, 95%, or approximately 720 mm Hg, were shown to have a powerful growth-inhibitory effect on cells that included a reduction in DNA, RNA, and protein synthesis. In addition, the rate of glucose consumption was greatly accelerated and the cells seemed to shift to a completely *anaerobic* pattern!

Balin et al. (1976) grew WI-38 cells under pO_2 values of about 7.8, 26, 44, 134, 291, and 560 mm Hg. At the lowest partial pressure (7.8 mm Hg) WI-38 cells had slower growth rates, lower saturation densities, and higher rates of glucose consumption and lactate production than did cells grown under a pO_2 of approximately 44 mm Hg. There was no significant difference in these parameters when cells were grown at pO_2 values of about 26, 44, or 134 mm Hg, although doubling times were slightly increased at 134 mm Hg. At 291 mm Hg, growth rate and saturation densities were severely depressed and lactic acid production increased 4 to 6 times, as compared to the 134-mm Hg group. WI-38 cells cultured at a pO_2 of 560 attached to the surface provided but did not proliferate. This study points out the wide optimum pO_2 range for WI-38 cells, but also demonstrates the severe consequences of growing these cells out of the optimum range.

The specific rate of oxygen utilization or oxygen uptake rate (OUR) has been determined for a variety of cultured cells. Some of these values are provided in Table 5–5.

As already mentioned, the carbohydrate source may greatly influence OUR values, at least in normal diploid cells (Fleischaker, 1982). It will therefore be critical that OUR determinations be conducted in cultures growing in the carbohydrate source that will be used during large-scale culture. In fact, all medium components should be optimized prior to determining OUR values if they are to be relevant.

5.5 MEDIUM DESIGN

The design of the medium for use in cell culture production systems depends on several factors. Many of these factors are interrelated, but all should be considered to develop an optimum medium for a given cell culture system.

5.5.1 Cell Characteristics

The most obvious and important factors when considering the optimum medium design for a particular cell culture system are the specific characteristics of the cell line being grown. Some important cell line characteristics

TABLE 5–5 Measured Oxygen-Demand Rates of Human Cells in Culture

Human	mmol O_2/ liter-hour at 10^6 cells/ml	Reference
HeLa	0.47	Danes et al. (1963)
	0.097	Phillips and McCarthy (1956)
	0.10	Phillips and McCarthy (1956) Phillips and Andrews (1960)
	0.39	Phillips and Andrews (1960) Green et al. (1958)
HLM (liver)	0.37	Danes et al. (1963)
LIR (liver)	0.30	
AM-57 (amnion)	0.13	Green et al. (1958)
	0.045	Green et al. (1958)
	0.059	Green et al. (1958)
Skin fibroblast	0.064	Danes et al. (1963)
Detroit 6 (bone marrow)	0.43	Phillips and Andrews (1960)
Conjunctiva	0.28	Phillips and Andrews (1960)
Leukemia MCN	0.22	Phillips and Andrews (1960)
Lymphoblastoid (Namalioa)	0.053	Katinger et al. (1978)
Lung To	0.24	Phillips and Andrews (1960)
Intestine	0.40	Phillips and Andrews (1960)
Diploid embryo		
WI-38	0.15	Cristofalo and Kritchevsky (1966)
MAF-E	0.38	Phillips and Andrews (1960)
FS-4	0.05	Fleischaker and Sinskey (1981)

Reprinted with permission from Fleischaker, R.J., and Sinskey, A.J. (1981) *Eur. J. Appl. Microbiol. Biotechnol.* 12, 193–197.

that may be helpful in defining an optimum medium are its species and tissue origin, whether or not it is a normal diploid or aneuploid cell line, and whether it grows in suspension or is anchorage-dependent. Knowledge of these characteristics will give insight into the specific needs of a cell, which might include a narrow pH optimum, a critical dissolved oxygen concentration, or an unusual requirement for a particular nutrient. Cells that have similar characteristics may have similar nutritional and environmental needs. By examining the literature, a "best guess" can be formulated for the particular cell line in question. A good starting point is to screen the available commercial media. Once a medium or a combination of media have been identified that provide the desired performance, a more refined optimization can be done. The clonal growth assay developed by Ham and co-workers (1978) can be used to establish basic nutritional and hormonal requirements and to define their optimal concentration range. This information can then be combined with utilization and production data for nutrients, generated preferably in the production-scale cell culture system, or a model of this system, to refine the optimum nutritional and hormonal environment. Utilization and production data can be used to either change initial concentrations of nutrients or to alter their method of delivery, which may alter the cell culture system itself. One caveat attends use of clonal assay systems: They do not account for cell-cell and cell-medium interactions by virtue of the limiting dilution of cells.

5.5.2 Cell Culture System

The proper medium design will also be a function of the cell culture system chosen. If cells are grown in a batch system in which no medium changes are made or medium components added, the essential nutrients that are utilized or disappear at the fastest rate should be contained in the medium in the highest concentrations. Two major disadvantages of this system are the concentration limits of some components like glutamine, due to toxicity (around 6 mM in some cells), and the increased rate of utilization of compounds like glucose, due to high initial concentrations. In a fed-batch system, medium components can be supplemented at lower, more physiological concentrations, and highly utilized compounds can be added as they are needed to prevent toxicity and wasting problems. If a system such as perfusion is chosen, in which fresh medium is continuously added to the culture environment and spent medium is continuously removed, the concentration of medium components will be a function of the perfusion rate. The ideal perfusion system would supply each nutrient at precisely the rate it is utilized. If this could be accomplished, then little nutrient wasting would occur and metabolic by-products could be removed before they reached potentially inhibitory concentrations. Before this system can be optimally employed, the precise nutrient requirements and utilization rates of the cells must be known. In addition, the rate of production of inhibitory cellular by-products should be known to properly set the perfusion rate. The success of a perfusion system will depend to a large degree on how carefully the medium is designed.

5.5.3 Method of pH Control

The method of pH control will also affect the design of the medium used. As discussed earlier, the carbohydrate chosen will greatly affect the amount of lactate produced (Imamura et al., 1982), which will affect pH. Fructose and galactose seem to be the best carbohydrates for decreasing lactate production and they are utilized at a somewhat slower rate than glucose. If bicarbonate (HCO_3^-) is used to control pH, its concentration should be related to the amount of buffering needed in the system. The major ions in the medium, such as sodium and potassium, will then need to be readjusted to maintain the proper osmolarity. In addition, the concentration of CO_2 in the gas phase will need to be adjusted according to the level of bicarbonate added. The reason for this relationship is expressed in the following equations:

Sodium bicarbonate will dissociate to form:

$$HCO_3^- + H^+ \rightleftharpoons H_2CO_3 \rightleftharpoons CO_2 \text{ (dissolved)} + H_2O \leftarrow CO_{2(g)}$$

The concentration of CO_2 far exceeds that of H_2CO_3, so the equilibrium constant (k) for the dissociation of carbonic acid (H_2CO_3) is:

$$k = [H^+] [HCO_3^-]/[CO_2 \text{ (dissolved)}]$$

When the equation is rearranged as the Henderson-Hasselbalch equation to solve for the hydrogen ion concentration $[H^+]$ we get:

$$pH = pk + \log [HCO_3^-]/[CO_2 \text{ (dissolved)}]$$

From these equations we can see that the pH of the medium in a bicarbonate-buffered solution will be inversely proportional to the CO_2 concentration of the gas phase at a given concentration of bicarbonate. For a more complete explanation of the bicarbonate-buffering system, read Umbriet (1972).

However, bicarbonate is not needed in culture media to maintain a stable pH. Kelley et al. (1960) and Leibovitz (1963) developed bicarbonate-free media by adding mono- and dibasic phosphates as buffers. In addition, Leibovitz's L-15 medium contains high levels of the basic amino acids arginine and histidine as well as galactose to reduce the level of lactate produced. Recently, Barngrover et al. (1985) found that when 10 mM fructose was substituted for galactose in L-15 medium, improved high-density growth was achieved with little pH change in Vero cells grown in microcarrier culture.

Different organic buffers such as HEPES or TES have been employed to buffer various culture media (Massie, 1972; Massie et al., 1974; McKeehan et al., 1977). In some cases these nonvolatile organic buffers have been shown to be superior to a bicarbonate-buffering system (Massie, 1972; Massie, 1974). Some cells, however, show growth inhibition in the presence of organic buffers; in general, it seems sounder strategy to prevent cell overproduction of lactic acid and ammonia than to try to maintain pH with buffers.

5.5.4 Production Kinetics

If the purpose of growing mammalian cells is to harvest a biologically active product, the production kinetics of this product will affect the design of the medium. For example, if a product is produced only in growing cells, the growth-limiting nutrient might be slowly fed into the culture to lengthen the growth phase of the culture. If the health or viability of the culture is not affected, this strategy might lead to a greater accumulation of the product. On the other hand, if the desired product is produced only when the cells are in stationary phase, a medium that can maintain a nondividing cell population for a long period of time would be desired. In the latter case, a growth medium to increase the number of producing cells would be desirable initially, followed by a maintenance medium. The maintenance medium might be missing a nutrient involved in DNA synthesis, or it might contain a reduced amount of serum or no serum at all. If the product desired is produced continuously whether the cells are growing or not, then the object would be to provide a medium that would support high-density cell growth and be able to maintain this cell density for as long a period as possible.

5.5.5 Purification Requirements

Finally, purification requirements can greatly influence the design of the medium. The level of serum that can be tolerated in the purification process is a large concern. If very low or no serum can be tolerated, the medium must be altered to support the growth of cells in this environment. This may mean going to more complete media with addition of growth factors and hormones. Chapter 4 presents a discussion of this type of growth environment.

REFERENCES

Arathoon, W.R., and Telling, R.C. (1982) *Develop. Biol. Stand.* 50, 145–154.

Bailey, J.M. (1966) *Biochim. Biophys. Acta* 125, 226–236.

Bailey, J.M., and Dunbar, L.M. (1973) *Exp. Molec. Path.* 18, 142–161.

Bailey, J.M., Howard, B.V., Dunbar, L.M., and Tillman, S.F. (1972) *Lipid* 7, 125–134.

Bailey, J.M., and Menter, J. (1967) *Proc. Soc. Exp. Biol. Med.* 125, 101–105.

Balin, A.K., Goodman, D., Rasmussen, H., and Cristofalo, V.J. (1974) *In Vitro* 10, 384.

Balin, A.K., Goodman, D.B.P., Rasmussen, H., and Cristofalo, V. (1976) *In Vitro* 12, 687–692.

Barngrover, D., Thomas, J.N., and Thilly, W.G. (1985) *J. Cell Sci.* 78, 173–190.

Barnes, D., and Sato, G. (1980) *Anal. Biochem.* 102, 255–270.

Barton, M.E. (1971) *Biotech. Bioeng.* 13, 471–492.

Bettger, W.J., and Ham, R.G. (1982) *Adv. Nutr. Res.* 4, 249–286.

Blaker, G.J., Birch, J.R., and Pirt, S.J. (1971) *J. Cell. Sci.* 9, 529–537.

Butler, M., Imamura, T., Thomas, J., and Thilly, W. (1983) *J. Cell Sci.* 61, 351–363.

Butler, M., and Thilly, W.G. (1982) *In Vitro* 18, 213–219.

Burns, R.L., Rosenberger, P.G., and Klebe, R.J. (1976) *J. Cell. Physiol.* 88, 307–316.

Chalifour, L.E., and Dakshinamurti, K. (1982) *Biochem. Biophys. Res. Commun.* 104, 1047–1053.

Chen, H.W., and Kandutsch, A.A. (1981) in *The Growth Requirements of Vertebrate Cells in Vitro* (Waymouth, C., Ham, R.G., and Chapple, P.J., eds.) pp. 328–342, Cambridge University Press, Cambridge.

Christophers, E. (1974) *J. Invest. Dermatol.* 63, 450–455.

Cristofalo, V.J. and Kritchevsky, D. (1965) *Proc. Soc. Exp. Biol. Med.* 118, 1109–1112.

Cristofalo, V.J., and Kritchevsky, D. (1966) *J. Cell. Physiol.* 67, 125–132.

Danes, S.B., Broadfoot, M.M., and Paul, J. (1963) *Exp. Cell. Res.* 30, 369–378.

Donnelly, M., and Scheffler, I.E. (1976) *J. Cell. Physiol.* 89, 39–51.

Eagle, H. (1955) *Science* 122, 501–504.

Eagle, H. (1958) *J. Biol. Chem.* 233, 551–558.

Eagle, H. (1959) *Science* 130, 432–437.

Eagle, H. (1973) *J. Cell. Physiol.* 82, 1–8.

Fleischaker (1982) Ph.D. Thesis, Massachusetts Institute of Technology, Cambridge.

Green, M., Henle, G., and Deinhardt, F. (1958) *Virology* 5, 206–219.

Griffiths, J.B., and Pirt, S.J. (1967) *Proc. R. Soc. Biol.* 168, 421–438.

Ham, R.G. (1981) in *The Handbook of Experimental Pharmacology* (Baserga, R., ed.) vol. 57, p. 13, Springer-Verlag, New York.

Ham, R.G., and McKeehan, W.L. (1978) in *Nutritional Requirements of Cultured Cells* (Katsuta, H., ed.) pp. 63–115, Japan Scientific Society Press, Tokyo.

Holmes, R., Helms, J., and Mercer, G. (1969) *J. Cell. Biol.* 42, 262–271.

Imamura, T., Crespi, C.L., Thilly, W.G., and Brunengraber, H. (1982) *Anal. Biochem.* 124, 353–358.

Katinger, H.W., Scheirer, W., and Kroemer, E. (1978) *Chem. Ing. Tech.* 50, 472–473.

Kelley, G.G., Adamson, D.J., and Vail, M.H. (1960) *Amer. J. Hyg.* 71, 9–14.

Kilburn, D.G., Lilly, M.D., Self, D.A., and Webb, F.C. (1969) *J. Cell Sci.* 4, 25–37.

Kilburn, D.G., and Webb, F.C. (1968) *Biotech. Bioeng.* 10, 801–814.

King, M.E., and Spector, A.A. (1981) in *The Growth Requirements of Vertebrate Cells In Vitro* (Waymouth, C., Ham, R.G., and Chapple, P.J., eds.) pp. 294–312, Cambridge University Press, Cambridge.

Kovacevic, Z., and Morris, H.P. (1972) *Cancer Res.* 32, 326–333.

Kruse, P.F., and Miedema, E. (1965) *Proc. Soc. Exp. Biol. Med.* 119, 1110–1112.

Kruse, P.F., Miedema, E., and Carter, H.C. (1967) *Biochem.* 6, 949–955.

Kuchler, R.J. (1967) *Biochim. Biophys. Acta* 136, 473–483.

Lambert, K., and Pirt, S.J. (1975) *J. Cell Sci.* 17, 397–411.

Lavietes, B.B., Regan, D.H., and Demopoulas, H.B. (1974) *Proc. Natl. Acad. Sci. USA* 71, 3993–3997.

Leffert, H.L., and Koch, K.S. (1980) *Ann. NY Acad. Sci.* 339, 201–215.

Leibovitz, A. (1963) *Am. J. Hyg.* 78, 173–180.

Levintow, L. (1957) *Science* 126, 611–612.

Levintow, L., Eagle, H., and Piez, K.A. (1957) *J. Biol. Chem.* 227, 929–941.

Lockart, R.Z., Jr., and Eagle, H. (1959) *Science* 129, 252–254.

Massie, H.R., Baird, M.B., and Samis, H.V. (1974) *In Vitro* 9, 441–444.

Massie, H.R., Samis, H.V., and Baird, M.B. (1972) *In Vitro* 7, 191–194.

McCarty, K. (1962) *Exp. Cell Res.* 27, 230–240.

McKeehan, W.L., and Ham, R.G. (1978) *In Vitro* 14, 11–22.

McKeehan, W.L., McKeehan, K.A., Hammond, S.L., and Ham, R.G. (1977) *In Vitro* 13, 399–416.

Mohberg, J., and Johnson, M.J. (1963) *J. Natl. Cancer Inst.* 31, 611–625.

Nielsen, F.H. (1981) in *The Growth Requirements of Vertebrate Cells In Vitro* (Waymouth, C., Ham, R.G., and Chapple, P.J., eds.) pp. 68–81, Cambridge University Press, Cambridge.

Pardridge, W.M., Davidson, M.B., and Casanello-Ertl, D. (1978) *J. Cell. Physiol.* 96, 309–318.

Pardridge, W.M., Duducgian-Vartavarian, L., Casanello-Ertl, D., Jones, M.R., and Kapple, J.D. (1981) *Am. J. Physiol.* 240, E203–E208.

Phillips, H.J., and Andrews, R.V. (1960) *Proc. Soc. Exp. Biol. Med.* 103, 160–163.

Phillips, H.J., and McCarthy, H.L. (1956) *Proc. Soc. Exp. Biol. Med.* 93, 573–578.

Reed, W.D., Zielke, H.R., Baab, P.J., and Ozand, P.T. (1981) *Lipids* 16, 677–684.

Reitzer, L.J., Wice, B.M., and Kennell, D. (1979) *J. Biol. Chem.* 254, 2669–2676.

Roberts, R.S., Hsu, H.W., Lin, K.D., and Yang, T.J. (1976) *J. Cell. Sci.* 21, 609–615.

Rubin, H. (1971) *J. Cell Biol.* 51, 686–702.

Rubin, H., and Sanui, H. (1977) *Proc. Natl. Acad. Sci. USA* 74, 5026–5030.

Rueckert, R.R., and Mueller, G.C. (1960) *Cancer Res.* 20, 944–949.

Sanui, H., and Rubin, H. (1977) *J. Cell. Physiol.* 92, 23–31.

Smith, J.R. (1981) in *The Growth Requirements of Vertebrate Cells In Vitro* (Waymouth, C., Ham, R.G., and Chapple, P.J., eds.) pp. 344–352, Cambridge University Press, Cambridge.

Spector, A.A. (1972) in *Growth, Nutrition and Metabolism of Cells in Culture* (Rothblat, G.H. and Cristofalo, V.J., eds.) vol. 1, pp. 257–296, Academic Press, New York.

Sporn, M.B., Clamon, G.H., Dunlop, N.M., Newton, D.L., Smith, J.M., and Saffiotti, U. (1975) *Nature* 253, 47–50.

Stoner, G.D., and Merchant, D.J. (1972) *In Vitro* 7, 330–343.

Umbriet, W.W. (1972) in *Manometric and Biochemical Techniques,* 5th ed. (Burris, R.H. and Stauffer, J.F., eds.) pp. 20–29, Burgess, Minneapolis.

Waymouth, C. (1981) in *The Growth Requirements of Vertebrate Cells In Vitro* (Waymouth, C., Ham, R.G., and Chapple, P.J., eds.) pp. 34–47, Cambridge University Press, Cambridge.

Whitfield, J.F., MacManus, J.P., Rixon, R.H., Boynton, A.L., Youdale, T., and Swierenga, S. (1976) *In Vitro* 12, 1–18.

Zetterberg, A., and Engstrom, W. (1981) *J. Cell. Physiol.* 108, 365–373.

Zielke, H.R., Ozand, P.T., Tildon, J.T., Sevdalian, D.A., and Cornblath, M. (1978) *J. Cell. Physiol.* 95, 41–48.

6

Substrata for Anchorage-Dependent Cells

Debra Barngrover

6.1 INTRODUCTION

Many mammalian and avian cells are anchorage dependent, which means they require a suitable surface to attach to before they can grow. The term anchorage dependence was first coined by Stoker and Rubin (1967) to describe an important distinction between transformed cells that would grow in suspension in soft agar and normal cells that would not. However, there are lines and strains of lymphoblastoid lines from various species that are anchorage independent and do not easily fit this classification. Since Stoker and Rubin, there has been much discussion of the types of substrata mammalian cells will grow on, as well as models to explain cell adhesion and the effects of substrata on cellular growth and metabolism. Yet, much still is not known about the precise chemistry of natural and artificial substrata and the needs of the cell. The mammalian cell technologist is forced to choose substrata based on empirical grounds (i.e., what has worked in the past) rather than on knowledge of the optimum substrata and the needs of the cell. This chapter reviews what is known about the adhesion of cells to surfaces, the chemistries of substrata, and the effects of substrata on cells, with a view toward outlining what remains to be investigated about the interaction of the cell with the surface it is attached to.

Cell adhesion is a phenomenon whose measurement depends on the definition used. Most commonly, cells are considered to be adhered when they cannot be dislodged from the surface by a gentle shaking or washing with liquid. A more precise measurement of the force of adhesion can be obtained by allowing the cells to attach to wells, then inverting and centrifuging the wells to determine the centrifugal force necessary to dislodge the cells (Guarnaccia and Schnaar, 1982). Cell spreading is a separate phenomenon in which the attached spherical cell flattens (such that the lengthwise dimension is 3–10× larger than the height), usually assuming a shape typical of the specific cell type. Folkman and Moscona (1978) have shown that DNA synthesis in three normal cell types (bovine aortic endothelial; human diploid fibroblasts, WI-38; and mouse fibroblasts, A-31) is inversely proportional to cell height, thus demonstrating the importance of cell spreading in normal cell growth. The only known way to overcome this need for attachment and spreading is to use high levels of serum (> 20%) (Peehl and Stanbridge, 1981), in which case normal human fibroblasts will grow suspended in methylcellulose medium, but slowly (doubling time of 60 + hours) and with a low plating efficiency compared to transformed cells. Cell separation, removal of the cell from the substratum, is not necessarily the reverse of cell attachment (Grinnell, 1976) and may involve different mechanisms, such as a separation within the cell surface rather than between the cell surface and the substratum (Weiss, 1961).

When viewed in cross sections by electron microscopy, the ventral surface of a spread cell is not a uniform distance from the substratum. The areas of closest approach are assumed to be most involved in attachment of the cell to the substratum. Two types of cell-substratum attachments are commonly seen in electron micrographs, and a third has recently been described (Chen and Singer, 1982). Focal adhesions or focal contacts are small pinpoint areas, usually located at the periphery of fibroblasts, separated from the substratum by 10–20 nm. They occupy only a small fraction of the cell surface but are the sites of strongest adhesion (Harris, 1973a; Chen, 1981). Close contacts are broader areas, often surrounding the focal contacts, with a cell-substratum separation of 30–50 nm. The third type has been named extracellular matrix sites, characterized by a wider separation of cell and substratum (> 100 nm) with sporadic filaments of extracellular matrix components connecting the two. These sites are seen mostly in late cultures of fibroblasts as confluence is reached, and their importance in cell adhesion has not yet been demonstrated.

Investigations of cell adhesion and spreading have used a wide variety of cell types and sources. Since different cells have different functions and growth rates in vivo as well as in vitro, it would not be unexpected to find that they interact with substrata in different ways. Thus, it is incorrect to generalize from a study of one cell type to all cells. This review mainly presents results from studies of fibroblasts, because this represents a majority of the literature. Otherwise, the cell type used is reported, and generalizations are drawn only where evidence exists for more than one cell type. In some cases, definite differences between cell types have been noted, and much more work needs to be done on comparisons among cells.

6.2 THEORIES OF CELL ADHESION

Theories have been advanced to explain both the how and the why of cell adhesion. How cells attach to a substratum is important in understanding the physical requirements necessary to promote attachment. Why cells attach is important in understanding cell behavior. Two theories of how cells adhere to the substrata are discussed here: (1) physical forces and (2) specific chemical binding. Existing information explaining why cells attach is also briefly outlined.

6.2.1 How Cells Attach: Physical Forces

The principal theories about the physical interactions between cell and substratum are based on the DLVO (Derjaguin and Landau, 1941; Verwey and Overbeek, 1948) theory of lyophobic colloid stability, since spherical cells have some physical similarities to lyophobic colloids. This theory was first applied to the adhesion of two cells and then extended to the adhesion between cell and substratum (Curtis, 1960; Gingell, 1967; Weiss and Harlos, 1972a; Dolowy, 1980; Gingell and Vince, 1980). Two forces are described that are involved in the interaction between two surfaces. The first is electrostatic repulsion between two like-charged surfaces. Since cells have an overall negative charge (Sherbet et al., 1972) and most substrata are also negatively charged (plastic, glass), they would repel each other. This force decreases exponentially with distance between the substratum and the cell. Positive ions in the medium would shield the negative charges and reduce the repulsive force, which may explain the often-noted requirement for divalent cations in attachment and spreading (for example, see Grinnell, 1976). The electrostatic force would of course be positive between positively charged substrata (e.g., DEAE-dextran, polylysine) and cells. The second force is an electrodynamic attraction due to the van der Waals forces between ions and dipoles. This force decreases more slowly as a power of the distance between cell and substratum. Thus, energy curves such as Figure 6–1a (for negatively charged substrata) and Figure 6–1b (for positively charged substrata) would result (Curtis, 1973). As the cell approaches a negative substratum, it first encounters the secondary minimum in which the attraction and repulsion forces are balanced. Because of the large energy barrier, closer approach is generally prevented. The distance corresponding to the secondary minimum has been estimated to range between 4 and 10 nm (Weiss and Harlos, 1972b; Parsegian, 1973; Bell, 1978; Dolowy and Holly, 1978; Dolowy, 1980), depending on the estimated relative strength of the forces. This range can be compared to the estimated 10–20 nm gaps seen

a)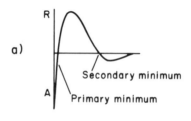

b)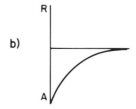

FIGURE 6–1 Force-distance relationships—theoretical possibilities. *R*, repulsion; *A*, attraction; ordinate, force; abscissa, distance between surfaces. (a) Conditions for the existence of primary and secondary minima, two types of adhesion. Note that the minima are normally used in reference to an energy-distance diagram and appear at zero force in this force-distance diagram. (b) Monotonic decrease in adhesive force. Reprinted by kind permission of A.S.G. Curtis and the Publishers from Curtis, A.S.G. (1973) in *Progress in Biophysics and Molecular Biology,* Vol. 27 (Butler, J.A.V., and Noble, D., eds.) pp. 315–386, Pergamon Press, Oxford.

in the focal contacts between fibroblasts and plastic (Chen and Singer, 1982). The strength of the adhesion could be modified by changing either of the two forces. Thus, if the surface charge of the cell was reduced, this would decrease the repulsive force. Experimentally, Gallin (1980) has demonstrated that human neutrophils have a reduced negative charge upon degranulation and an increased adhesiveness to plastic surfaces. This change is assumed to be due to the release of a cationic protein that is found in high levels in granules of neutrophils (Oseas et al., 1981). Cells in a regenerating liver (after partial hepatectomy) can also alter their surface charge within 30 minutes after the hepatectomy (Eisenberg et al., 1962). The strength of the van der Waals forces can also be modified by changing the surface components, since the magnitude of the interactions depends on the components present. Nir and Andersen (1977) derived the parameters of the van der Waals forces from the refractive index of solutions of the various components and found the following sequence: water < phospholipid < cholesterol, protein < sugar. This means that replacing one of these components on the cell surface with a component to the left in the sequence would reduce the attractive force, with similar changes in the extracellular medium leading to the opposite effect. Thus, stripping glycoproteins from the cell surface would reduce the attractive force. However, since glycoproteins contain much of the negative charge of the cell surface (from the terminal sialic acid), the actual effect on cell adhesion would depend on the interaction between the two forces.

The calculated physical force holding the cell to the substratum is well within the measured range of adhesive forces (Gingell and Vince, 1980), mainly because the measured range is so broad ($10-10^{-6}$ dynes/cm^2). The physical theory of cell adhesion has at least two major deficiencies. Most estimates of the force between the cell and the surface assume a uniform distribution of negative charge. Familiarity with cell membrane biology leads one to suspect that charges would not be uniformly distributed, and in fact Borysenko and Woods (1979) found that negative charges on the surface of BALB/c embryonic fibroblasts are present as large, discrete clusters with an average separation of 0.47 μm when the cells are labeled with polycationic ferritin. The interactive forces would be quite different between these negative clusters on the cell surface and the intervening neutral areas and the substratum, which would lead to different estimates of the adhesive forces. A second deficiency is that most discussions of the theory ignore the adsorption of protein to the substratum. Most cell culture and adhesion studies are carried out in the presence of protein (usually serum). This protein rapidly adsorbs to the substratum, resulting in a layer 2–5 nm thick (Rosenberg, 1960; Grinnell et al., 1976), and the substratum takes on many of the properties of the adsorbed protein layer, with hydrophobic substrata becoming more wettable and hydrophilic substrata less wettable (Vroman, 1967). The charge structure of the substratum would also be modified, especially for positive substrata, since most serum proteins are negatively charged. The physical forces discussed are active over the long range (up to 100 nm) (Parsegian, 1973), so analysis of the physical forces of adhesion needs to be extended to include this protein layer to determine if it completely masks the physical characteristics of the underlying surface or just modulates the physical interaction.

One point to emphasize in discussing physical adhesion theory is that adhesion does not depend on the presence of specific molecules, only general classes. For example, the effect of glycoproteins on cell adhesion is due to their general charge characteristics and dipole moments rather than any specific binding between a glycoprotein present on the cell surface and the substratum or vice versa. Many cell surface reactions do involve rather specific recognition and binding reactions (antibody-antigen, hormone-receptor, and so on), however, which has led many researchers to speculate that such reactions are involved in cell adhesion as well.

6.2.2 How Cells Attach: Specific Chemical Binding

The distinction between physical forces and chemical binding in this section is purely semantic, since on the molecular level, chemical interactions do involve physical forces. This includes not only the two forces discussed above, but also hydrogen-bonding and hydrophobic interactions. This distinction is made because, as discussed, the physical theory of cell adhesion does not depend on the presence of any specific molecule, while the chemical binding theory does require the presence of one or more molecules recognized by receptors in the cell surface. One example of such a cell adhesion molecule (CAM) that has received much attention in the literature is fibronectin. Fibronectin is found on the surface of many cells (Kleinman et al., 1981) and in perhaps a slightly different form in serum. It is an elongated molecule, and after proteolytic digestion, separate domains have been isolated that bind collagen and cells (for review, see Yamada, 1981). After it is attached to the substratum, fibronectin has been shown to promote the spreading of a number of cells (for reviews, see Olden et al., 1980; Kleinman et al., 1981; Ruoslahti et al., 1982), including transformed cells that otherwise do not spread normally. Fibronectin in solution, however, does not bind to cells or promote spreading (Pearlstein, 1978). This model is summarized in Figure 6–2 (Hughes et al., 1980), in which cell-surface receptors are shown fitting substratum-bound fibronectin (circles) but not albumin (squares) or soluble fibronectin (triangles). This lock-and-key mechanism is analogous to that proposed for many biological reactions that show specificity, such as enzyme-substrate, hormone-receptor, or antibody-antigen reactions.

The major criticism of the specific binding theory of cell adhesion is that cell-substratum interactions are not as specific as the preceding reactions cited. Fibroblasts will bind to a large number of polymers in the absence of fibronectin (using fibronectin-depleted serum, or antibodies to fibronectin).

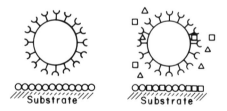

FIGURE 6–2 Adsorbed fibronectin molecules (O) interact directly with cell-surface receptors (carbohydrate chains of glycoproteins). Subsequently, flattening is induced by the formation of many such contacts. The interaction is relatively specific since adsorbed albumin molecules (□) are inactive and prevent cell attachment. Neither albumin nor fibronectin (Δ) in the solution phase inhibit interaction of the cells with adsorbed fibronectin molecules. Either fibronectin undergoes, or is stabilized in, some conformational change to a biochemically active form after adsorption, or the interaction of a cell with fibronectin-coated substrata requires cooperative binding of multiple contacts, each of individually weak affinity. Reprinted with permission from Hughes, R.C., Pena, S.D.J., and Vischer, P. (1980) in *Cell Adhesion and Motility* (Curtis, A.S.G. and Pitt, J.D., eds.) pp. 329–359, Cambridge University Press, Cambridge and New York.

Examples include native collagen (Grinnell and Minter, 1978; Rubin et al., 1981), various random copolypeptide films (Soderquist et al., 1979), various plant lectins such as concanavalin A, ricin, or wheat-germ agglutinin (Hughes et al., 1979; Oppenheimer-Marks and Grinnell, 1981; Aplin and Hughes, 1981), antibodies raised against the cell surface that do not interact with fibronectin (Aplin and Hughes, 1981; Grinnell and Hays, 1978), polycationic ferritin (Grinnell and Hays, 1978), and other proteins isolated from serum (Barnes et al., 1980; Knox and Griffiths, 1980; Hayman et al., 1982; Couchman et al., 1983). For cells other than fibroblasts, they appear to adhere to glycoproteins other than fibronectin, such as laminin (Terranova et al., 1980) or other peptides isolated from serum (Barnes et al., 1980; Knox and Griffiths, 1980). Furthermore, the location of fibronectin on the cell surface or in the cell matrix, often cited as supporting the role of fibronectin in cell adhesion, is not sufficient evidence. As pointed out by Barondes (1980) in Table 6–1, all of the established criteria for a cell adhesion molecule can generate false positives, that is, the proposed molecule has no specific role in adhesion even though it meets the criteria. The broad specificity for attachment suggests that a lock-and-key mechanism is not involved in cell adhesion and that the primary adhesion mechanism is comprised of the nonspecific physical forces discussed previously. However, if cell-surface

TABLE 6–1   Expected Characteristics of (Criteria for) a Cell Adhesion Molecule (CAM); and False Positives and Negatives

Expected Characteristics of CAM	Reasons for:	
	False Positive	False Negative
Located on cell surface	Coincidental	Overlooked Inaccesible
Appearance of CAM correlates with development of adhesiveness	Coincidental	CAM present before adhesiveness but other factor is limiting
Complementary receptor on cell surface (if CAM is isolated as polyvalent molecule it may agglutinate test cells)	Binding has other function or is nonspecific	CAM binds poorly when solubilized Receptors saturated
Binding univalent antibodies or haptens to CAM blocks adhesion	Nonspecific effect	Affinity of univalent antibodies or haptens for CAM relatively low
Mutant with impaired cell adhesion has defective CAM	Indirect effect	Defect in CAM not detected by the measurements used

Reprinted with permission from Barondes, S.H. (1980) in *Cell Adhesion and Motility* (Curtis, A.S.G., and Pitts, J.D., eds.) pp. 309–328, Cambridge University Press, Cambridge and New York.

molecules are present that do bind to fibronectin (see Yamada et al., 1981), a role for specific binding cannot be entirely ruled out.

The mechanism of cell adhesion and spreading becomes important when trying to design an optimal substratum for in vitro cell culture. If specific binding is important, then the cell adhesion molecules or appropriate analogues must be provided for the specific cell type of interest. If only the longer-range physical forces are important in adhesion, then substrata with the correct physical conditions could be formulated from a wide variety of polymers. Even though the forces discussed are nonspecific, different cell types with their different surfaces would vary in their interaction with such substrata. Thus, with sufficient knowledge about the physical interactions of specific cells with substrata, specific substrata could be designed.

6.2.3 Why Cells Attach

One of the main differences between attached and suspended cells is their surface-to-volume ratio. Spherical suspended cells have a minimum surface-to-volume ratio, while a flattened cell has much more surface area corresponding to the same volume. Increasing the serum concentration in the medium causes hamster and mouse fibroblasts to round up until, at 66% serum, they have the same surface area as suspended cells (O'Neill et al., 1979). At 5% serum, attached cells have three times the surface area in contact with the medium (not including the ventral cell surface next to the substratum) when compared to suspended cells; they also have eight times the growth rate (O'Neill, ibid.) At 66% serum, with both attached and suspended cells having the same surface area, they also have the same growth rate. These results suggest the main reason for cell spread is to provide more surface area for mitogenic factors from serum to bind and perhaps be taken up. When the concentration of the mitogenic factor or factors is high, less surface area is necessary. If these factors can be identified, reasonable suspension growth of normally anchorage-dependent cells may be possible, which would simplify large-scale culture of mammalian cells. Much work has been done on serum-free growth of cells, but as yet a combination of factors that would allow for serum-free suspension growth of normal cells has not been identified (see Chapter 4).

6.3 SUBSTRATA USED FOR ANCHORAGE-DEPENDENT CELLS

This section examines the various natural and artificial substrata to which anchorage-dependent cells attach and spread. Comparisons of substrata characteristics are made in an attempt to understand the important parameters for cell adhesion.

6.3.1 Natural Substrata

In vivo, cells are attached either to other cells or to a wide variety of structures generally termed "extracellular matrix." This matrix not only provides structural support for the tissue, but also affects the metabolism and differentiation of the cell (Hay, 1981a). With the exception of connective tissue cells (fibroblasts and chondrocytes), this matrix is condensed into layers that can be distinguished microscopically and that are loosely termed "basement membranes" (Grant et al., 1981). Since different tissues have different structures and functions, it would not be unexpected to find that these basement membranes and extracellular matrices vary with the tissue studied. Indeed, with the electron microscope differences can be noted between basement membranes, with a translucent lamina rara next to the cell, a denser lamina densa, and a fibrous reticular layer (Figure 6–3; Heathcote and Grant, 1981); the corneal endothelial (Descemet's) membrane, which has no lamina rara (Grant et al., 1981); and the glomerular basement membrane of the kidney, which has no reticular layer, but instead two lamina rarae bounding a central lamina densa (Farquhar, 1981). Biochemically, even more differences have been noted between basement membranes; morphology, composition, and organization of the basement membrane are affected by the species, the organ, the site within the organ, the age of the animal, and any pathology present (Grant et al., 1981). The differences among basement membranes offer many fruitful research possibilities in attempts to understand how cells differentiate into a wide variety of organs and interact with other cells. Because there has been little work done in identifying the distinguishing characteristics of specific basement

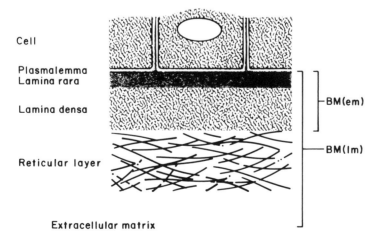

FIGURE 6–3 Organization of basement membrane. [em, electron microscopy; lm, light microscopy] Reprinted with permission fron Heathcote, J.G., and Grant, M.E. (1981) *Int. Rev. Connective Tissue Res.* 9, 191–264.

membranes, this chapter presents only a brief review of the components known to be present in extracellular matrices and possible ways in which the structure and composition can be varied.

6.3.1.1 Collagens. Collagens are a family of proteins with a characteristic triple helix and a high proportion of glycine, proline, and hydroxyproline, with the typical repeating sequence Gly-X-Y. At least five genetically distinct collagens are now recognized: I—found in skin, bone, and tendon; II—cartilage; III—blood vessels, skin, and parenchyma of internal organs; IV—basement membrane of epithelial cells; V—skin, smooth muscle, placenta, and bone (Kleinman et al., 1981). Types I–III are the more fibrillar collagens and are generally arranged as parallel quarter-staggered molecules in the microfibril (Hay, 1981b). The overlap is not complete, however, leaving gaps that appear as bands in the fibrils when the fiber is stained with negative staining. When the fibrils are stained with metal salts (positive staining), charged residues are localized in the overlap region, which means that the collagen fibril has a repeating pattern of charges and holes spaced regularly 67 nm apart (Hay, 1981b). Type IV collagen is not as fibrillar, and a continuous network model has been proposed based on electron micrographs of the various regions of the molecule (Figure 6–4; Timpl et al., 1981). This collagen would present a different pattern of charges and molecular domains to the cell.

6.3.1.2 Proteoglycans. Proteoglycans are structures consisting of a variable number of glycosaminoglycans attached to a core protein. Glycosaminoglycans are large polyanionic chains of repeating disaccharide units containing hexosamine and another sugar. Some of them are highly sulfated

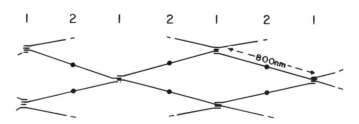

FIGURE 6–4 Two-dimensional model of the association of type IV collagen molecules in the basement-membrane matrix. The length between two identical cross-linking sites (800 nm) comprises the length of two stretched type IV collagen molecules. Cross-linking sites: (1) 7-S collagen domain; (2) noncollagenous domain. Reprinted with permission from Timpl, R., Wiedemann, H., Van Delden, V., Furthmayr, H., and Kuhn, K. (1981) *Eur. J. Biochem.* 120, 203–211.

(from 0 to 3 sulfates per disaccharide unit), which increases the negative charge in the molecule. Four main types of glycosaminoglycans are recognized: hyaluronic acid (glucuronate-N-acetyl-glucosamine), chondroitin sulfate (glucuronate or iduronate-N-acetyl-glucosamine-[4 or 6]-sulfate), keratin sulfate (N-acetyl-glucosamine-6-sulfate-galactose-6-sulfate), and heparan sulfate/heparin (glucuronate or iduronate-2-sulfate-N-sulfate-[or acetate-]glucosamine-6-sulfate) (Hascall and Kimura, 1982). The proteoglycan structures are even more complex. The only one that has been completely described is from cartilage and consists of a large core protein (250,000 MW), which is only 5–10% of the total weight of the proteoglycan; about 80 chondroitin sulfates ($\sim$ 20,000 MW each) attached by glycosidic bonds to serine residues on the core protein; about 100 keratin sulfate chains and O-linked oligosaccharides attached to serine and threonine residues; and a glycosaminoglycan-free region on one end of the core protein that has a highly specific binding site for hyaluronic acid (Hascall and Hascall, 1981). Variations in the amounts and types of glycosaminoglycans attached to the core protein would present the cell with very different structures, and proteoglycans isolated from different sources have very different contents (see Hay, 1981b, for a partial review).

6.3.1.3 Other proteins.   Other proteins found in extracellular matrix include fibronectin, laminin, chondronectin, elastin, entactin, and various unnamed glycoproteins. Again, variations in content and amount of these various glycoproteins occur with different extracellular matrices, and the different proteins have been proposed as providing specific attachment molecules for different cells (e.g., fibronectin for fibroblasts and laminin for epithelial cells).

In summary, the extracellular matrix is a highly complex structure that is only beginning to be investigated. Various components of the matrix have been used to derivatize artificial substrata to enhance cell attachment and growth. The use of collagen-coated surfaces, either native or denatured, is well established in the culture of various primary cells or cell lines (Grinnell, 1982). Typically, Type I collagen from skin or rat tails is used, though Type IV collagen purified from EHS sarcomas is now also being studied (Kleinman et al., 1982). A mixture of all the fibrous proteins present in an organ, termed biomatrix, produced by solubilizing away all the other components (proteins or other components soluble in NaCl or water, lipids, and nucleic acids) has also been used to maintain long-term cultures of differentiated epithelial cells (Rojkind et al., 1980; Reid et al., 1981). The use of these natural components will lead to understanding the role of the matrix in cell growth and differentiation, but the components are too difficult and expensive to prepare for large-scale culture. Therefore, various artificial substrata are substituted for the natural matrix.

6.3.2 Artificial Substrata

6.3.2.1 Glass. The first artificial substratum used was glass, and the term in vitro means "in glass." Studies by Rappaport et al. (1960) of the attachment and growth of HeLa cells, primary monkey kidney cells, and mouse L cells in serum-free medium showed that amount of negative charge present (as measured by cationic dye binding) could be manipulated by alkali treatment of the glass, and cell attachment and growth were improved by increasing the negative charge to a level specific for each cell type.

6.3.2.2 Plastic. To the cell culturist, plastic means polystyrene, and tissue culture plastic denotes polystyrene that has been treated to increase the negative charge. Studies by Maroudas (1975; 1977) using sulfuric acid to sulfonate the polystyrene showed that a maximum number of cells was spread when the substratum had 2–5 negatively charged groups/nm^2. This roughly corresponded to sulfonation of every benzene in the surface layer of the substratum.

6.3.2.3 Positively charged polymers. Cells will also adhere and grow on positively charged polymers such as DEAE-dextran (van Wezel, 1967; Levine et al., 1979); polylysine, polyornithine, polyarginine, polyhistidine, protamine, and histone (McKeehan et al., 1981); polyionenes (Rembaum et al., 1977); polyacrylamide (Monthony et al., 1980); and copolypeptides of lysine and either leucine or phenylalanine (Soderquist et al., 1979). Again, charge density is an important parameter, as shown by Levine et al. (1979) using a series of DEAE microcarriers with different degrees of DEAE substitutions (Figure 6–5).

6.3.2.4 Other substrata. Other substrata that have been used to grow cells include FEP-Teflon, which is gas-permeable (Jensen, 1981) and glycine-derivatized polystyrene (Kuo et al., 1981). Many other substrata have been used experimentally to test parameters involved in cell adhesion. These include various metals (Harris, 1973b; Dolowy et al., 1982), microporous membranes (McCall et al., 1981; Kondo et al., 1979), surfaces with immobilized carbohydrates (Guarnaccia and Schnaar, 1982), as well as the various polymers discussed under the theory of specific chemical binding.

6.3.3 Characteristics of Adhesive Substrata

Necessary to the design or selection of suitable substrata is an understanding of the essential parameters of adhesive substrata. Though some generalizations can be drawn from the above list of substrata, obviously the specific optimum characteristics are not known and probably vary with cell type and

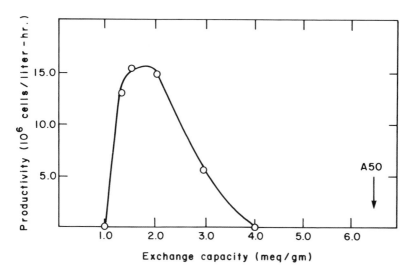

FIGURE 6–5 Productivities of normal diploid human fibroblasts HEL 299 on micro-carriers of varying degrees of DEAE substitution at carrier concentrations of 5-g cross-linked dextran/liter. (A50, charge density of Sephadex A50 resin). Reprinted with permission from Levine, D.W., Wang, D.I.C., and Thilly, W.G. (1979) *Biotechnol. Bioeng.* 21, 821–845.

production goal. The three common characteristics of suitable substrata are (1) solidity, (2) charge density, and (3) wettability.

6.3.3.1   Solidity.   Cells will adhere to solid but not fluid phospholipid substrata (Margolis et al., 1978). Maroudas (1979) has speculated that this is due to a requirement for small, dense, rigid adhesive sites in the substratum to match the focal contacts of the cells. Fluid substrata would not allow the stable aggregation of such adhesive sites.

6.3.3.2   Charge density.   The importance of charge density has been shown for both positively charged (DEAE-dextran) and negatively charged sub-strata (sulfonated polystyrene). Though this may be due to electrostatic attraction or repulsion between the substratum and cell surface, the presence of adsorbed proteins on the substratum (either from the medium or from the cells) complicates the picture. Charge density may be more important in causing the proteins to be adsorbed in a suitable concentration and pattern. As pointed out in the discussion of natural substrata (section 6.3.1), collagens in the extracellular matrix present a very ordered array of charges and polar domains to the cell. The highly anionic proteoglycans have also been shown to be arrayed in regular patterns in at least five separate basement membranes: in the glomerular basement membrane (Farquhar, 1981) where the proteoglycans are arranged in a lattice at 60-nm intervals; in chick embryonic cornea basement membrane (Trelstad et al., 1974), where they are arrayed along the collagen fibrils with 60-nm spacing; in embryonic lens capsule and neural tube basement membrane with the same arrangement (Hay and Meier, 1974); and in the adult aorta basement membrane (Wight and Ross, 1975). The importance of the pattern of protein adsorption was demonstrated by the observation that cells did not grow at all on surfaces coated first with bovine serum albumin and then the IgG antibody to albumin, although they did grow on albumin and somewhat on IgG alone (Giaever and Ward, 1978). The specifically attached IgG molecules would present an ordered array of their Fc portions to the cell, which presumably is a nonadhesive pattern. By varying the size of positively charged islands in a hydrophobic sea (by varying the proportion of the charged side chains attached to a hydrophobic polymer backbone), Kataoka et al. (1982) were able to affect the spreading of platelets on the substratum. These findings all suggest that cells require a specific density and pattern of polymers on the substratum, which would in turn be influenced by the underlying charge density and pattern of the substratum.

6.3.3.3   Wetting.   Wetting is the ability of a drop of water to spread on a substratum and is indicated by the contact angle (θ) of the drop (Figure 6–6; Baier et al., 1968). In general, cells attach and spread better as the wettability of the substratum increases (Harris, 1973b), though there are the notable exceptions of agar and poly(hydroxyethylmethacrylate) (HEMA) that are both wettable and completely nonadhesive (Klebe et al., 1981). This requirement is probably related to the van der Waals attraction forces that are stronger for more polar substrata.

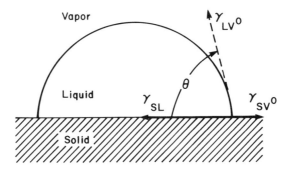

FIGURE 6–6   Schematic diagram of a finite contact angle formed by a sessile drop resting on a solid surface. Reprinted with permission from Baier, R.E., Shafrin, E.G., and Zisman, W.A. (1968) *Science* 162, 1360–1368, copyright 1968 by the American Association for the Advancement of Science.

This summary of characteristics of adhesive substrata ignores the specific requirements of the individual cell depending on the species, organ, site within the organ, and age of animal, all of which have been shown to affect the basement membrane and presumably the cell's interaction with it (Grant et al., 1981). The effects of different substrata on cells are briefly considered in the next section.

6.4 EFFECTS OF SUBSTRATUM ON CELL DIFFERENTIATION AND METABOLISM

The influence of substrata on cells, beyond the initial effect of permitting attachment and growth, presents an area of much diversity. A few examples are presented here in order to give a flavor of the possibilities.

Many instances have been reported of the effect of collagen substratum in maintaining differentiated function of epithelial cells when compared to culturing the cells on plastic. Examples include the presence of secretory granules and maintenance of casein secretion in mammary epithelial cells cultured on collagen rafts (Emerman et al., 1979) and differentiation of epidermal cells into squamous epithelium when grown on Type IV collagen (Murray et al., 1978). Cells maintained on collagen often have reduced needs for certain hormones in serum-free medium (Reid et al., 1981). The basal level of tyrosine aminotransferase (an enzyme characteristic of the adult liver) was 1.5- to 2.5-fold higher in various rat liver epithelial cell lines maintained on collagen rafts than in the same cells maintained on plastic (Malan-Shibley and Iype, 1981).

Differences between the various artificial substrata have also been noted. Rat peritoneal macrophages have a reduced ability to bind thymocytes and glutaraldehyde-treated sheep red cells when plated on plastic as compared with those plated on glass coverslips, though their ability to bind some other particles was not changed (Garrouste et al., 1982). Incorporation of labeled glucosamine was three to four times higher in BHK fibroblasts grown on glass than in those grown on plastic, although there was no difference in growth rate or incorporation rate of fucose (Warren et al., 1982). Electrophoresis of extracted glycopeptides labeled with radioactive glucosamine from the two cell populations showed different concentrations of many of the peaks. Most strikingly, Wahrmann et al. (1981) showed that myogenic cells of a skeletal muscle line differentiate and fuse to form myotubes when grown on negatively charged substrata (bovine serum albumin, BSA, non-treated or treated with polyglutamic acid), but do not form myotubes when grown on positively charged substrata (BSA treated with polylysine). Cloning experiments on cells taken from the substrata at various times show that cells on the negatively charged substrata switch from a proliferative state as confluency is reached, but a significant number of cells on the positively charged substrata do not. This result suggests that substratum charge could be used to maintain the cells in a differentiated or proliferative state.

The mechanisms for these examples and the many others noted for the effects of substrata on cells await further work on the exact nature of the interactions. These examples suggest that someday it will be feasible to select an optimum substratum based on the cell type grown and the desired goal (cell growth, cell differentiation, specific protein production, and so forth). The types of information needed to design such substrata are outlined in the next section.

6.5 DIRECTIONS FOR FUTURE RESEARCH

Now that many general characteristics of cell surfaces and substrata (such as overall charge density) are known, future research needs to focus on a detailed examination of such surfaces and a comparison of specific cell-matrix interactions. Examples include:

1. Documentation of the physical characteristics of specific basement membranes and comparisons to determine the essential characteristics.
2. Design and synthesis of substrata that mimic these essential characteristics.
3. Delineation of how the substrata affect cell differentiation, growth, and metabolism.
4. Design of substrata for specific production goals, such as continued cell proliferation versus cell differentiation.

REFERENCES

Aplin, J.D., and Hughes, R.C. (1981) *J. Cell Sci.* 50, 89–103.

Baier, R.E., Shafrin, E.G., and Zisman, W.A. (1968) *Science* 162, 1360–1368.

Barnes, D., Wolfe, R., Serrero, G., McClure, D., and Sato, G. (1980) *J. Supramol. Struct.* 14, 47–63.

Barondes, S.H. (1980) in *Cell Adhesion and Motility* (Curtis, A.S.G., and Pitts, J.D., eds.) pp. 309–328, Cambridge University Press, Cambridge and New York.

Bell, G.I. (1978) *Science* 200, 618–627.

Borysenko, J.Z., and Woods, W. (1979) *Exp. Cell Res.* 118, 215–227.

Chen, W.-T. (1981) *J. Cell Biol.* 90, 187–200.

Chen, W.-T., and Singer, S.J. (1982) *J. Cell Biol.* 95, 205–222.

Couchman, J.R., Hoeoek, M., Rees, D.A., and Timpl, R. (1983) *J. Cell Biol.* 96, 177–183.

Curtis, A.S.G. (1960) *Amer. Natural.* 94, 37–56.

Curtis, A.S.G. (1973) *Prog. Biophys. Mol. Biol.* 27, 315–386.

Derjaguin, B., and Landau, L. (1941) *Acta Physicochem. USSR* 14, 633–662.

Dolowy, K. (1980) in *Cell Adhesion and Motility* (Curtis, A.S.G., and Pitts, J.D., eds.) pp. 39–63, Cambridge University Press, Cambridge and New York.

Dolowy, K., and Holly, F.J. (1978) *J. Theor. Biol.* 75, 373–380.

Dolowy, K., Moran, K.A., and Holly, F.J. (1982) *J. Bioelect.* 1, 1–12.

Eisenberg, S., Ben-Or, S., and Doljanski, F. (1962) *Exp. Cell Res.* 26, 451–461.

Emerman, J.T., Burwen, S.J., and Pitelka, D.R. (1979) *Tissue Cell* 11, 109–119.

Farquhar, M.G. (1981) in *Cell Biology of the Extracellular Matrix* (Hay, E.D., ed.) pp. 335–378, Plenum Press, New York.

Folkman, J., and Moscona, A. (1978) *Nature* 273, 345–349.

Gallin, J.I. (1980) *J. Clinic. Investig.* 65, 298–306.

Garrouste, F., Capo, C., Benoliel, A.-M., Bongrand, P., and Depieds, R. (1982) *J. Reticuloendothel. Soc.* 31, 415–422.

Giaever, I., and Ward, E. (1978) *Proc. Natl. Acad. Sci. USA* 75, 1366–1368.

Gingell, D. (1967) *J. Theor. Biol.* 17, 451–482.

Gingell, D., and Vince, S. (1980) in *Cell Adhesion and Motility* (Curtis, A.S.G., and Pitts, J.D., eds.) pp. 1–37, Cambridge University Press, Cambridge and New York.

Grant, M.E., Heathcote, J.G., and Orkin, R.W. (1981) *Biosci. Reports* 1, 819–842.

Grinnell, F. (1976) *Exp. Cell Res.* 97, 265–274.

Grinnell, F. (1982) *Methods Enzymol.* 82, 499–503.

Grinnell, F., and Hays, D.G. (1978) *Exp. Cell Res.* 116, 275–284.

Grinnell, F., and Minter, D. (1978) *Proc. Natl. Acad. Sci. USA* 75, 4408–4412.

Grinnell, F., Tobleman, M.Q., and Hackenbrock, C.R. (1976) *J. Cell Biol.* 70, 707–713.

Guarnaccia, S.P., and Schnaar, R.L. (1982) *J. Biol. Chem.* 257, 14288–14292.

Harris, A. (1973a) *Dev. Biol.* 35, 97–114.

Harris, A. (1973b) *Exp. Cell Res.* 77, 285–297.

Hascall, V.C., and Hascall, G.K. (1981) in *Cell Biology of the Extracellular Matrix* (Hay, E.D., ed.) pp. 39–64, Plenum Press, New York.

Hascall, V.C., and Kimura, J.H. (1982) *Methods Enzymol.* 82, 769–800.

Hay, E.D. (1981a) in *Cell Biology of the Extracellular Matrix* (Hay, E.D., ed.) pp. 1–4, Plenum Press, New York.

Hay, E.D. (1981b) *J. Cell Biol.* 91, 205s–223s.

Hay, E.D., and Meier, S. (1974) *J. Cell Biol.* 62, 889–898.

Hayman, E.G., Engvall, E., A'Hearn, E., Barnes, D., Pierschbacher, M., and Ruoslahti, E. (1982) *J. Cell Biol.* 95, 20–23.

Heathcote, J.G., and Grant, M.E. (1981) *Int. Rev. Connect. Tis. Res.* 9, 191–264.

Hughes, R.C., Pena, S.D.J., Clark, J., and Dourmashkin, R.R. (1979) *Exp. Cell Res.* 121, 307–314.

Hughes, R.C., Pena, S.D.J., and Vischer, P. (1980) in *Cell Adhesion and Motility* (Curtis, A.S.G., and Pitts, J.D., eds.) pp. 329–356, Cambridge University Press, Cambridge and New York.

Jensen, M.D. (1981) *Biotechnol. Bioeng.* 23, 2703–2716.

Kataoka, K., Okano, T., Sakurai, Y., Nishimura, T., Maeda, M., Inoue, S., and Tsuruta, T. (1982) *Biomaterials* 3, 237–240.

Klebe, R.J., Bentley, K.L., and Schoen, R.C. (1981) *J. Cellular Physiol.* 109, 481–488.

Kleinman, H.K., Klebe, R.J., and Martin, G.R. (1981) *J. Cell Biol.* 88, 473–485.

Kleinman, H.K., Woodley, D.T., McGarvey, M.L., Robey, P.G., Hassell, J.R., and Martin, G.R. (1982) in *Extracellular Matrix* (Hawkes, S., and Wang, J.L., eds.) pp. 45–55, Academic Press, New York.

Knox, P., and Griffiths, S. (1980) *J. Cell Sci.* 46, 97–112.

Kondo, S., Aso, K., and Namba, M. (1979) *J. Invest. Dermatol.* 72, 85–87.

Kuo, M.J., Lewis, C., Jr., Martin, R.A., Miller, R.E., Schoenfeld, R.A., Schuck, J.M., and Wildi, B.S. (1981) *In Vitro* 17, 901–906.

Levine, D.W., Wang, D.I.C., and Thilly, W.G. (1979) *Biotechnol. Bioeng.* 21, 821–845.

Malan-Shibley, L., and Iype, P.T. (1981) *Exp. Cell Res.* 131, 363–371.

Margolis, L.B., Dyatlovitskaya, E.Y., and Bergelson, L.D. (1978) *Exp. Cell Res.* 111, 454–457.

Maroudas, N.G. (1975) *J. Theor. Biol.* 49, 417–424.

Maroudas, N.G. (1977) *J. Cell. Physiol.* 90, 511–519.

Maroudas, N.G. (1979) *J. Theor. Biol.* 79, 101–116.

McCall, E., Povey, J., and Dumonde, D.C. (1981) *Thromb. Res.* 24, 417–431.

McKeehan, W.L., McKeehan, K.A., and Ham, R.G. (1981) in *Requirements of Vertebrate Cells in Vitro* (Waymouth, C., Itam, R.G., and Chapple, P.G., eds.) pp. 118–130, Cambridge University Press, Cambridge.

Monthony, J.F., Schwartz, N.D., Hollis, D.F., and Polastri, G.D. (1980) U.S. Patent 4,237,218.

Murray, J.C., Stingl, G., Kleinman, H.K., Martin, G.R., and Katz, S.I. (1978) *J. Cell Biol.* 80, 197–201.

Nir, S., and Andersen, M. (1977) *J. Membrane Biol.* 31, 1–18.

O'Neill, C.H., Riddle, P.N., and Jordan, P.W. (1979) *Cell* 16, 909–918.

Olden, K., Hahn, L.-H.E., and Yamada, K.M. (1980) in *Cell Adhesion and Motility* (Curtis, A.S.G., and Pitts, J.D., eds.) pp. 357–408, Cambridge University Press, Cambridge and New York.

Oppenheimer-Marks, N., and Grinnell, F. (1981) *Europ. J. Cell Biol.* 23, 286–294.

Oseas, R.S., Allen, J., Yang, H.-H., Gaehner, R.L., and Boxer, L.A. (1981) *Infect. Immun.* 33, 523–526.

Parsegian, V.A. (1973) *Annu. Rev. Biophys. Bioeng.* 2, 221–225.

Pearlstein, E. (1978) *Int. J. Cancer* 22, 32–35.

Peehl, D.M., and Stanbridge, E.J. (1981) *Proc. Natl. Acad. Sci. USA* 78, 3053–3057.

Rappaport, C., Poole, J.P., and Rappaport, H.P. (1960) *Exp. Cell Res.* 20, 465–510.

Reid, L., Morrow, B., Jubinsky, P., Schwarz, E., and Gatmaitan, Z. (1981) *Ann. N.Y. Acad. Sci.* 372, 354–370.

Rembaum, A., Senyei, A.E., and Rajaraman, R. (1977) *J. Biomed. Mat. Res. Symp.* 8, 101–110.

Rojkind, M., Gatmaitan, Z., Mackensen, S., Giambrone, M.-A., Ponce, P., and Reid, L.M. (1980) *J. Cell Biol.* 87, 255–263.

Rosenberg, M.D. (1960) *Biophys. J.* 1, 137–159.

Rubin, K., Hoeoek, M., Oebrink, B., and Timpl, R. (1981) *Cell* 24, 463–470.

Ruoslahti, E., Hayman, E.G., Pierschbacher, M., and Engvall, E. (1982) *Methods Enzymol.* 82, 803–839.

Sherbet, G.V., Lakshmi, M.S., and Rao, K.V. (1972) *Exp. Cell Res.* 70, 113–123.

Soderquist, M.E., Gershman, H., Anderson, J.M., and Walton, A.G. (1979) *J. Biomed. Mat. Res.* 13, 865–886.

Stoker, M.G.P., and Rubin, H. (1967) *Nature* 215, 171–172.

Terranova, V.P., Rohrbach, D.H., and Martin, G. (1980) *Cell* 22, 719–726.

Timpl, R., Wiedemann, H., Van Delden, V., Furthmayr, H., and Kuehn, K. (1981) *Eur. J. Biochem.* 120, 203–211.

Trelstad, R.L., Hayashi, K., and Toole, B.P. (1974) *J. Cell Biol.* 62, 815–830.

van Wezel, A.L. (1967) *Nature* 216, 64–65.

Verwey, E.J., and Overbeek, J.T.G. (1948) *Theory of the Stability of Lyophobic Colloids,* Elsevier, Amsterdam.

Vroman, L. (1967) in *Blood Clotting Enzymology* (Seegers, W.H., ed.) pp. 279–322, Academic Press, New York.

Wahrmann, J.P., Delain, D., Bournoutian, C., and Macieira-Coelho, A. (1981) *In Vitro* 17, 752–762.

Warren, I., Blithe, D.L., and Cossu, G. (1982) *J. Cell. Physiol.* 113, 17–22.

Weiss, L. (1961) *Exp. Cell Res.* 8, 141–153.

Weiss, L., and Harlos, J.P. (1972a) *Progress Surface Sci.* 1, 355–405.

Weiss, L., and Harlos, J.P. (1972b) *J. Theor. Biol.* 37, 169–179.

Wight, T.N., and Ross, R. (1975) *J. Cell Biol.* 67, 660–674.

Yamada, K.M. (1981) in *Cell Biology of the Extracellular Matrix* (Hay, E.D., ed.) pp. 95–115, Plenum Press, New York.

Yamada, K.M., Kennedy, D.W., Grotendorst, G.R., and Momoi, T. (1981) *J. Cell. Physiol.* 109, 343–351.

Growth and Maintenance of Anchorage-Dependent Mammalian Cells in Perfused Systems and Metabolism of Nutrients

Ara T. Nahapetian

7.1 INTRODUCTION

Growth and maintenance of anchorage-dependent mammalian cells in vitro is affected by nutrient supply, accumulation of metabolic end products, growth stimulators (conditioning factors), growth inhibitors (toxicity factors), dissolved oxygen, pH, temperature, shear forces, osmolarity, and attachment surface. Currently, mammalian cells are grown and maintained in both batch and perfused systems. In most laboratories, however, batch procedures are preferred because of their simplicity, ease of preparation, and availability of material. Tissue culture was considered to be a valuable tool for metabolic studies and production of homogeneous cell populations under defined conditions resembling those present in vivo. Batch cultures do not fulfill this requirement due to wide fluctuations in the environmental components (Graff and McCarty, 1957; Kruse et al., 1963; Knazek et al., 1972; Jensen et al., 1974). Graff and McCarty (1957) have stated that a batch culture provided a "feasting and fasting" environment for cells maintained in vitro.

Both excesses and deficiencies of nutrients and metabolic end products could result in unphysiological extremes in culture pH, osmolarity, and gas tensions that could exert detrimental effects on cell growth and survival.

7.2 PERFUSED SYSTEMS

The original perfused systems were developed for morphological examination of mammalian cells in vitro. Christiansen et al. (1953) have described construction of a culture chamber for continuous phase contrast microscopic examination of growing cells. A glass microslide was used for the construction of the chamber. Culture medium could pass through the system without optical interference and was periodically replaced by air for oxygenation. The cells were maintained in this system for as long as three days.

The first perfused systems designed for production of anchorage-dependent mammalian cells were developed in the 1960s (Kruse et al. 1963; Kruse and Miedema, 1965; Miedema and Kruse, 1965; Kruse et al., 1967; Weiss and Schleicher, 1968; Schleicher and Weiss, 1968; Kruse et al., 1969; Kruse et al., 1970; Rose et al., 1970). Kruse et al. (1963) used T-60 flasks fitted with medium and gas inflow and outflow lines (Figure 7–1). The culture vessels were perfused at 0.7 to 14 ml/h rates with gravity-flow culture media supplied from separatory funnel reservoirs. The growth curves of Jensen sarcoma cells of the rat were characterized by an initial logarithmic rate of increase for two to three days, followed by a period of density-dependent retardation of cell growth. After inoculation of a single T-60 flask with 2.3×10^6 cells, over 1.4×10^8 cells were produced in eight days. The same perfused system was used for production of 6.7×10^7 WHISH human amnion, 6.2×10^7 HEP-2 human carcinoma, 2.9×10^7 WI-38 human diploid, 1.3×10^8 DON Chinese hamster, and 1.3×10^8 Jensen sarcoma cells (Kruse and Miedema, 1965). Multicell layers were observed in the perfused cultures. The term "monolayer equivalents" (ME) was introduced and defined as the number of cells per culture divided by the number of cells in a monolayer. Monolayer equivalents of five and 17 were obtained for WI-38 and DON cells, respectively, following a nine-day perfusion period. Production of multiple-layered dense cultures in T-60 and T-75 flasks (Kruse et al., 1969) and roller bottle-perfused systems (Kruse et al., 1970) were reported for a number of other cell types.

In the perfused systems described, the cells were presumably provided with an adequate supply of nutrients, while accumulation of metabolic end products was prevented by constant removal of the spent medium. It was assumed that accumulation of the metabolites would generally retard cell growth. However, mammalian cells could produce vital metabolites necessary for their growth and survival, and constant removal of spent medium would naturally lead to a loss of endogenous growth factors. Rose et al. (1970) designed a system that would retain endogenously synthesized large

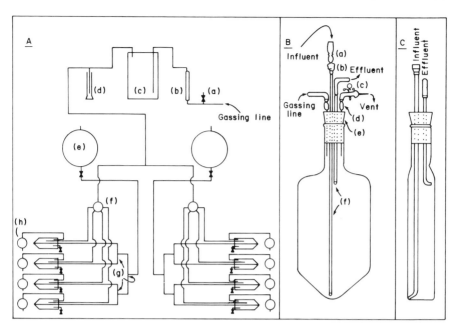

FIGURE 7–1 Replicate culture perfusion system. *(A)* line drawing of apparatus (without timer and motor-clamp assembly); (a) pressure vent pinch clamp; (b) gas flow rate tube (viz., Ace Glass, Inc., Vineland, N.J., metering tube, TRU-TAPER tube size 2-15-3); 12-liter pyrex gas reservoir bottle; (d) 500-ml water-filled graduated cylinder gas pressure stabilizer; (e) 1-liter influent media separatory funnel reservoirs (cotton-plugged); (f) 125-ml inverted filter flasks for gas line connections; (g) 6-mm outside diameter glass U-tube connectors; (h) 125- or 250-ml filter flask effluent media containers (cotton-plugged). All influent and effluent media connections were made with Silatube [Labtician Products Co., Hollis, N.Y., inside diam., outside diam., wall thickness: 1/4 × 1/2 × 1/8 in. from funnels to (g), 1/8 × 7/22 × 3/64 in. from (g) to (h)]; (a)–(d) are on top of the incubator.

(B) T-60 flask connections: (a) 27-gauge, ⅜-inch hypodermic needle with 6-mm outside diameter × 89-mm glass connector tube; (b) sleeve-type, red rubber serum stopper with 6-mm outside diameter plug; (c) cotton-plugged pressure vent with pinch clamp; (d) 20-gauge 1½-inch hypodermic needles; (e) silicone rubber stopper (The West Co., Phoenixville, PA., S-103, #2 stopper); (f) 4-mm outside diameter glass tubing.

(C) position of influent and effluent medium lines in T-60(side view).

Reprinted with permission from Kruse, P.F., Jr., Myhr, B.C., Johnson, J.E., and White, P.B. (1963) *J. Natl. Cancer Inst.* 31, 109–123.

molecular weight metabolites by separating the circulating nutrient from the tissue culture environment by using nonperforated cellophane membranes (Figure 7–2). Furthermore, the spent medium was recirculated, and the system, which was called circumfusion instead of perfusion, was used for maintenance and differentiation of chick embryo tissues for extended pe-

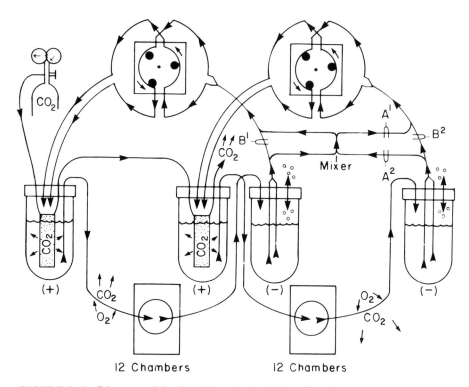

FIGURE 7–2 Diagram of the fluid flow in the 24-chamber dual-rotary circumfusion system. This diagram is 2 superimposed 12-chamber units, with the exception that the 2 polyvinyl leads from each of the 2 negative pressure bottles are joined at various points to form the mixer harness. Clamps placed at A^1 and A^2 direct the flow of nutrient from the negative pressure bottles through their respective pumps to the positive pressure bottle of the same 12-chamber units; this pattern maintains 2 separate culture systems. Clamps placed at B^1 and B^2 direct the fluid from both negative pressure bottles through the mixer segment of the harness and redistribute the fluid to both pumps. Thus, the fluid passing into the 2 positive pressure bottles is a mixture from both negative pressure bottles, and a single 24-chamber system is effected. The CO_2 is shown passing through the CO_2 coil of the second positive pressure bottle and then to air. In the dual-rotary unit, as in the original circumfusion system, the CO_2 is monitored with a bubble flowmeter as it passes to air. The double-ended arrows in the negative pressure bottles represent air vents made with covered 18-gauge needles inserted through the rubber gaskets in the bottle tops. Reprinted with permission from Rose, G.G., Kumegawa, M., Nikai, H., Bracho, M., and Cattoni, M. (1970) *Microvascular Res.* 2, 24–60.

riods. In 1972 Knazek and co-workers introduced a cell culture technique using two types of artificial capillary units (hollow fibers) in a circumfused system (Figure 7–3). One of the units was made of 100 cellulose acetate capillaries sealed in a glass T-shaped tube. It provided 46 cm² of surface

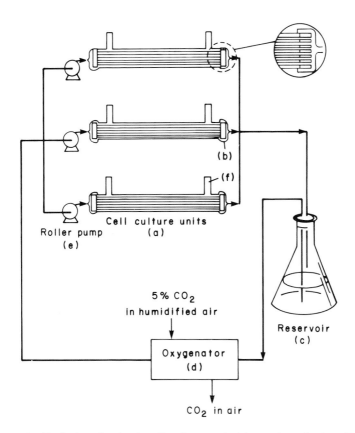

FIGURE 7–3 Perfusion circuit. A cell culture unit (a) consists of a bundle of one or more types of hollow fibers (capillaries) sealed into each end of an 8-mm glass shell by silicone rubber or epoxy resin (b). Units may be arranged in parallel as shown or in series. Nutrient medium stored in a 125-ml reservoir flask (c) was oxygenated and brought to the appropriate pH by exposure to a humidified mixture of 5% CO_2 and air in a Dow Corning Mini-lung (d) before being pumped through each capillary bundle (pump RL-175, Holter) (e). Components were connected by silicone rubber tubing (3.2-mm outer diameter). Cells were inoculated onto the capillary bundles through shell side ports (f). Reprinted with permission from Knazek, R.A., Gullino, P.M., Kohler, P.O., and Dedrick, R.L. (1972) *Science* 178, 65–67, copyright 1972 by the American Association for the Advancement of Science.

area in 1.5 cm³ volume. Diffusion through the capillary wall was limited to substances with less than 30,000 molecular weight. The other unit was constructed with a combination of 30 polymeric (XM-50, Amicon) and 30 silicone polycarbonate (Dow Chemical) capillaries in a 90- by 8-mm glass shell with two side ports. The XM-50 capillary was not permeable to substances with higher than 50,000 molecular weight. The silicone polycarbonate capillary was permeable to gases. It was used for aeration of the unit mainly for exchange of oxygen and carbon dioxide. After inoculation with 2×10^5 mouse fibroblasts (L-929) in the extracapillary space, the unit was circumfused with culture medium supplied by a reservoir with the help of a roller pump at a rate of 0.7 ml/min (1000 ml/24 h). The reservoir medium was replaced every one to four days and the extracapillary medium was replaced weekly. About 1.7×10^7 cells were produced by the end of two weeks. With human choriocarcinoma cells (JEG-7), a cell density close to that of tissue (2.17×10^8 cells in 3 cm^3 culture space) was obtained. Similar to earlier systems, the circumfused environment favored formation of multicell layers (Knazek, 1974). The same technique with minor modifications was used for production of a number of other cell lines in high densities (Knazek et al., 1977; Fike et al., 1977; Rutzky et al., 1977; Ehrlich et al., 1978; Rutzky et al., 1979).

The hollow-fiber technique is especially useful for production of cell products. It was used for production of human chorionic gonadotrophin (Knazek et al., 1972; Knazek et al., 1974), insulin (Chick et al., 1975; Sun and Macmorine, 1976; Chick et al., 1977; Tze and Chen, 1977), and carcinoembryonic antigen (Quarles et al., 1978; Quarles et al., 1980). Two major shortcomings in almost all perfused anchorage-dependent cell cultures were the limitation of surface for attachment and the lack of an accurate monitoring procedure for cell enumeration during the experimental period. Cell growth was estimated either indirectly by determination of glucose utilization (Schleicher and Weiss, 1968) or by daily termination of single perfused cultures (Kruse et al., 1967). Frequent sampling of single homogenous cell populations for direct observation, biochemical testing, and enumeration was made possible by the discovery of microcarriers (van Wezel, 1967). However, DEAE-Sephadex A-50 microcarriers at concentrations higher than 1 g/liter were found to be toxic for the cells, which limited their potential as a means of increasing surface area for cell attachment. The potential value of the microcarriers together with the toxicity problem raised the interest of investigators in our laboratory. A microcarrier not toxic to diploid human fibroblasts (HEL 299) (at a 2-g/liter concentration) was developed (Levine et al., 1977). The cells proliferated and reached a density higher than 1×10^6 cells/ml. The same cells could not grow on DEAE-Sephadex A-50 at the higher concentration of the microcarrier.

Butler et al. (1983), who continued the studies in our laboratory at the Massachusetts Institute of Technology, have described the design of a perfused system for production of anchorage-dependent mammalian cells on microcarriers (Figure 7–4). A silicone inflow tube together with a peristaltic pump maintained a steady flow of medium from a reservoir at 1 ml/min for a 500-ml culture. A column separator at the culture surface controlled the outflow of spent medium into a second reservoir via silicone tubing with the help of a second peristaltic pump. The dimensions of the separator and sedimentation rate of microcarriers were such that the systems ensured complete separation of the medium by steady removal. The microcarrier

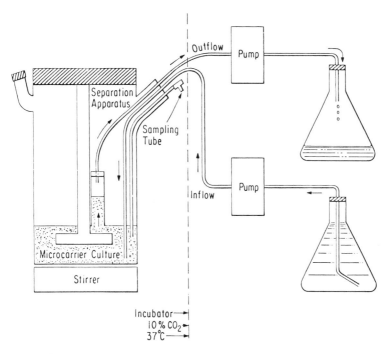

FIGURE 7–4 Perfusion apparatus for microcarrier cultures: *sa*, separation apparatus; *mc*, microcarrier culture; *Out, In*, outflow and inflow; *st*, sampling tube. Reprinted with permission from Butler, M., Imamura, T., Thomas, J., and Thilly, W.G. (1983) *J. Cell Sci.* 61, 351–363, copyright 1983, The Company of Biologists, Ltd.

concentration in the culture was 7.5 g/liter. A final cell density close to 10^7 cells/ml was obtained for Madin-Darby canine kidney (MDCK) cells by the end of a six-day experimental period. After the formation of a monolayer of MDCK cells on the microcarriers, the rate of growth was reduced, which resulted in a biphasic pattern of cell growth similar to that reported in an earlier investigation (Kruse et al., 1963).

Recently, following an 18-day circumfusion period, high cell densities (10^7 cells/culture unit) for two strains of human foreskin fibroblasts were attained in a hollow-fiber unit (Vita fiber 3S 100, Amicon Corp.) only when microcarriers (Cytodex-1, Pharmacia Fine Chemicals, and Polyacrylamide Bio-carriers, Bio Rad Laboratories) were added to the culture chamber. The cells did not grow in the unit without the carriers (Strand et al., 1984a). Moreover, the total interferon production in the circumfused system was significantly higher than from a monolayer cell culture (Strand et al., 1984b).

More recently, Butler et al.'s (1983) microcarrier perfused system was modified in our laboratory (Nahapetian et al., 1986) by placing a probe in the culture for monitoring the dissolved oxygen (Figure 7–5). In addition,

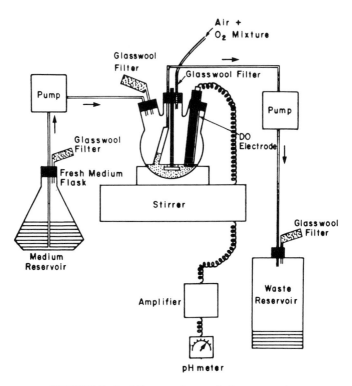

FIGURE 7–5   Microcarrier perfusion apparatus.

the culture vessel was equipped with gas inflow and outflow lines for maintenance of culture dissolved oxygen between 8 and 12% of saturation level prior to inoculation by using a mixture of oxygen and room air. Concentration of microcarriers (Superbeads, Flow Laboratories) in a 100-ml culture was 20 g/liter, which provided a surface area for attachment of cells equivalent to about 22 standard size (490 cm^2) roller bottles. The culture was perfused at the rate of 0.35 ml/min (about 5 vol/day) for 12 days. For Vero, a cell line originating from African green monkey kidney cells, cell densities in excess of 10^7 cells/ml were attained. The high cell densities for Vero cells (3 × 10^7 cells/ml) were reproduced in the same system by perfusing it with a 50% culture medium in phosphate-buffered saline (PBS) at a rate of 8 vol/day for 16 days (Nahapetian et al., 1986) (Figure 7–6). Vero cell-growth curves had a clear biphasic pattern. In general, the cells proliferated with a 24-h doubling time until day six when the microcarriers were covered with a monolayer of Vero cells. A density-dependent retardation of cell growth similar to that reported for perfused cultures of rat Jensen sarcoma (Kruse et al., 1963) and MDCK cells (Butler et al., 1983) was observed following day six. Both the data on cell densities and visual examination of the

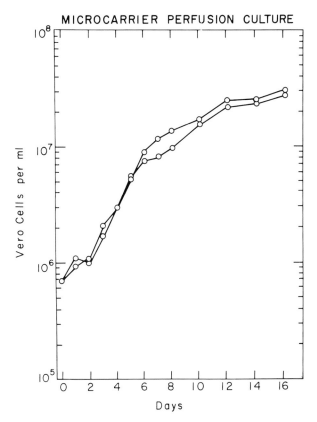

FIGURE 7–6   Growth curves of Vero (monkey kidney) cells in perfused microcarrier culture. Perfusion of the cultures (100 ml) commenced 24 h following cell innoculation at 8 vol/day. Microcarrier concentration was 20 g/l. Experimental medium was modified L15 (4 mM glutamine, 10 mM fructose instead of galactose) plus 5% fetal bovine serum diluted 1:1 with phosphate buffered saline. Each circle represents a single observation from each of two independent cultures.

microcarrier cultures indicated formation of multicell layers in the perfused microcarrier cultures during the second week of the experimental period.

7.3 MEDIA

Perfusion media used in most of the investigations were originally developed and optimized for batch cultures (Table 7–1). It was assumed that either nutrient requirements under the two conditions were similar or an excess of nutrients would not impair growth and maintenance of cells under the continuous feeding condition. Our studies have provided evidence to the contrary. Vero cells in batch cultures grew best in a modified L15 medium

TABLE 7–1   List of References Together with Their Reported Choice of Culture Medium for Growth and Maintenance of Mammalian Cells in Perfused Systems

Graff and McCarty, 1957	Composition of experimental medium was tabulated, and it was stated, "This mixture is certainly overgenerous in some ingredients and just barely sufficient in others."
McCarty, 1962	Eagle's minimal essential medium (MEM)
Miedema and Kruse, 1965	Medium 7a
Kruse et al., 1967	Medium 7a
Rose, 1967	Fischer's V-614 nutrient
Kruse et al., 1969	McCoy's 7a medium
Knazek et al., 1972, 1974, 1977	Eagle's MEM and Ham's F-10 medium
Fike et al., 1977	RPMI 1640
Rutzky et al., 1977	Eagle's MEM
Tze and Chen, 1977	Medium 199
Ehrlich et al., 1978	Dulbecco's MEM
Gebhardt and Mecke, 1979	Waymouth's MB 752/1 medium
Rutzky et al., 1979	Eagle's MEM
Quarles et al., 1980	L15
Knop et al., 1984	F12
Strand et al., 1984a, b	Eagle's MEM

(containing 4 mM glutamine and 10 mM fructose instead of galactose and 5% fetal bovine serum, FBS), while supplying the culture with 50% L15 in a PBS at a rate of 8 vol/day provided the optimum microenvironment for the same cell line in a perfused system (Nahapetian et al., 1986). This study is discussed in more detail in the following section.

7.3.1   Nutrient Utilization and Metabolism for Production of Energy and Nucleic Acid Synthesis

Most media currently in use for cell culture are similar to or a modification of the original formulation reported by Eagle (1955). They contain glucose as the main source of carbohydrate and, presumably, energy. It has been suggested, however, that the level of the monosaccharide in the original formulation (5 mM) was too high, so that it was wasted due to its rapid conversion to lactic acid (Graff and McCarty, 1957). In addition, since lactate is known to be one of the main sources of nonvolatile acid equivalents in mammalian cell cultures, the excessive rise in concentration of the metabolite could be the main cause of the decrease in culture pH, which inhibits cell growth. Even though fructose was found to be a more efficient source of carbohydrate than glucose for growth of cells in vitro (Eagle et al., 1958), the latter monosaccharide is still the most widely used source of carbohydrate in culture media. Reitzer et al. (1979) have reported that 80% of glucose was anaerobically oxidized to lactate, 8% was metabolized through the pentose phosphate pathway, and 5% or less was oxidized aerobically in HeLa cell cultures. Almost all of the medium fructose (90%) was metabolized through the pentose phosphate pathway. It was suggested that either fructose or low concentrations of glucose in culture medium were essential for nucleic acid synthesis, while the major portion of energy requirement of mammalian cells (30–50%) in culture was met by aerobic oxidation of glutamine (Zielke et al., 1984). It was proposed that glutamine was the sole source of energy when glucose concentration was low or when it was replaced by fructose. In contrast, Nagle and Brown (1971) had previously demonstrated that mouse L and HeLa cells could grow in a chemically defined glutamine-free medium containing glucose as the major source of carbohydrate.

Studies in our laboratory demonstrated that when glucose in DMEM was replaced with fructose, both carbohydrates seemed equally effective in terms of cell production for MDCK cells. However, the rate of fructose depletion from the culture medium was much slower than that for glucose (Imamura et al., 1982). Moreover, lactate production decreased and culture pH was relatively more stable when the experimental medium was supplied with fructose. It was also found that Vero cells could grow and reach confluence both on microcarriers (Thilly, Varunsatian, and Nahapetian, unpublished data) and in standard (490-cm^2) roller bottles (Nahapetian and Thilly, unpublished data) containing a glutamine-deficient, modified L15 medium, which was supplemented with 10 mM fructose and 10% FBS. The results were recently confirmed by others (Wolfrom et al., 1984). In both investigations, following a slow growth period (one to two weeks), there was a significant increase in cell proliferation in the group lacking the amino acid. There were no significant differences between the final cell numbers of test and control cultures supplemented with glutamine. Since the test media were supplemented with neither glutamine nor glucose, then fructose was the only major source, aside from other amino acids and pyruvate, that the cells could have utilized for production of energy and synthesis of triglycerides and nucleic acids required for cell proliferation.

Data available in the literature concerning utilization and metabolism of nutrients in perfused cultures are quite limited. Kruse and Miedema (1965) measured the concentration of glucose in fresh and spent media in perfused systems and calculated utilization of the monosaccharide by using data on rates of inflow and outflow and duration of the perfusion period. For perfused WISH human amnion cell cultures, glucose concentration in the influent medium was 280 mg% (15.5 mM) while concentration of the sugar in the effluents collected daily ranged between 249 (13.8 mM) and 168 mg% (14.9 mM). Rates of glucose utilization were found to be related to cell number and proliferation. The glucose level in suspended perfused spin-filter cultures of murine leukemia L1210 cells (Himmelfarb et al., 1969) was reduced to near zero at high population densities (10^7 cells/ml).

In a study recently completed in our laboratory (Nahapetian et al., 1986) for optimization of culture environment, the effects of nutrient supply and removal of spent medium were studied by monitoring cell growth, medium pH, dissolved oxygen (DO), utilization of glucose, fructose, pyruvate, and glutamine, and production of lactate, ammonia, and glutamate during the course of the study. Cultures of Vero cells on microcarriers were perfused with 100%, 50%, 25% and 12.5% modified L15 media (galactose was replaced with 10 mM fructose; the medium contained 4 mM glutamine and 5% FBS) in phosphate-buffered saline at either 4 or 8 vol/day for 16 days.

Nutrient supply and conditioning factors were found to be the most probable growth-limiting factors in cultures perfused with 12.5% and 25% L15 media, while multilayering and limitation of available oxygen accumulation of metabolic end products in the cellular microenvironment were the most probable causes of a density-dependent inhibition of cell growth observed under optimized (supply of 50% L15 medium in PBS at the rate of 8 vol/day) and overfed (supply of 100% L15 medium at the rate of 8 vol/day) culture conditions.

An extremely high rate of glucose utilization, which resulted in almost complete depletion of the monosaccharide within the first 24 hours, confirmed the data reported in the earlier investigations (Graff and McCarty, 1957; Himmelfarb et al., 1969). Under the optimized environmental condition, glutamine was most probably the major source of energy during the first week. However, significant utilization of fructose became evident at higher cell densities ($> 10^7$ cells/ml) during the second week, when lactate production dramatically declined, reaching an almost undetectable level, and respiration progressively acquired the predominant role in energy production.

7.3.2 Nutrient Utilization and Metabolism for Protein Synthesis

Kruse et al. (1967) reported high rates of methionine, serine, asparagine, glutamine, isoleucine, leucine, and lysine utilization in perfused cultures of Jensen sarcoma cells. In contrast, extracellular concentrations of alanine, aspartate, and glutamate were increased. More recently (Butler et al., 1983), daily changes in concentrations of isoleucine, leucine, valine, lysine, histidine, cytidine, methionine, phenylalanine, tyrosine, arginine, glutamic acid, glycine, alanine, glutamine, and ammonia in perfused microcarrier cultures of MDCK cells were monitored for six days. Excluding alanine, glycine, and glutamic acid, which showed a net increase in concentration following an initial decrease, concentrations of most of the amino acids were maintained between 60 and 70% of their original value in the fresh inflow media. The decline in concentration of glutamine (25% of its original value on day six) was significantly greater than for other amino acids, and ammonia concentration in the culture was elevated to a toxic level (2.3 mM) despite the continuous removal of spent medium in the perfused system.

Green and Goldberg (1963) have demonstrated that collagen synthesis in a culture of a mouse fibroblast cell line, 3T6, was greatest in a period when the cells had reached their highest density following a period of rapid cell growth. It was suggested (Kruse and Miedema, 1965) that cell cultures could have a threshold density below and above which proliferation and extracellular protein (such as collagen) synthesis, respectively, could predominate. Subsequently, Kruse et al. (1967) demonstrated that despite a progressively slower rate of proliferation at higher density of Jensen sarcoma cells in a perfused system, rates of utilization of amino acids (expressed in picomoles/hour/microgram of cell protein) were quite constant. It was shown that the decrease in growth rate and increase in cell density led to increasing amounts of extracellular protein in the culture media.

More recently, Strand et al. (1984b) found that interferon yield per cell in perfused cultures of human foreskin fibroblasts was 4- to 10-fold greater than in a monolayer culture.

7.4 NEED FOR FURTHER RESEARCH

While the significance of perfused systems as a means of producing cells and cell products and as a powerful tool for metabolic investigations of high-density homogenous cell populations has been recognized, such production and studies have not actually been widely implemented. The major obstacles have been the commercial unavailability of the systems and technical difficulties involved in maintenance, sampling, and harvesting of the anchorage-dependent mammalian cells in the earlier designs of perfused apparatuses. As discussed earlier, the sampling and harvesting problems were partially solved by the discovery and development of microcarriers. However, the design of perfusion systems currently available does not allow removal of undesirable metabolic end products without loss of conditioning factors (endogenously produced metabolites necessary for cell growth and maintenance) in the outflow medium. The perfused and circumfused systems either remove or retain, respectively, both toxic and vital metabolic end products. The perfused microcarrier system (Figure 7–5) could be improved by a combination of perfusion and recirculation of the spent medium after passage through a hollow-fiber unit (Figure 7–7), provided the latter could selectively retain the useful metabolites.

Moreover, as mentioned earlier, media currently in use in most of the perfused systems were originally developed and optimized for batch cultures. They could certainly be overgenerous in some and inadequate in other ingredients. Further research is required for optimization and development of media especially designed to meet the requirements of individual mammalian cells in perfused systems.

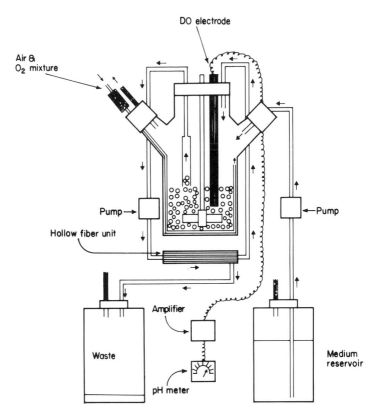

FIGURE 7–7 Proposed microcarrier perfusion apparatus.

REFERENCES

Butler, M., Imamura, T., Thomas, J., and Thilly, W.G. (1983) *J. Cell Sci.* 61, 351–363.

Chick, W.L., Like, A.A., and Lauris, V. (1975) *Science* 187, 847–848.

Chick, W.L., Perna, J.J., Lauris, V., Low, D., Galletti, P.M., Panol, G., Whittemore, A.D., Like, A.A., Colton, C.K., and Lysaght, M.J. (1977) *Science* 197, 780–782.

Christiansen, G.S., Danes, B., Allen, L., and Leinfelder, P.J. (1953) *Exp. Cell Res.* 5, 10–15.

Eagle, H. (1955) *Science* 122, 501–504.

Eagle, H., Bartan, S., Levy, M., and Schultze, H.O. (1958) *J. Biol. Chem.* 233, 551–558.

Ehrlich, K.C., Stewart, E., and Klein, E. (1978) *In Vitro* 14, 443–450.

Fike, R.M., Glick, J.L., and Burns, A.A. (1977) *In Vitro* 13, 170 (abstract).

Gebhardt, R., and Mecke, D. (1979) *Exp. Cell Res.* 124, 349–359.

Graff, S., and McCarty, K.S. (1957) *Exp. Cell Res.* 13, 348–357.

Green, H., and Goldberg, B. (1963) *Nature* 200, 1097–1098.

Himmelfarb, P., Thayer, P.S., and Martin, H.E. (1969) *Science* 167, 555–557.

Imamura, T., Crespi, C.L., Thilly, W.G., and Brunengraber, H. (1982) *Anal. Biochem.* 124, 353–358.

Jensen, M.D., Wallach, D.F.H., and Lin, P.S. (1974) *Exp. Cell Res.* 84, 271–281.

Knazek, R.A. (1974) *Fed. Proc.* 33, 1978–1981.

Knazek, R.A., Gullino, P.M., Kohler, P.O., and Dedrick, R.L. (1972) *Science* 178, 65–67.

Knazek, R.A., Kohler, P.O., and Gullino, P.M. (1974) *Exp. Cell Res.* 84, 251–254.

Knazek, R.A., Lippman, M.E., and Chopra, H.C. (1977) *J. Natl. Cancer Inst.* 58, 419–422.

Knop, R.H., Chen, C.W., Mitchell, J.B., Russo, A., McPherson, S., and Cohen, J.S. (1984) *Biochim. Biophys. Acta* 804, 275–284.

Kruse, P.F., Jr., Keen, L.N., and Whittle, W.L. (1970) *In Vitro* 6, 75–88.

Kruse, P.F., Jr., and Miedema, E. (1965) *J. Cell Biol.* 27, 273–279.

Kruse, P.F., Jr., Miedema, E., and Carter, H.C. (1967) *Biochemistry* 6, 949–955.

Kruse, P.F., Jr., Myhr, B.C., Johnson, J.E., and White, P.B. (1963) *J. Natl. Cancer Inst.* 31, 109–123.

Kruse, P.F., Jr., Whittle, W., and Miedema, E. (1969) *J. Cell Biol.* 42, 113–121.

Levine, D.W., Wong, J.S., Wang, D.I.C., and Thilly, W.G. (1977) *Somatic Cell Genet.* 3, 149–155.

McCarty, K. (1962) *Exp. Cell Res.* 27, 230–240.

Miedema, E., and Kruse, P.F., Jr. (1965) *Biochem. Biophys. Res. Commun.* 20, 528–534.

Nagle, S.C., Jr., and Brown, B.L. (1971) *J. Cell Physiol.* 77, 259–264.

Nahapetian, A.T., Thomas, J., and Thilly, W.G. (1986) *J. Cell Sci.* (in press).

Quarles, J.M., Morris, N.G., and Leibovitz, A. (1978) *In Vitro* 14, 335.

Quarles, J.M., Morris, N.G., and Leibovitz, A. (1980) *In Vitro* 16, 113–118.

Reitzer, L.J., Wice, B.M., and Kennel, D. (1979) *J. Biol. Chem.* 254, 2669–2676.

Rose, G.G., Kumegawa, M., Nikai, H., Bracho, M., and Cattoni, M. (1970) *Microvascular Res.* 2, 24–60.

Rutzky, L.P., Tomita, J.T., Calenoff, M.A., and Kahan, B.D. (1977) *In Vitro* 13, 191 (abstract).

Rutzky, L.P., Tomita, J.T., Calenoff, M.A., and Kahan, B.D. (1979) *J. Natl. Cancer Inst.* 63, 893–899.

Schleicher, J.B., and Weiss, R.E. (1968) *Biotechnol. Bioeng.* 10, 617–624.

Strand, J.M., Quarles, J.M., and McConnell, S. (1984a) *Biotechnol. Bioeng.* 26, 503–507.

Strand, J.M., Quarles, J.M., and McConnell, S. (1984b) *Biotechnol. Bioeng.* 26, 508–512.

Sun, A.M., and Macmorine, H.G. (1976) *Diabetes* 25, 339 (abstract).

Tze, W.J., and Chen, L.M. (1977) *Diabetes* 26, 185–191.

van Wezel, A.L. (1967) *Nature (Lond.)* 216, 64–65.

Weiss, R.E., and Schleicher, J.B. (1968) *Biotechnol. Bioeng.* 10, 601–615.

Wolfrom, C., Polini, G., Decimo, D., and Gautier, M. (1984) *Bio. Cell.* 52, A35.

Zielke, H.R., Zielke, C.L., and Ozand, P.T. (1984) *Fed. Proc.* 43, 121–125.

Mammalian Cell Culture Technology: A Review from an Engineering Perspective

Wei-Shou Hu
Daniel I. C. Wang

8.1 INTRODUCTION

Many perceive engineering as being mainly involved in the scale-up or in the large-scale operation of processes, but this is only partly correct. Engineering studies can certainly contribute to the scale-up of bioprocesses, but the contribution to process optimization is not restricted only to "large-scale" operation. The first problem to be examined concerns nutrient supply and metabolite removal from the culture medium. This seemingly strictly biological problem is one that can be profitably examined from an engineering perspective and needs to be addressed even if the bioreactor used is relatively small in size. We also will review the effects of oxygen transfer and shear force in the cultivation of mammalian cells. These two problems are genuinely related to scale-up, since their effect on cell growth varies with the scale of operation.

One of the authors, W.-S.H., wishes to acknowledge support from the Economics Laboratory, Inc., St. Paul, Minnesota.

8.2 MEDIUM DESIGN FROM A KINETIC POINT OF VIEW

8.2.1 Well-Mixed versus Plug-Flow Reactor

Idealized bioreactors are generally categorized similarly to chemical reactors—according to their mixing characteristics. In a well-mixed bioreactor, complete mixing is assumed to occur instantaneously; that is, upon the injection of a pulse of tracer into the reactor, the tracer is instantaneously blended and distributed uniformly throughout the reactor. In a batch-mixing process, this gives rise to a steady concentration of the tracer (Figure 8–1A). In a continuous mixing process with fluid flowing in and out at a constant rate and the liquid level in the reactor maintained at a constant level, the pulse addition of a tracer results in an instantaneous rise of tracer concentration. This is followed by an exponential decay (Figure 8–1B). In contrast with a well-mixed reactor, it is assumed that the fluid flow in a

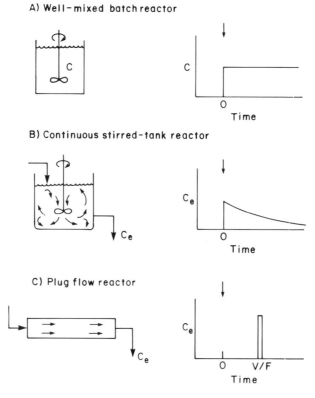

A) Well-mixed batch reactor

B) Continuous stirred-tank reactor

C) Plug flow reactor

FIGURE 8–1 Mixing in different types of reactors. (A) Well-mixed batch reactor. C, tracer concentration in the reactor. (B) Continuous stirred-tank reactor. Ce, tracer concentration in the effluent stream. (C) Plug-flow reactor. Ce, tracer concentration in the effluent stream; F, flow rate of inlet and effluent stream; V, volume of the reactor; ↓, pulse addition of tracer into the reactor.

plug-flow reactor resembles that of piston movement, i.e., there is no back-mixing. The pulse of tracer in the inlet stream results in a sharp band of tracer moving toward the outlet at a constant rate (Figure 8–1C). Because of the difference in mixing characteristics, the transport of nutrients, cell growth, and metabolism in plug-flow and well-mixed reactors can also be different.

The stirred vessels are used in both continuous and batch fashions in biochemical processes. Except for a few cases, most bioreactors for mammalian cell cultivation are operated in a batch fashion: The cell concentration in the reactor increases with time. The kinetics of cell growth, nutrient consumption, and product formation in a batch well-mixed bioreactor can be expressed in the following equations:

$$\frac{dx}{dt} = \mu x \tag{8.1}$$

$$\frac{ds_i}{dt} = \frac{-\mu x}{y_i} - m_i x \tag{8.2}$$

$$\frac{dp_j}{dt} = q_j x \tag{8.3}$$

In the preceding equations, x, s_i, and p_j are the concentrations of cell, nutrient i, and product j, respectively. The specific growth rate (h^{-1}) is μ, y_i is cell yield based on substrate i or the amount of cell mass produced per unit amount of substrate i consumed (gram cell mass or number of cells produced/gram substrate i consumed), and q_j is the specific productivity for product j (gram product/cell-h). In Equation 8.2, m_i is the maintenance coefficient as postulated by Pirt (1965). Pirt proposed that the substrate consumed by cells be divided into two categories, a portion for cell growth and a portion for so-called maintenance. Basically, maintenance is a term referring to substrate utilized but not directly attributed to cell growth. This may include turnover of cellular materials, maintaining osmotic gradient across cell membrane, and so on. The cell growth rate of mammalian cells in culture, μ, is generally affected by the concentrations of serum, other medium components, and metabolite(s). For the cultivation of microbial cells, the Monod model, which assumes that cell growth is limited solely by the concentration of a single substrate, is often used for cell growth (Monod, 1949). This model assumes that the specific growth rate can be expressed as Equation 8.4.

$$\mu = \frac{\mu_{max}s}{(s + k_s)} \tag{8.4}$$

In Equation 8.4, μ_{max} is the maximum specific growth rate, k_s is the Mechalis-Menten constant, and s is the concentration of the limiting substrate. According to the Monod model, cells grow at their maximum rate with an abundance of the limiting substrate, and the growth rate decreases as the concentration of the limiting substrate decreases. This model predicts the growth of microorganisms reasonably well in both batch and continuous cultures in which the growth-limiting substrate is known. It has been proposed to apply the Monod model to express the growth of mammalian cells in suspension (Tovey and Brouty-Boye, 1976). Using a chemostat operated under glucose-limiting conditions, Tovey (1980) examined the growth kinetics of a cancerous cell line as a function of dilution rate. A general agreement exists between the prediction of the Monod model and the experimental results over a range of dilution rates. However, at high dilution rates the experimental results deviate from the Monod model significantly. The Monod model as expressed in Equation 8.4 is for cell growth limited solely by a single substrate. For microbial growth in a chemically defined medium, such limiting substrates can often be clearly identified. However, for the cultivation of mammalian cells, the medium used usually includes a variety of amino acids, vitamins, and many undefined growth factors or hormones in the serum. Although glucose is consumed most rapidly among the components of the cell culture medium, it is not yet clear if it is the sole limiting substrate in most circumstances. Given the complexity of the growth medium for mammalian cells and the vast difference in cell metabolism between microorganisms and mammalian cells, it may not be surprising to learn that the Monod model is not adequate to predict cell growth over a wide range of dilution rates. For the cultivation of anchorage-dependent mammalian cells, there have been few studies on the mathematical model for cell growth, and the development of a growth model can be further complicated by the interaction of cells according to their spatial relationship. For many cell types that exhibit contact inhibition and form a monolayer after reaching confluence, the cell growth rate is also a function of spatial cell density. The specific growth rate, μ, decreases gradually as cells approach confluence. Many continuous cell lines can grow as multilayers, and their growth rate is less affected by the spatial crowding. However, even for those cells the apparent growth rate can be greatly reduced after reaching confluence. This may be due to the limitation of nutrient diffusion through multiple layers of cells. It is also possible that cells form associations that define new states of biochemical behavior at high spatial cell density. For mammalian cells the rates of nutrient utilization (ds/dt) and metabolite accumulation (dp/dt) are not necessarily the functions only of cell concentration and growth rate, but may also be affected by the medium composition. For instance, the glutamine consumption rate and thus the ammonium accumulation rate are affected by glucose concentration in the medium (Zielke et al., 1984). The exponential growth in a batch culture is typically followed by a transition stage and subsequently a stationary stage in which growth is limited by nutrient limitation, product inhibition, or high cell density (Figure 8–2A). The kinetics of nutrient consumption and product or

A) Batch

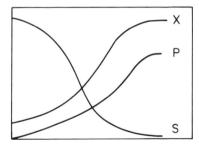

B) Plug flow

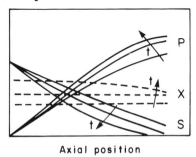

Axial position

FIGURE 8–2 Idealized growth kinetics in (A) batch and (B) plug-flow reactor. X, cell concentration; S, substrate concentration; P, product or metabolite concentration.

metabolite production vary to a great extent with the medium composition. The rates of nutrient consumption and product accumulation often decrease as cells approach stationary stage (Figure 8–2). However, for some nutrients for which the maintenance coefficients are large, or for some products whose formation is non–growth-associated, the rate may not be substantially reduced even after cell growth ceases. One such example is the glucose consumption rate of FS-4 cells, a normal diploid fibroblastic strain, in Dulbecco's modified Eagle's medium (Fleischaker, 1982). The growth of FS-4 cells on microcarriers proceeded until confluence and the rates of glucose consumption and lactate production increased with cell concentration during growth. However, both the glucose consumption and lactate production continued at a constant rate even after cells ceased multiplying in the confluent stage.

For cell cultivation in a plug-flow reactor, the concentrations of nutrients and metabolites are affected not only by time but also by spatial position. For anchorage-dependent cells, it can be assumed that the fluid flow through the reactor does not change the spatial position of cells. If cells are uniformly distributed after inoculation in the reactor, and the composition of the inlet stream remains constant throughout the cultivation period, then the concentrations of cell, nutrient, and product in the reactor can be expressed as the following equations:

$$\frac{dx(z,t)}{dt} = \mu x(z,t) \tag{8.5}$$

$$\frac{dS_i(zt)}{dt} = \frac{dJ_i}{dz} - \frac{\mu x}{y_i} - m_i x \tag{8.6}$$

$$\frac{dP_j(z,t)}{dt} = \frac{dJ_j}{dz} - q_j x \tag{8.7}$$

In the above equations, z is the axial distance from the inlet of the stream along the reactor, and J_i and J_j are the fluxes, or the mass flow rates per unit cross-section area, of nutrient i and product j respectively. The flux terms in Equations 8.6 and 8.7 are thus functions of the medium flow rate. The nutrient concentration decreases and the product concentration increases as the medium moves downstream (Figure 8–2b). The gradient of the concentrations of nutrients and products along the axial position of the reactor increases with cultivation time as the cell concentration increases. Due to the nature of plug-flow, the growth limiting effect of low nutrient concentration and high product concentration can be severe toward the exit end of the reactor. As the cell concentration increases, a gradient of specific growth rate thus eventually can occur along the axial distance of the reactor. The overall growth rate in the reactor gradually slows down as a result of nutrient limitation and/or product inhibition. The extent of the gradients is affected by the flow rate used, and the maximum axial length of the reactor is limited by the adverse effect of nutrient limitation and product inhibition.

8.2.2 Kinetics of Mammalian Cell Cultivation in Bioreactors

The kinetics of mammalian cell cultivation illustrated in Figure 8–2 are somewhat idealized. Most mammalian cell cultivations are operated under a modified version of batch or continuous culture. One reason for the need for modification is the medium composition currently used in most processes. A typical animal cell culture medium is a balanced salt solution containing sugar, amino acids, and other nutrients. In order for animal cells to grow, it is necessary to supplement the medium with 5–10% serum. The media presently used in cell culture were mostly developed for cell growth on a conventional cultivation apparatus such as a Petri dish or roller bottle. For the production of biological molecules in a bioreactor, a higher cell concentration than that attainable in conventional vessels is desirable. At a high cell concentration, both the concentrations of nutrients and the buffer capacity of the traditional cell culture media are not sufficient to support a high metabolic rate. Supplementation of the growth-limiting nutrient to the culture often has only limited success due to the resulting high concentration of metabolites accumulated in the medium.

8.2.3 Plug-Flow Reactors

For cell cultivation in bioreactors in which fluid flow resembles plug-flow, such as hollow-fiber or stationary glass-bead systems, the problem of metabolite accumulation can be complicated by oxygen limitation due to the low solubility of oxygen in aqueous solution. In such a system, the operating parameters, including medium flow rate and reactor length, are chosen to avoid the adverse effect on cell growth near the exit end of the reactor. In a plug-flow bioreactor it is not unusual to find that an adverse environment of growth exists downstream due to the depletion of one nutrient or the accumulation of some metabolites while most other nutrients are still abundant. In order to utilize the medium efficiently, especially to salvage serum in the medium, the effluent stream is often recycled to a medium reservoir. The dissolved oxygen or the limiting nutrient can be replenished in the medium reservoir before the medium is recirculated back to the reactor. Alternatively, the axial concentration gradient of dissolved oxygen can be also reduced by the use of an oxygen-permeable membrane in the reactor. In such systems, air flows along the membrane, usually in tubular form, and oxygen is allowed to diffuse into the culture medium through the membrane. With such an arrangement axial oxygen concentration gradient can be reduced; however, the metabolite concentration gradient still exists, making medium recirculation necessary. The metabolite concentration from the effluent stream is reduced by mixing with the bulk medium before recirculating into the reactor. Such medium recirculation has been in use in packed-glass sphere (Whiteside and Spier, 1981) and in hollow-fiber systems (Gullino and Knazek, 1979). As an alternative to medium recirculation, a shallow bed-depth and relatively high flow rate can be used. In one such system, a high concentration of metabolite (lactate, in this case) in the effluent stream was avoided and presumably the growth of cells in the downstream region of the reactor was not inhibited by high lactate concentration (Ku et al., 1981).

8.2.4 Stirred Vessels: Intermittent Medium Exchange
versus Continuous Perfusion

For cell cultivation in a stirred vessel, typically part of the medium is periodically withdrawn and replaced with fresh medium in order to sustain cell growth in the culture. Figure 8–3 shows the growth kinetics of the lymphoblastoid cells JY in such a fed-batch culture. In this culture cells grew exponentially after the short lag phase. To sustain the exponential growth

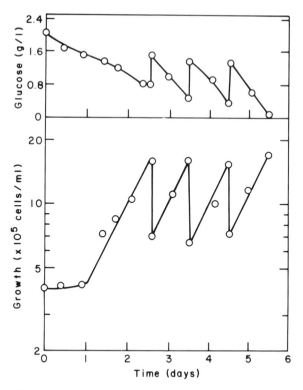

FIGURE 8–3 Kinetics of growth of lymphoblastoid cells, JY, in a suspension culture. Growth medium was RPMI supplemented with 10% fetal calf serum.

50% of the medium was withdrawn and replenished with fresh medium periodically. Because the cells were cultivated in suspension, 50% of cells were withdrawn during medium exchange. In a microcarrier culture, the medium exchange is typically operated in a different fashion: Cells are allowed to settle with microcarriers and be retained in the reactor during medium exchange, thus achieving a higher final cell concentration. The kinetics of a typical microcarrier culture are shown in Figure 8–4. The growth of FS-4, a normal diploid fibroblastic strain, proceeded until reaching confluence on the sixth day with a final cell density of 1.2×10^6 cells/ml. The microcarrier concentration used was 5 g/l. The medium exchange on the third day of cultivation is reflected in the step change in the concentrations of glucose and lactate. The kinetics of the production of fibronectin, a large extracellar glycoprotein, were determined using radioimmunoassay. A portion of the fibronectin produced was withdrawn together with medium during medium exchange. Fibronectin concentration increased with cell number, and a final concentration of 7 μg/ml was reached when the culture reached confluence.

Another mode of medium change is often called "perfusion." The word

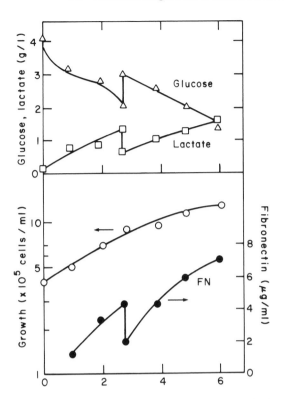

FIGURE 8–4 Kinetics of growth and fibronectin production of FS-4 cells in micro-carrier culture. (○) cell concentration; (●) fibronectin concentration; (Δ) glucose concentration; (□) lactate concentration. The microcarrier concentration was 5 g/l.

perfusion is used in two different contexts: It refers to medium recirculation through a reservoir, as in the study by Griffiths and Thornton (1982), or it denotes a cultivation method that employs continuous removal and replenishment of culture medium (Tolbert et al., 1981; Butler et al., 1983). In a continuous flow or perfusion system, means must be devised to retain cells in the reactor. This can be achieved by the use of a spin filter (Thayer et al., 1970; Thayer, 1973). Recently such a filter was applied to the cultivation of suspension cells in a 40-liter vessel (Tolbert et al., 1981). The filter has also been used for the cultivation of mammalian cells on microcarriers (Griffiths and Thornton, 1982). A spin filter was often installed along the agitation shaft so that the problem of filter clogging was alleviated by the rotating motion; thus, the medium could be withdrawn from the cell- or microcarrier-free region. Eventually, clogging occurred and the operation was terminated. In a microcarrier culture, cells can even be retained in the reactor without the use of any filter when cells along with microcarriers are allowed to separate from the effluent stream and settle back to the reactor by sedimentation. It has been reported that both cell growth and cell yield per unit amount of medium consumed or per unit serum used is higher in the perfused culture than in unperfused culture (Tolbert et al., 1981; Griffiths and Thornton, 1982). It was suggested that lower lactate concentration in the culture contributed to the improvement. However, little kinetic information is available to determine the cause of such improvement conclusively. Tolbert et al. (1981) compared the growth of a rat tumor cell line in a conventional batch culture to that in a perfused culture equipped with a spin filter. In the batch culture, cells grew exponentially until about 50% of the glucose was utilized. Subsequently, cell concentration increased at a much slower rate and the viability of the culture also decreased drastically. In the perfused culture, cells grew exponentially over an extended period and reached a much higher cell density with, of course, the use of a larger volume of medium. However, when the maximum amount of cells produced in the culture was divided by the amount of medium used, the researchers found a 2- to 2.5-fold improvement with the perfused culture. From the batch culture the cell yield on glucose during exponential growth can be calculated to be 7.1×10^5 cells/mg glucose. The perfusion rate used in the Tolbert study was between 10 to 20 ml/10^9 cells·h. If we assume cell yield is constant during exponential growth, then the quasi–steady state concentration of glucose can be estimated. This concentration ranges from 0.5 mg/ml at 15 ml/10^9 cells·h to 1.5 mg/ml at 20 ml/10^9 cells·h. At 10 ml/10^9 cells·h the supply of glucose would not be sufficient to sustain the calculated consumption rate. However, the glucose concentrations reported in the perfusion experiment were significantly higher than the calculated results. A similar calculation for lactate also showed that the lactate concentration in the perfused culture was lower than that calculated from the batch culture. A possible explanation was that the cell yield on glucose was higher in the perfused culture, thus giving rise to a higher residual glucose concentration and low lactate concentration. Since the exponential growth rates in both batch and perfused cultures were similar, and the growth in the batch culture during the exponential stage was apparently not inhibited by a high metabolic concentration, it is not clear why the yield was different under the two cultivation conditions. Nevertheless, the improvement gained by the use of the spin filter with perfusion is quite apparent. In the suspension cell culture, cells would be withdrawn together with the fluid if perfusion were performed without the use of a spin filter, resulting in a lower attainable cell concentration. At a high perfusion rate, cells could even be washed out. The use of a spin filter allows a high flow rate to be used, as in the study by Tolbert et al. (1981) previously discussed.

8.2.5   Kinetic Considerations for Medium Design and Medium Exchange

In the cultivation of mammalian cells in bioreactors, the cell concentration can often be one to two orders of magnitude higher than that achievable with conventional cultivation methods. However, the media used for mammalian cell culture processes are still based on those designed for conventional cultivation. The necessity of medium exchange or perfusion for achieving maximum growth has been documented (Butler et al., 1983; Tolbert and Feder, 1983). However, by and large, the important parameters in devising a medium exchange scheme, such as the interval between medium changes and the fraction of the total medium volume to be changed each time, or the flow rate in the case of perfusion, have been determined empirically. There has not been a systematic study to acquire the kinetic data and to develop a rational means of optimizing those operating parameters.

One problem posed to medium replenishment is efficient utilization of serum and other growth factors. The concentration of serum, or of growth factors in the case of serum-free culture, is usually the growth-rate-limiting factor in a culture medium. The relative cost of serum or growth factors in an animal cell culture is staggering to those familiar with costs of microbial fermentation medium. Too-frequent medium exchange or the use of an unnecessarily high perfusion rate would result in a waste of this valuable medium component. This was illustrated by the study of Morandi and Valeri (1982), who observed that in the cultivation of human diploid fibroblasts, MRC5, medium exchange at the third day of cultivation was necessary for the cells to reach the maximum cell concentration of about 2×10^6 cells/ml. Without medium exchange, the final growth attainable was only about 50% of the confluent density. To avoid discarding fetal calf serum, a component in their medium, during the cultivation they dialysed the culture medium against a large volume of medium without serum and examined cell growth under such conditions. The molecular weight cut-off of the dialysis membrane used in their study was not mentioned; nevertheless, as a result of dialysis the glucose concentration was sustained at a higher level and lactate concentration was reduced. Presumably the concentrations of some low molecular weight nutrients were also restored, while those of other low molecular weight metabolites reduced. Both the growth rate and the extent of final growth in the continuously dialysed culture are similar to the one with medium exchange. Although it was speculated that the low glucose and high lactate levels were the growth-limiting factors, other possibilities, including the accumulation of an as yet unidentified, dialysable growth inhibitory substance in the culture cannot be discounted. Above all, the results support the notion that medium exchange or perfusion practiced in mammalian cell culture may well be wasteful in terms of serum consumption.

Another adverse effect of medium replenishment is its effect on the attainable product concentration. For suspension-cell culture, medium exchange results in a low maximum attainable cell concentration. If a medium for high-density cell culture can be developed to eliminate or reduce the need for frequent medium exchange, possibly the cell concentration in a suspension culture can be increased to the same level as that attainable with a spin filter. High cell concentration can often be translated into high product concentration, and thus a lower recovery cost. For instance, in the experiment that gave rise to the results shown in Figure 8–4, if the need for medium exchange was eliminated, the final concentration of fibronectin would be increased by 40 to 50%. The magnitude of increase in product concentration would be even greater for those cultures that require even more frequent medium exchange.

The growth-limiting factor(s) that renders the medium change necessary has not yet been identified conclusively. It could be unfavorable pH, the depletion of essential nutrient(s), the accumulation of inhibitory metabolite(s), or a combination of some of these factors. Glucose and lactate are often suggested as the primary effector compounds affecting cell growth in a bioreactor. If glucose is the growth-limiting factor in the culture medium, one may speculate that the addition of glucose in the medium would increase growth. However, supplementation of glucose to the culture only is not the solution to the problem of medium design for high-density cell culture. Under normal conditions, with an initial glucose concentration in the range of 1–4 g/l, most of the glucose molecules consumed by mammalian cells in culture are converted to lactate. Supplementing glucose in the culture without taking measures to reduce lactate production merely increases the lactate level and further reduces pH in the medium. To minimize the need for medium exchange, it is necessary to reduce the lactate formation. Possibly this can be achieved by the use of fructose or galactose as the source of carbohydrate (see Chapter 5). The cellular energy metabolism is also affected by glucose concentration. At a glucose concentration of 80 μM, the glucose utilized by human diploid fibroblasts is only 7% of that utilized by cultures initially at 5 mM (Zielke et al., 1984); thus, possibly, lactate formation in the culture can be reduced by controlling glucose concentration at a low level. The reduction of lactate formation may not eliminate the need for medium exchange, but it will certainly help maintain the pH of the culture and perhaps lead to reduction of the amount of medium required for a given culture. Such an improvement will be advantageous not only for cultures in stirred vessels but also for those in plug-flow reactors. The minimization of the formation of inhibitory metabolites will allow a lower flow rate or a longer bed-depth to be used, possibly giving rise to a higher product concentration in the effluent stream.

8.2.6   Medium Design: A Multidisciplinary Task

In the development of medium for mammalian cell culture processes it is important to keep the design criteria in mind. A desirable medium should provide cells with optimum environment to sustain maximum cell growth rate or maximum product formation rate. The word "optimum" should not be restricted to the initial conditions. Practically speaking, the high metabolic rate of cells can cause the growth medium to deviate from the initial optimum conditions quickly. Means must be developed to sustain optimum conditions over an extended period to allow for a high level of growth and a high product concentration. Thus, the optimization of mammalian cell culture medium involves not only manipulation of medium composition, the concentrations of serum, and/or growth factors, but also balancing of the rates of supply and consumption of nutrient as well as of removal and accumulation of metabolites.

From this discussion one may speculate that a better mode of cell culture operation is probably to feed key nutrients at a prescribed rate, thereby controlling cell metabolism and leading to a minimum of medium replenishment. In a plug-flow reactor, one may need to feed limiting nutrient(s) at multiple points along the axial dimension of the reactor. However, such feeding at a prescribed rate is possible only if there is sufficient knowledge to formulate the system mathematically as a growth model. Such a model would allow us to analyze the system and to predict the response of cells to the change of environmental conditions. In addition, the bioreactor must have sufficient instrumentation and an on-line data acquisition system to permit adjustment for model prediction error. Furthermore, even if the model is available, one has to identify which set of conditions would allow us to achieve our objective, namely optimum cell growth at minimum medium expenditure. To define the optimum condition for cell growth, the constraints imposed on the system include the acceptable ranges of the concentrations of nutrients, the kinetics of the metabolism of a number of nutrients, as well as the acceptable operating ranges of osmolality, pH, and the concentrations of metabolites. The manipulatable parameters are the mode of operation (e.g., intermittent versus continuous medium changes) and the feeding rates of various nutrients. It is desirable to reduce the rate of metabolite accumulation in the manipulation of medium composition. On the other hand, in devising the means of sustaining the optimum growth conditions over an extended period, it is desirable to minimize the residence time of metabolite while maximizing that of serum or other growth factors. With the great number of variables involved, it is difficult, if not impossible, to exhaustively examine all possible combinations by trial and error to define the optimal conditions. It is necessary to apply a kinetic model to optimize the operating parameters and then test it experimentally. Kinetic studies and control of cell metabolism require knowledge of physiology and cell biology, whereas instrumentation, modeling, and process simulation and optimization need engineering training and insight. The design of cell culture medium should be a collective effort among engineers, chemists, and biologists.

8.3 OXYGEN TRANSFER IN CELL-CULTURE VESSELS

The requirement of oxygen for the cultivation of vertebrate cells in vitro has been discussed in Chapter 5. Because of its low solubility in aqueous solution, about 0.2 mmoles/l at 37° C, oxygen in the medium can be quickly depleted unless it is constantly replenished. The oxygen transfer rate in the bioreactor must be sufficient to meet the oxygen consumption requirement to sustain optimum cell growth. The rate of oxygen transfer from gas phase into the culture can be described by Equation 8.8.

$$OTR = K_L a (C^* - C_L) \tag{8.8}$$

In Equation 8.8, OTR is the oxygen transfer rate per unit culture volume (mmoles/l·h), K_L is the mass transfer coefficient (cm/h), a is the interfacial area per unit volume (cm^{-1}), C^* is the oxygen concentration (mmoles/l) at equilibrium and C_L is the dissolved oxygen concentration in the bulk liquid. The mass transfer coefficient is a measurement of the oxygen transfer resistance. The larger the transfer coefficient, the smaller is the resistance. $C^* - C_L$ is the concentration difference across the "film" at the interface, a measure of the driving force that allows oxygen to be transported into the liquid phase. In microbial cultivation, oxygen transfer is achieved by sparging air into the culture. In contrast to microbial fermentation, oxygen is often supplied to growing animal cells simply by diffusion through the liquid surface. This is especially true for the cultivation of animal cells in conventional vessels, such as roller bottles. In conventional vessels the cell concentration is typically lower than that achievable in bioreactors; thus, the volumetric oxygen consumption rate in the conventional vessels is relatively low. However, in conventional vessels the liquid gas interfacial area per unit volume is large. It is conceivable that under such conditions, ample oxygen can be supplied for cell growth by diffusion through the interface. In a bioreactor, oxygen can easily become the growth-limiting factor. The stirred vessels used for cell cultivation often have a liquid height to diameter ratio of about one. The liquid surface per unit volume is thus about 0.9 V$^{-1/3}$. Since the ratio of interfacial surface area to liquid volume decreases as reactor volume increases, the limitation of oxygen transfer will be more pronounced in large-scale operation. Continuous sparging of air into liquid has been used in the cultivation of cells grown in suspension (Acton and Lynn, 1977), but it is not a common practice in cell culture. In general, direct sparging of air into serum-containing medium causes foaming. In a microcarrier culture, foaming can result in the agglomeration and flotation of microcarriers on the surface of the foam. In most cases, oxygen is supplied by surface aeration, resulting in limited oxygen transfer capability; there have been numerous reports of oxygen as the growth-limiting factor in cell culture. Telling and Radlett (1970) reported that oxygen supply was the limiting factor in the cultivation of baby hamster kidney cells growing in suspension in a 4-liter vessel. At a dissolved oxygen level below 5% of saturation, both the growth rate and the yield based on glucose was decreased. In a study of chick embryo fibroblast cultivation on microcarriers, Sinskey et al. (1981) reported a decrease in maximum growth extent when culture volume was increased from 100 ml to 1000 ml. The reduction in growth extent was attributed to oxygen transfer limitation in the 1-liter culture.

To sustain optimum cell growth, not only must the rate of oxygen supply meet the oxygen consumption rate of cells, but also the dissolved oxygen concentration must be maintained above a critical value. There have been a few attempts to determine such a critical concentration of dissolved oxygen for cell growth. In some early studies of the effect of oxygen, cell growth was correlated to the oxygen partial pressure in the gas phase. However, in a culture with a high oxygen consumption rate, the oxygen concentrations in the liquid phase and gas phase are typically not in equilibrium. Often the measurement of oxygen partial pressure in the gas phase does not reflect the critical oxygen concentration for cell growth. In order to determine the critical dissolved oxygen concentration for cell growth, it is necessary to measure the dissolved oxgyen concentration rather than the partial pressure of oxygen in the gas phase. Van Wezel and van der Velden-de Groot (1978) compared the growth of primary monkey kidney cells on microcarriers at two different dissolved oxygen concentrations. In one case, the dissolved oxygen was maintained between 15–70% of the saturation level of air at one atmosphere; in the other, dissolved oxygen was controlled at 5% of the saturation level. The growth rate of the culture with the low dissolved oxygen concentration was significantly slower than that with a higher dissolved oxygen level. In an earlier study with suspension-grown cells, Telling and Radlett (1970) observed that maximum cell growth extent was achieved with the dissolved oxygen controlled between 20–45% of saturation. Sinskey et al. (1981) studied the effect of dissolved oxygen concentration on the oxygen consumption rate of chick embryo fibroblasts. Cells on microcarriers were placed in a sealed, agitated beaker devoid of head gas space. The initial dissolved oxygen was raised to about 60% of saturation. As cellular respiration proceeded, the dissolved oxygen concentration decreased. The rate of decrease in oxygen concentration was used as a measure of oxygen consumption rate. It was observed that the oxygen consumption rate decreased gradually as the dissolved oxygen concentration fell below 35% of saturation. It was concluded that a dissolved oxygen level above 35% of saturation is necessary for optimum cell growth. However, under similar experimental conditions, we examined the oxygen consumption rate of both Vero cells and MDCK cells but did not observe the effect of oxygen concentration on its own consumption at a concentration above 15% of the saturation level. Therefore, there seems to be a wide range of "optimal" concentrations of dissolved oxygen for cell growth. However, from the published literature it is reasonable to assume that for most mammalian cells an oxygen concentration between 30–70% of saturation is unlikely to be growth-limiting.

An obvious method of improving oxygen transfer is to increase the driving force. This is usually achieved by enriching air with oxygen, a practice often seen in both suspension and microcarrier culture. In their cultivation of chick embryo fibroblast cells on microcarriers in a 140-liter vessel, Scattergood et al. (1983) avoided oxygen limitation by injecting oxygen-enriched air through the liquid surface. Relying solely on surface aeration, they were able to maintain dissolved oxygen concentration above 30% of the saturation level until cell density reached 4×10^6 cells/ml. It has been noted that too high an oxygen concentration can be growth-inhibitory to mammalian cells (Kilburn et al., 1969). Therefore, when using oxygen-enriched air, care should be taken to avoid overshooting.

8.3.1   Use of Surface Aerators to Improve Oxygen Transfer

The agitation rate is relatively slow for the cultivation of mammalian cells in stirred vessels. Under such agitation conditions little turbulence occurs at the liquid surface, thus the resistance to mass transfer at the gas-liquid interface is high. Therefore, oxygen transfer by surface aeration is limited by the low degree of fluid mixing in the gas-liquid interface. A simple method to improve oxygen transfer would be to increase the surface turbulence, which can be achieved by injecting air into the fermentor head space through a series of outlets placed directly above the liquid surface (van Wezel, 1982). Such an apparatus allowed monkey kidney cells to be cultivated in a 350-liter fermentor to about 10^6 cells/ml. Oxygen transfer through surface aeration could also be improved by the use of a surface aerator. Surface aerators of various types are often used in waste treatment (Zlokarnik, 1979). To test the effect of a surface aerator, we installed one in a 1-liter culture vessel. The schematic diagram of the vessel is shown in Figure 8–5. The oxygen transfer coefficients of the culture vessel are shown in Table 8–1. A more than 4-fold increase in the oxygen transfer rate was attained with a surface aerator in both a 1-liter vessel with 500-ml liquid volume and an 8-liter vessel with 5-liter working volume.

We have used the surface aerator in both microcarrier and suspension cultures in vessels of different volume, ranging from 1 to 8 liters. Shown in Figure 8–6 are the growth kinetics of a lymphoblastoid cell line, JY, in 8-liter vessels with surface aeration as the only oxygen transfer mechanism. In one case, the vessel was equipped with a surface aerator; in the other, no aerator was used. The growth medium was RPMI supplemented with 10% fetal calf serum. Without the surface aerator, the oxygen consumption rate quickly exceeded the supply rate. The dissolved oxygen concentration decreased at a relatively fast rate despite the fact that the gas mixture of air and 5% carbon dioxide was constantly blown over the liquid surface. Cell growth was retarded by oxygen limitation, as evident by the decreased growth rate. In the vessel with the surface aerator, the dissolved oxygen concentration decreased at a much slower rate and the period of exponential growth was considerably longer than that without a surface aerator. The final growth extent was also higher in the vessel equipped with a surface

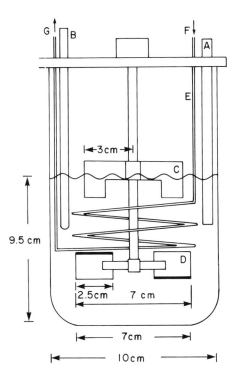

FIGURE 8–5 Schematic diagram of the 1-liter vessel with surface aerator. The dimensions are described in the figure. A, pH electrode; B, dissolved oxygen electrode; C, surface aerator; D, impeller with two 45-degree pitched blades; E, silicone rubber tubing; F, air inlet; G, air outlet.

aerator. A similar improvement in cell growth was also obtained with the monkey kidney cell line Vero, grown on microcarriers.

The oxygen transfer coefficient (K_L) for surface aeration is on the order of 0.005 cm/s. The specific oxygen consumption rate of mammalian cells ranges from 4 to 15 $\times$ 10^{-11} mmoles/cell·h (see Chapter 5). The maximum cell concentration for cell lines such as Vero cells at 15 g/l of microcarriers is about 1 $\times$ 10^7 cells/ml. The oxygen consumption rate in a culture can

TABLE 8–1   Oxygen Transfer Coefficient in Vessels with and without Surface Aerator

	Mass Transfer Coefficient (K_L)	
	1-liter vessel	*8-liter vessel*
Vessel	*(500-ml medium)*	*(5-l medium)*
Without aerator	6.4 cm/h	3.3 cm/h
With aerator	26.2 cm/h	13.5 cm/h

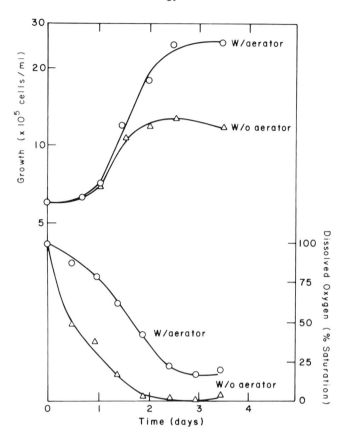

FIGURE 8–6   Effect of surface aerator on the growth of JY cells. (○) with surface aerator; (△) without surface aerator.

therefore be as high as 1.5 mmole/l·h. For a 100-liter vessel with a liquid height equal to the diameter, the specific surface area is 0.02 cm⁻¹. The solubility of oxygen at atmospheric pressure is about 0.18 mM. Thus, the oxygen transfer rate is less than 0.06 mmoles/l·h. Apparently, oxygen transfer would be severely limiting in such a reactor. The use of a surface aerator alone will surely not solve the oxygen transfer problem for large-scale operation; however, for any vessel in which surface aeration plays an important role in oxygen transfer, a surface aerator will certainly have an enhancing effect.

8.3.2   Improvement of Oxygen Transfer by Using Gas-Permeable Membranes

An effective means of improving oxygen transfer in cell culture is to use nonwettable, gas-permeable membranes to increase the transfer area. Such membranes are often used in blood oxygenation in artificial lung (Kolobow et al., 1968). The membrane used in this and many other laboratories is in the form of tubing with different diameters and wall thicknesses. The oxygen transfer rate through the membrane is affected by the diffusion coefficient of oxygen through the membrane, the concentration gradient across the membrane, and thus the wall thickness. This is described by Equation 8.9.

$$J = \frac{DH(C^o(z) - C)}{l} = \frac{DH\Delta C(z)}{l} \tag{8.9}$$

In Equation 8.9, J is the local oxygen flux through the membrane, D is the oxygen diffusion coefficient, l is the membrane thickness, and H is the partition coefficient. As air flows downstream, the fraction of oxygen decreases due to the transport into the liquid side. Thus, the concentration of oxygen, C^o, on the gas side is not a constant but a function of the distance from the gas inlet, z. The concentration of oxygen on the liquid side can be assumed to be constant throughout the whole length of membrane. The equation can also be expressed in terms of the driving force across the membrane, ΔC. Since the membrane is in tubular form, the gas flow in the tubing resembles that of a plug-flow reactor. The oxygen concentration on the tube side decreases as the gas flows downstream, as does the driving force for oxygen transfer. The concentration of oxygen in the tube side at any point in the tubing is expressed as Equation 8.10.

$$F\left(\frac{d\Delta C}{dz}\right) = \frac{-DH\Delta C(z)}{l} \tag{8.10}$$

It is apparent from Equation 8.10 that the overall oxygen transfer rate in any tubing is affected by the gas flow rate, F. Oxygen transfer is feasible only in the region where the concentration on the tube side is greater than that in the bulk medium. The length of tubing that can be employed is also dependent on the gas flow rate. The higher the gas flow rate, the longer the tubing can be.

Using silicone rubber tubing with an inner diameter of 0.058 in. and a wall thickness of 0.02 in., Fleischaker and Sinskey (1981) measured the oxygen transfer rate across the membrane; this was estimated to be 0.5 mmole/l·meter·h in one atmosphere of air. The flow rate used in the measurement was not specified, and it was not clear if the concentration gradient along the tube side was significant or not. Nevertheless, it provides us with a reasonable estimate of the oxygen transfer capability through the membrane. With this oxygen transfer capability we estimate that a relatively long tubing, in the range of meters, can be employed before the driving force is significantly reduced. Nevertheless, it is probably more desirable to have multiple tubings in parallel for gas transfer in large-scale operations. In our laboratory the silicone rubber tubing is routinely used to improve oxygen transfer. Although such tubings can sustain repeated autoclaving, pinholes do appear at times, but the resulting air bubbles make them easy to detect.

It is probably desirable to use a cartridge-type device for membrane installation in a large-scale operation to facilitate replacement of defective membranes.

8.3.3   Oxygen Transfer through External Oxygenators

Medium recirculation is often used as a means of supplying oxygen in cell culture. In such systems, medium is continuously withdrawn from the cultivation vessel or chamber and pumped to an "oxygenator" before it is recirculated back into the cultivation apparatus. The oxygenator can be membranous in nature or simply a stirred vessel. The use of an external oxygenator is most common in systems in which cells are cultivated in a stationary phase and medium is partially or totally recirculated. For such systems the culture vessel is not in direct contact with air or oxygen and medium circulation is often the major mechanism of oxygen supply. Cells are retained in the culture vessel, and thus a more vigorous method of supplying oxygen can be used in the oxygenator and cell damage can be avoided. Medium recirculation has been used in hollow-fiber (Ehrlich et al., 1978; Knazek et al., 1972), packed-glass beads (Whiteside and Spier, 1981), and ceramic-cylinder systems (Marcipar et al., 1983). In such systems oxygenation by aeration in the culture vessel is difficult, if not impossible.

In stirred vessels, improving oxygen transfer by circulating the medium through an external oxygenator poses another problem. Because of the low solubility of oxygen in the culture medium, a very high circulation rate is needed. With an oxygen consumption rate of 1.5 mmole/l·h in the culture, a medium recirculation rate of nearly 8 volumes per hour is required to avoid oxygen limitation. In order to avoid cell damage through pumping and flowing through piping, it is desirable to recirculate medium only and to retain cells in the culture vessel. Although this can possibly be achieved with spin filters (van Wezel, 1982; Tolbert and Feder, 1983), with the high medium recirculation rate required a large filtration area is necessary. Such constraints will certainly cause difficulty, especially for large-scale operations.

8.3.4   Direct Sparging

For the cultivation of mammalian cells, a relatively low agitation rate is used to avoid the excessive shear force caused by fluid flow. When air is sparged into the culture vessel, the entrapment and break-up of air bubbles due to agitation is minimal. Thus, the residence time of the air bubbles in the liquid is short and the interfacial area for oxygen transfer is small. As a result, the volumetric oxygen transfer coefficient ($K_L a$) is much smaller than that in microbial fermentations for a given air space velocity. To achieve a significant improvement in oxygen transfer a high airflow rate is necessary, especially in small culture vessels where the residence time of air bubbles is very short. Excessive aeration by sparging, however, causes serious foaming and may also be detrimental to cells. This is particularly problematic for microcarrier cultures where the agglomeration and flotation of cells or microcarriers on top of the foam can result in cell death.

In suspension-cell culture, direct sparging of air into the culture vessel has been reported. In the work reported by Acton and Lynn (1977), air was directly sparged into 14-liter fermentors at a rate of 0.008 vvm (volume air/volume liquid·min). An airflow rate in the range of 0.015 to 0.03 vvm was used for a 70-liter fermentor. Neither airflow rate was detrimental to cell cultures. However, in a study by Telling and Radlett (1970) a detrimental effect was observed when air was sparged continuously even at a slow rate of 6 ml/l·min. The direct cause of cell death in the sparged culture was unclear. Telling and Radlett also reported that such detrimental effects could be avoided by sparging air intermittently to maintain dissolved oxygen concentration at 25% of saturation level. It is difficult to assess the effect of sparging on cell growth from the published literature, because the oxygen transfer rate and the hydrodynamic effect are related to the agitation conditions, reactor configuration, design of sparger, and airflow rate. It appears that the effect of direct sparging on cell growth also varies with the cell types used. However, it is probable that sparging of air can be used for most suspension cell culture if the proper conditions are defined. This is supported by the implementation of a bubble-column reactor for cell culture.

In a bubble-column reactor the power input needed to keep cells in suspension is provided by the sparging of air from near the bottom of the reactor. Katinger et al. (1979) used two bubble-column reactors of 8 and 80 liters, respectively, to study the effect of superficial gas velocity on oxygen transfer and cell growth. The oxygen transfer rate at a given superficial velocity is affected by the type of sparger used and the reactor size. At a given gas flow rate per unit reactor volume, the superficial velocity increases linearly with the diameter of the reactor. The results of Katinger et al. showed that the gas flow rate per unit volume required to provide the same oxygen transfer rate decreases with increasing reactor volume. They found a superficial velocity in the range of 5 to 10 cm/min sufficient to keep cells in suspension. This velocity is almost one order of magnitude smaller than that typically used in bubble-column reactors for microbial cells. Under such operating gas flow rates, their bubble-column reactors were capable of supplying oxygen at a rate of about 0.6 to 1.0 mmole/l·hr, which is sufficient for the cultivation of most cell types. For some cell types having higher oxygen demand, the use of a higher airflow rate to improve oxygen transfer is probable. Using such bubble-column reactors, they were able to cultivate BHK cells to nearly 8×10^6 cells/ml. Bubble-column fermentors are an attractive alternative to stirred vessels for the cultivation of mammalian cells; whether they are suitable for most cell types remains to be tested. Nevertheless, it is most likely that bubble-column bioreactors will be used more widely in the near future.

For microcarrier cultures, direct sparging poses a more difficult problem; however, it would probably be the most effective method of oxygen transfer if the drawbacks involved with that method could be overcome. Past failures in supplying oxygen by sparging should not be interpreted as proof of its impossibility. Possibly, foaming caused by sparging can be suppressed by proper selection of an antifoaming agent. We have tested the effect of a few antifoaming agents on the growth of Chinese hamster ovary cells grown on Petri dishes and microcarriers. Cell growth was not affected by the presence of either FG-10 or P-2000 at a concentration of 400 parts per million. However, care should be taken to assess the effect of sparging on cell growth. The terminal rising velocity of air bubbles is much higher than the terminal settling velocity of microcarriers; the shear generated by air bubbles may well be detrimental to cells if microcarriers surrounding the air bubbles are entrained by them. For some cell types, the maximum growth rate can often be maintained even at relatively low levels of dissolved oxygen concentration. Controlling dissolved oxygen at an arbitrarily high level by continual sparging would require a higher aeration rate, which may in turn generate excessive shear and foaming problems. A better understanding of the effect of dissolved oxygen concentration on cell growth and metabolism is also necessary for the solution of the oxygen supply problem.

8.4   EFFECT OF SHEAR

Another parameter sensitive to scale-up is the shear force exerted on cells by fluid flow. It has been noted that animal cells are sensitive to this force (Nevaril et al., 1968; Augenstein et al., 1971); excessive shear force can lead to cell death. To avoid this detrimental effect of shear force, a low agitation rate is usually used in cell culture. The major purpose of agitation in mammalian cell culture is to suspend cells or microcarriers and achieve fluid mixing, not to disperse air bubbles to enhance oxygen transfer, as in microbial cultures. In scaling up mixing processes, the maximum shear rate increases with impeller diameter at a constant impeller speed, while the average shear rate remains about the same at a given impeller speed regardless of impeller size (Oldshue, 1966; Nagata, 1975). Using shear-sensitive protozoa as a model system, Midler and Finn (1966) found that extensive shear caused cell disruption. Their data showed a correlation between survival versus impeller tip speed. Neither Reynolds number nor power input per unit volume seemed to be appropriate parameters. Augenstein et al. (1971) pumped HeLa S3 and mouse L929 cells through capillary at high-pressure drops to study the effect of shear. They found that cell damage could be correlated to wall shear and to power dissipation in the liquid while in the capillary shear section. Although the effect of shear exerted by fluid flow in the reactor is often a concern in the scale-up of mammalian cell culture, there have been few systematic studies to examine the effect of hydrodynamic shear in bioreactors. There is clear evidence that mammalian cells are sensitive to the shear exerted by fluid flow, more so than microorganisms. However, the question is whether the hydrodynamic stress is damaging to cells under normal operating conditions. If it is, then we must determine the important parameter(s) for quantifying the effect of shear and the critical range of operation. Most of the reports on large-scale operation of suspension-cell culture employed vessels of hundreds of liters in volume (Acton and Lynn, 1977; Lazar et al., 1982; Arathoon and Telling, 1982; Beale, 1981). There appears to be no adverse effect of mechanical agitation on cell growth provided the agitation rate used is not excessive. The word "excessive" is used here, but as mentioned previously, there has been little quantitation of the effect of shear on cell growth, so that no line can be drawn as to what range is excessive. The need for avoiding vigorous agitation was pointed out by Telling and Radlett (1970), who suggested that the stirring speed be reduced from that used in microbial fermentation. They found that the agitation speed used in vessels stirred by a single turbine impeller was usually in the range of 200 to 400 rpm. The agitation rate by itself, without reference to the vessel volume, impeller size, and other geometric factors, is not a quantification of hydrodynamic stress; nevertheless, that range of agitation rate indicates what agitation speed is excessive. In other studies the agitation rates used seem to fall in this range. An agitation speed of 300 rpm was used in a 14-liter fermentor, and 100 rpm in both 70- and 200-liter fermentors to cultivate suspension-cell lines (Zwerner et al., 1975; Acton and Lynn, 1977). The growth rate of cell line S49.1 in the 14-liter fermentor appeared to be comparable to that in the 50-ml spinner flask, even though the agitation rate used was as high as 300 rpm (Zwerner et al., 1975). The range of agitation speed used in those studies was apparently much greater than necessary to suspend cells. In contrast, the agitation speed routinely used in the 5-liter vessels at the Massachusetts Institute of Technology Cell Culture Center is in the range of 40–60 rpm for various types of cells (Giard, personal communication). Fazekas de St. Groth (1983) examined the effect of stirring speed on the growth of hybridoma cell lines in a specially designed laboratory vessel. The vessel's unique feature is the positioning of its two paddles, one near the bottom and the other close to the liquid surface. It was observed that excessive agitation resulted in both reduced growth rate and growth extent, but did not appear to affect the proportion of dead cells. A stirring rate of 10 to 30 rpm was needed to keep the cell line in suspension. Depending upon each individual cell line, the critical agitation rate ranged from 60 to 100 rpm. Cells grew equally well as long as the agitation speed was maintained below the critical rate. However, when cell growth was compared to that under stationary conditions, a consistent 15% longer doubling time was observed in the stirred culture for all cell lines tested. It is possible that the higher growth rate observed in stationary culture was due to a localized concentration of conditioning factors. However, the possibility that mechanical shear caused by agitation resulted in a lower growth rate in the stirred culture cannot be excluded.

Although the stirred tank is most widely used in suspension cell culture, other types of bioreactors, such as Vibromixers (Ulrich and Moore, 1965; Moore et al., 1968) and bubble-column bioreactors (Katinger et al., 1979), have also been employed. Few studies of hydrodynamic effect on cell growth in those reactors have been reported. Though a study by Katinger et al. (1979) did not compare the cell growth in the bubble-column reactor with that in a conventional vessel, no apparent adverse effect was reported. The use of a bubble-column reactor also demonstrated that the shear caused by continuous air sparging is not necessarily detrimental to cells, as has been suggested by Telling and Radlett (1970). Katinger et al. (1979) compared the growth of Namalwa and BHK 21 cells in 8- and 80-liter bubble-column reactors to that in a 2-liter Vibromixer. An inferior cell growth was consistently observed in the Vibromixer. With Namalwa cells grown in low serum medium, cell growth was often retarded. Although one successful attempt in growing Namalwa cells in the Vibromixer was achieved, a high proportion of trypan-stainable or presumably nonviable cells was observed in the culture. With BHK 21 cells the Vibromixer could be used for either batch or continuous culture; however, the maximum growth rate attainable was considerably lower than that in the bubble-column reactor. The Vibromixer's adverse effect was attributed to the mechanical damage resulting from the vibration of the plate. It is not clear from the results reported by Katinger et al. whether the adverse effect observed with a Vibromixer could have been avoided were the amplitude or frequency of vibration reduced. In contrast to the results of Katinger et al., Moore et al. (1968) reported the use of Vibromixers in 200-liter vessels in a pilot plant. Tolbert et al. (1982) have also successfully used a Vibromixer in a 100-liter reactor to cultivate a number of tumor cell lines. Although in their studies the growth rate and growth extent were not compared with those in conventional mechanically agitated reactors, no adverse effect of mixing using a Vibromixer was reported.

In a study of the effect of shear on cell death, Augenstein et al. (1971) calculated the power input needed to give measurable cell death to be 10,000 W/l. Since this power dissipation is several orders of magnitude higher than that typically observed in the fermentor, they suggested that cultured cells may be more mechanically resistant to shear than some investigators have assumed. One word of caution is that the criterion used in that study was cell death, while the study of Fazekas de St. Groth (1983) indicated that shear can affect cell growth rate without affecting the proportion of dead cells in the culture. The sensitivity of cells in suspension to the shear caused by impeller agitation probably varies greatly with each cell line. Nevertheless, from the studies discussed it is reasonable to believe that most cell lines can be successfully cultivated in bioreactors while avoiding the detrimental effect of shear.

The use of microcarriers in cell culture poses somewhat different agitation requirements than for free cell suspension. The diameter of microcarriers is in the range of 150 to 200 micrometers as opposed to 10 to 20 micrometers for free cells. The terminal settling velocity of microcarriers in cell culture medium is thus almost two orders of magnitude higher than that of free cells. Since the development of microcarriers for the cultivation of anchorage-dependent animal cells, there have been several studies concerning different types of vessels for microcarrier culture, among which are fluidized-bed reactors and spinners with different mixing mechanisms (Hirtenstein et al., 1982). At present the impeller-agitated stirred-tank reactor is still the type most widely used in microcarrier culture.

In our studies of the growth of FS-4 cells in microcarrier culture, we examined the effect of the agitation conditions on cell growth in laboratory-scale vessels. An experiment was carried out to assess the effect of shear force in spinner vessels. The spinners used were each equipped with a suspended, teflon-coated cylindrical magnetic rod as impeller. Cells were inoculated into 250-ml vessels, each with 100 ml of culture volume. The microcarrier used was dextran beads with a controlled charge density of 2.0 meq/g dextran with a median diameter of 180 μm. The microcarrier concentration was 5 g/l for all cases studied. An inoculum cell concentration of 3.5×10^5 cells/ml was used for each culture. Impellers of different diameters were used. After inoculation, the minimum agitation required for complete suspension of microcarriers was used for each spinner to allow cells to attach and spread out. Twenty-four hours later, different agitation speeds were applied to the vessels in order to compare different agitation conditions. The cultures in which normal growth occurred reached confluence in five days. At higher agitation rates, a decreased growth extent was observed. The final growth extent under different agitation conditions is plotted against the impeller tip speed in Figure 8–7. It can be seen that higher impeller tip speeds correlated with lower growth extents. In two cases the high impeller tip speed resulted in cell death. However, the validity of this correlation is apparently restricted to this culture vessel size. A similar study was carried out in 2-liter vessels with 1-liter culture volumes. In this case high agitation speeds again resulted in cell death, but the correlation of growth extent to agitation speed was different from the case of the 100-ml cultures.

Sinskey et al. (1981) studied the effect of shear force on the growth of chick embryo fibroblasts and their use for virus production. Their results indicated that cells in the stage after attachment to microcarriers were more shear-sensitive than during subsequent growth. At high agitation rates both cell growth extent and virus productivity were impeded. However, the production of Sindbis virus was affected at an agitation speed that did not affect cell growth. Thus, in considering the effect of shear, it is necessary to keep in mind the possible differential effect on cell growth and product formation.

It was noted that the growth extent of chick embryo fibroblasts under

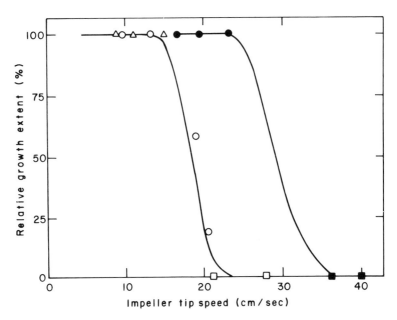

FIGURE 8–7 Effect of impeller tip speed on the growth extent of FS-4. (Δ) 250-ml vessel with 3.2-cm diameter impeller; (○) with 4.1-cm diameter impeller; (□) with 5.1-cm diameter impeller; (●) 2-l vessel with 7.5-cm impeller; (■) with 8.5-cm impeller.

different shear conditions could be correlated to an integrated shear factor (Sinskey et al., 1981). This integrated shear factor was defined as $(2\pi n D_i)/(D_t - D_i)$, where D_t is the vessel diameter, D_i is the impeller diameter and n is the agitation speed. In the integrated shear factor, nD_i represents the impeller tip speed and $(D_t - D_i)/2$ the distance between the impeller tip and the wall of the vessel. Since the fluid velocity at the wall is zero, the integrated shear factor is thus an indication of the magnitude of the velocity gradient in the horizontal plane of the impeller. The results from Figure 8–7 can be replotted to correlate the growth extent and the integrated shear factor. There appears to be good correlation throughout the range of experimental conditions tested (Figure 8–8).

The results shown in Figures 8–7 and 8–8 as well as those of Sinskey et al. (1981) demonstrate that the growth of FS-4 cells and chick embryo fibroblasts on microcarriers is sensitive to agitation conditions. However, in normal culture conditions, for instance, a 4.1-cm diameter impeller in a 250-ml spinner flask agitated at 60 rpm, the agitation conditions fall well below the region in which a detrimental effect was observed for both types of cells. For the growth of FS-4 cells and chick embryo fibroblasts, the important parameter in the assessment of the effect of agitation appears to be the integrated shear factor rather than the impeller tip speed. Under the con-

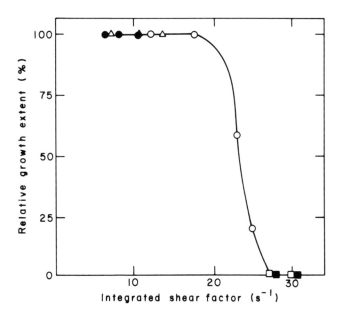

FIGURE 8–8   Correlation between shear factor and growth extent. Symbols are the same as those in Figure 8–7.

straint of geometric similarity, $D_i/(D_t - D_i)$ in the integrated shear factor is constant for reactors of different scale; thus the scale-sensitive parameter is the impeller speed, n. When the power input per unit volume is held constant, the impeller speed as well as the average shear rate decrease with increasing scale (Nagata, 1975). It has been noted that the power per unit volume requirement for the suspension of solids decreases when the scale is increased (Zwietering, 1958). Under the operating conditions tested, the shear force exerted by mechanical agitation has no negative effect on the growth of FS-4 and chick embryo fibroblast cells. Further studies using reactors of different scale are necessary to obtain more reliable correlation for scale-up. Nevertheless, our results and those of Sinskey et al. indicate that shear force caused by impeller agitation is not likely to affect cell growth in larger-scale reactors for microcarrier culture.

Microcarrier culture has been practiced in production scale. Van Wezel and van der Velden-de Groot (1978), reporting the cultivation of monkey kidney cells in 150-liter vessels, emphasized the need for low stirring speed and suggested a range of 50 to 150 rpm depending on the geometry and size of vessel. Scattergood et al. (1983) have also grown secondary chick embryo cells in a 140-liter vessel. The primary culture was grown in a 9-liter vessel and later trypsinized to inoculate the 140-liter vessel. In the 9-liter vessel the stirring speed was initially set at 38 rpm and later increased to 52 and 79 rpm to control microcarrier clumping. In the 140-liter vessel the stirring speed was initially 27 rpm and later increased to 50 rpm. No apparent difference in growth rate could be seen in the two vessels. In both reports of larger-scale operation, a single impeller was used. Although no detail was given, the impellers appeared to be either pitched blades or marine impellers. All the vessels used were round-bottomed. The vessels used in the study by Scattergood et al. had a liquid-height-to-vessel-diameter ratio of about one. These features of round bottom, inclined impeller blades, and unity height-to-diameter ratio are all consistent with those proposed by Nagata (1975) for the suspension of light solids in liquid. The design criteria of solid-liquid mixing have been reviewed by Oldshue (1983). In general, marine impellers or inclined large paddles are preferred to the various types of turbines often used in microbial fermentation. The preference for large impellers was taken to an extreme in a Monsanto group design in which two flexible sheets of sail-shaped agitators, extending from near the bottom of the vessel to almost the liquid surface, were used in a 40-liter flat-bottom vessel (Tolbert and Feder, 1983). As a result of the increased pumping capacity of the agitation system, an agitation speed as low as 5 to 10 rpm could be used. This system may offer an advantage for any cells that might be extremely sensitive to impeller tip speed. In comparing the results from different research groups, one should be aware of the fact that the micro-carriers used in those studies are often different. Van Wezel and van der Velden-de Groot (1978) used celloidin-coated DEAE-Sephadex beads, Scat-tergood et al. (1983) employed gelatin-coated dextran beads, while Tolbert and Feder (1983) used polyacrylamide-based microcarriers. Although the cells used in those studies were from different species, they all seemed to be normally diploid. Besides exerting shear force on the cell surface, agi-tation can also affect cell attachment or cause cell detachment from micro-carriers. Cell adhesion to the surface is greatly affected by the surface properties. Whether the sensitivity of cells to shear force is affected by the type of microcarrier used is still not clear. However, as demonstrated by the preceding studies, agitation by impeller is not likely to be damaging to cells, at least in vessels of a few hundred liters for dextran-based microcar-riers.

It has been speculated that the collision of microcarriers in a stirred vessel may be detrimental to cells at a high microcarrier concentration (Tolbert and Feder, 1983). The microcarrier concentration most often seen in the literature ranges from 1 to 5 g/l. Again, this range cannot be taken literally, since the settled microcarrier volume varies widely depending on the type as well as the size distribution of the microcarriers used. If one assumes a 40% bead volume is to be used in a microcarrier culture, this gives the equivalent of about a 15–20 g/l bead concentration for most commonly used dextran-based microcarriers. We tested the effect of micro-carrier concentration on cell growth by inoculating FS-4 cells into two identical cultures at a microcarrier concentration of 5 g/l. After cells attached to the microcarriers, excess empty microcarriers were added to one of the cultures to give a microcarrier concentration of 15 g/l. If, as had been speculated, the collision of beads was detrimental to cells, a difference in growth kinetics would be expected. However, the two cultures grew at identical rates to the same confluent cell density (Figure 8–9) (Hu et al., 1985). Using the sail-shaped agitation system, Tolbert and Feder also grew human cells at 12 g/l. Therefore, there is reason to believe that microcarrier culture can be applied to a 100-liter-scale vessel with relatively high microcarrier concentration without agitation causing detrimental effects on cells.

8.5 CONCLUDING REMARKS

We have reviewed three aspects of mammalian cultivation from an engineering point of view. The media used in conventional cell culture do not support cell growth to the high density that is, in principle, achievable in a bioreactor (in the range of 10^7 cells/ml), at least not economically. A better means of supplying the nutrients and removing the metabolites would probably give rise to a more efficient use of serum or other growth factors. The supply of one nutrient, oxygen, can be particularly problematic, especially for large-scale operations. The shear caused by excessive agitation can result

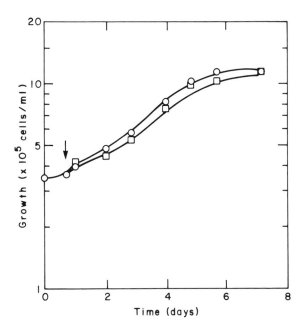

FIGURE 8–9 Effect of addition of new beads to microcarrier culture. Microcarrier concentration was initially 5 g/l. (□), at 16 h (↓) new microcarriers were added at 10 g/l, thus giving rise to a final microcarrier concentration of 15 g/l. (○), control, no new microcarriers were added.

in cell death or reduced growth rate. However, under the operating conditions most likely to be used in a reactor up to several liters in volume, shear force is not likely to cause any detrimental effect on cells. Although better cell culture media for high cell density growth and a better means of oxygen transfer are very desirable, the existing media and current methods of supplying oxygen are adequate to meet the requirements of most cell cultivation in bioreactors.

REFERENCES

Acton, P.T., and Lynn, J.D. (1977) *Adv. Biochem. Eng.* 7, 85–110.

Arathoon, W.R., and Telling, R.C. (1982) *Develop. Biol. Standard.* 50, 145–154.

Augenstein, D.C., Sinskey, A.J., and Wang, D.I.C. (1971) *Biotechnol. Bioeng.* 13, 409–418.

Beale, A.J. (1981) *Develop. Biol. Standard.* 47, 19–23.

Butler, M., Imamura, T., Thomas, J., and Thilly, W. (1983) *J. Cell Sci.* 61, 351–363.

Ehrlich, K.C., Stewart, E., and Klein, E. (1978) *In Vitro* 14, 443–450.

Fazekas de St. Groth, S. (1983) *J. Immunol. Methods* 57, 121–136.

Fleischaker, R.J., Jr. (1982) Ph.D. Thesis, Massachusetts Institute of Technology, Cambridge.

Fleischaker, R.J., Jr., and Sinskey, A. (1981) *Eur. J. Appl. Microbiol. Biotechnol.* 12, 193–197.

Griffiths, B., and Thornton, B. (1982) *J. Chem. Technol. Biotechnol.* 32, 324–329.

Gullino, P.M., and Knazek, R.A. (1979) in *Methods in Enzymology* (Jacoby, W.B. and Pastan, I.H., eds.) vol. 58, pp. 178–184, Academic Press, New York.

Hirtenstein, M.D., Clark, J.M., and Gebb, C. (1982) *Develop. Biol. Standard* 50, 73–80.

Hu, W.S., Meier, J., and Wang, D.I.C. (1985) *Biotechnol. Bioeng.* 27, 585–595.

Katinger, H.W.D., Scheirer, W., and Kromer, E. (1979) *Ger. Chem. Eng.* 2, 31–38.

Kilburn, D.G., Lilly, M.D., Self, D.A., and Webb, F.C. (1969) *J. Cell Sci.* 4, 25–37.

Knazek, R.A., Gullino, P.M., Kohler, P.O., and Dedrick, R.L. (1972) *Science* 156, 65–66.

Kolobow, T., Zapol, W., and Marcus, J. (1968) in *Organ Perfusion and Preservation* (Folkman, J., Hardison, W.G., Rudolf, L.E., and Veith, F.J., eds.) pp. 155–175, Appleton-Century-Crofts, New York.

Ku, K., Kuo, M.J., Delente, J., Wildi, B.S., and Feder, J. (1981) *Biotechnol. Bioeng.* 23, 79–95.

Lazar, A., Reuveny, S., Traub, A., Minai, M., Grosfeld, H., Feinstein, S., Gez, M., and Mizrahi, A. (1982) *Dev. Biol. Stand.* 50, 167–171.

Marcipar, A., Henno, P., Lentwojt, E., Rosento, A., and Broun, G. (1983) *Ann. NY Acad. Sci.* 413, 416–420.

Midler, M., Jr., and Finn, R.K. (1966) *Biotechnol. Bioeng.* 8, 71–84.

Monod, J.C. (1949) *Annu. Rev. Bacteriol.* 3, 371.

Moore, G.E., Hansenpusch, P., Gerner, R.E., and Burns, A.A. (1968) *Biotechnol. Bioeng.* 10, 625–640.

Morandi, M., and Valeri, A. (1982) *Biotechnol. Lett.* 4, 465–468.

Nagata, S. (1975) *Mixing: Principles and Applications*, p. 446, Kodansha Ltd., Tokyo.

Nevaril, C.G., Lynch, E.C., Alfrey, C.P., and Hellums, J.D. (1968) *J Lab. Clin. Med.* 71, 784–790.

Oldshue, J.Y. (1966) *Biotechnol. Bioeng.* 8, 3–24.

Oldshue, J.Y. (1983) *Fluid Mixing Technology,* McGraw-Hill, New York.

Pirt, S.J. (1965) *Proc. R Soc. Lond. Ser. Bull.* 163, 224.

Scattergood, E.M., Schlabach, A.J., McAleer, W.J., and Hilleman, M.R. (1983) *Ann. NY Acad. Sci.* 413, 333–339.

Sinskey, A.J., Fleischaker, R.J., Tyo, M.A., Giard, D.J., and Wang, D.I.C. (1981) *Ann. NY Acad. Sci.* 369, 47–59.

Telling, R.C., and Radlett, P.J. (1970) *Adv. Appl. Microbiol.* 13, 91–119.

Thayer, P.S. (1973) in *Tissue Culture Methods and Applications* (Kruse, P.F., Jr., and Mo, K., Jr., eds.) pp. 345–351, Academic Press, New York.

Thayer, P.S., Himmelfarb, P., and Roberts, D.W. (1970) *Cancer Res.* 30, 1709–1714.

Tolbert, W.R., Feder, J., and Kimes, R.C. (1981) *In Vitro* 17, 885–890.

Tolbert, W.R., and Feder, J. (1983) *Annu. Rev. Ferm. Processes* 6, 35–74.

Tolbert, W.R., Schoenfeld, R.A., Lewis, C., and Feder, J. (1982) *Biotechnol. Bioeng.* 24, 1671–1679.

Tovey, M.G. (1980) *Adv. Cancer Res.* 33, 1–37.

Tovey, M.G., and Brouty-Boye, D. (1976) *Exp. Cell Res.* 101, 346–354.

Ulrich, K., and Moore, G.E. (1965) *Biotechnol. Bioeng.* 7, 507–515.

van Wezel, A.L., and van der Velden-de Groot, C.A.M. (1978) *Process Biochem.* 13, 6–8.

van Wezel, A.L. (1982) *J. Chem. Technol. Biotechnol.* 32, 318–323.

Whiteside, J.P., and Spier, R.E. (1981) *Biotechnol. Bioeng.* 23, 551–565.

Zielke, H.R., Zielke, C.L., and Ozand, P.T. (1984) *Fed. Proc.* 43, 121–125.

Zlokarnik, M. (1979) *Adv. Biochem. Eng.* 11, 157–180.

Zwerner, R.K., Runyan, C., Cox, R.M., Lynn, D., and Acton, R.T. (1975) *Biotechnol. Bioeng.* 17, 629–657.

Zwietering, T.N. (1958) *Chem. Eng. Sci.* 8, 244–253.

Practical Matters in Instrumentation for Mammalian Cell Cultures

Robert J. Fleischaker, Jr.

9.1 INTRODUCTION

Instrumentation for use in mammalian cell culture is subject to a very different set of constraints than that encountered in microbial fermentations. Most notably, the lower rates of metabolism combined with the lower densities obtained in culture require a higher degree of sensitivity and stability in the sensors used. Furthermore, because the nutritional requirements of animal cells are much more complex than those of the microbial organisms, a very different approach must be used in developing strategies to monitor and control growth. In this chapter I review some of the instrumental methods currently used in cell culture and discuss the implementation and limitation of process control technology as applied to these systems.

9.2 CULTURE VESSEL CONFIGURATION

From the viewpoint of instrumentation and process control, current methodologies for large-scale cell culture can be divided into two groups—stirred-tank and column designs. The difference is that a homogeneous environment exists in a stirred tank. Consequently, the sensors are placed within the vessel where control action occurs (e.g., addition of base to neutralize excess acid). In contrast, the environment in a column reactor will always show a gradient. Thus, the sensors are usually placed before and after the device; in addition, controlling actions usually occur in a reservoir external to the growth chamber. To illustrate this, consider the determination of the oxygen uptake by a culture. In a stirred tank, this can be accomplished by momentarily turning off the oxygen controller and then measuring the rate at which oxygen is removed during that time. Alternately, in a column the difference in oxygen concentration between fluid entering and leaving the column is examined in conjunction with the flow rate of fluid through the column.

9.3 CHARACTERIZATION OF SENSORS

The choice of an appropriate sensor depends, of course, not only on what is to be measured, but also on the design and limitations of the sensor. Of particular importance are the concepts of response time, gain, specificity, signal-to-noise ratio, and drift.

Sensors function to translate information about the physical or chemical environment around them into an electric signal. The electric signal can be either a voltage (as with a pH probe) or a current (as with a dissolved oxygen electrode). Generally, when the signal is a current some chemical reaction occurs within the sensor. In order to utilize these signals, it is important to develop a good understanding of the relationship between the observed electric signal and the environment observed by the sensor. There are two primary means by which this understanding is developed. The first is the "analytical" approach. This involves modeling the sensor by examining the entire sequence of reactions that occur within the sensor. The second methodology is the "black box" approach, which largely ignores the internal operations of the sensor and models the output as a function of the input from the experimental data. These functions are generally assumed to consist of a steady state and a transient component. While the analytical approach may be more elegant, the black box approach is better suited to our purpose. In addition, the results of the black box approach are often more accurate, perhaps partly because many of the equations generated in the analytical process must be simplified to generate solutions.

One experiment often used to characterize a sensor is its response to a step change. An example is given in Figure 9–1, where x is the input and e is the output. Typically, sensors respond to such a change by exhibiting little or no change at first, followed by a period of rapid change, then asymptotically settling to a steady state value. Here, both the gain and the response time of the sensor can be examined. If we examine first the steady state value, the gain is defined as the change in the output for a given change in the input. Notably, the gain may not be constant over the entire range of

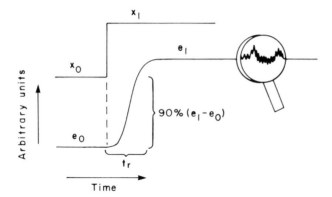

FIGURE 9-1 Transfer function and transducer output.

expected input value, and the construction of a calibration curve is highly recommended. There are a number of different definitions of response time, although in essence they are very similar. The particular convention we follow is defined as the time required for the output following a step change to reach 90% of the steady state value. This definition serves two purposes. First, it gives a measurable number in that, as the curve approaches the steady state value, its slope is essentially zero, and consequently any measurement of the time required to reach steady state is subject to very large errors. Second, it provides a number that correlates well with what we observe.

Regarding the limitations of sensors in general, we need to address signal to noise and drift. Any electrical signal will appear noisy when examined under sufficient magnification (as suggested in Figure 9-1). Noise is standardly measured as the root mean square value (rms) of the fluctuations about the time average of the signs. There are many sources of noise. A very common one is the 60-Hz power signal that almost any wire will pick up by acting as an antenna. Also, certain electrical components, such as carbon composition resistors, add noise, and the environment actually being measured may not be perfectly stable. To some extent the level of noise can be reduced by filtering techniques and time averaging of the signal. However, reducing noise by these techniques comes at the cost of increasing the response time of the sensor, and as always a compromise must be sought. Ultimately, noise does determine the smallest-level signal we can measure. In general, the signal needs to exceed the noise level (the S/N ratio) by at least a factor of 10 if the information that the sensor provides is to be useful for control purposes.

The slow steady change of sensors with time is known as drift. Typically, drift is measured as the change in percent of the full scale reading per day, and may or may not be a problem, according to how frequently sensors need to be recalibrated. For example, with external analyzers such as an external gas analyzer, recalibration is a simple procedure. However, with sensors physically within the growth vessel such as dissolved oxygen probes, recalibration is quite difficult. For these instruments, the drift over the course of the experiment must be within an acceptable limit.

Finally, other considerations in sensor selection need to be addressed. First, there is the specificity of the sensor, i.e., to what other chemical species does the sensor respond? And in addition, are these chemicals present in the culture broth at levels that will interfere with the principal measurement? Second, there is the question of maintaining culture sterility. Sensors that can be autoclaved in situ are most preferred. Otherwise, we need to ensure that samples can be regularly removed from the vessel and brought to the sensor. Alas, there is as always the consideration of cost.

9.4 INSTRUMENTS AND SENSORS USED IN MAMMALIAN CELL CULTURE

Many sensors have been used to monitor the growth and metabolism of microbial cells in culture, some of which have also been used in conjunction with animal cell cultures. In this section, I share with the reader some observations and opinions about three of the commonly used, and perhaps also more valuable, sensors: those for temperature, pH, and dissolved oxygen. I then briefly comment on some more exotic instruments that we may see in the near future.

9.4.1 Temperature

Temperature is clearly one of the more important variables to monitor and control in cell culture. The sensors we use for this need to be accurate over the range of 0–150°C, to be used both in work with animal cells and in sterilization of the culture vessel. Probably the sensors best suited for this work are platinum wire resistors. They are linear, change little with age, are interchangeable, and very reliable. Alternatively, one might want to consider thermistors. They are semiconductor devices and in fact are more sensitive to temperature changes than platinum. Generally, they are nonlinear devices and not readily interchangeable. Notably, some manufacturers (Yellow Spring Instruments and Thermometrics) have developed composite devices (consisting of two or more thermistors) whose output is essentially linear and displays an absolute accuracy of 0.15°C. However, if one does not need the greater sensitivity to small changes in the temperature that thermistors offer, platinum is the preferred choice.

9.4.2 pH

The pH will determine the ionization state of many organic acids and bases and consequently has a profound effect upon many biochemical processes.

Typically, pH is measured with a combined glass-reference electrode. Steam sterilizable electrodes are commercially available. There are two points to remember when using steam sterilizable electrodes. The first is that these are very high impedence devices. In order for the glass electrode to withstand several autoclaving cycles, a special and thicker glass is used, so that these probes typically have resistance on the order of 500–800 megaohms. Such probes require special input amplifiers, which are not used in many lab pH meters. The second point is that because these probes may be used for extended periods of time, one needs to worry about their drift. In our experience, fouling of the junction on the reference electrode has been a major source of such error. A number of substances in the culture fluid are not soluble in the reference electrolyte (for example, cysteine) and hence tend to precipitate at that junction. This fouling of the reference junction causes a shift in the reference potential, which results in a drift of the measured pH. However, this problem can be largely eliminated by using pH probes with a fluid bridge (such as those manufactured by Ingold). These probes separate the reference electrolyte from the culture broth with a second electrolyte (for example, 1M KCl plus 1% tylose).

Animal cells grow well over a narrow pH range, which varies among cell types. Typically, we are looking at a pH range of $\pm$ 0.2 pH units around an experimentally determined optimum, although some applications may have narrower ranges. For large-scale cell culture, this is generally accomplished by one of three means. The first is to adjust the CO_2 concentration as organic acids accumulate in the culture broth. The second method is to eliminate the bicarbonate buffer and maintain pH by the direct addition of base to the culture. An added benefit of the latter approach is that the total production of acids by the culture can be measured by simply monitoring the amount of base added to the vessel. One convenient means of monitoring base addition is to mount the base reservoir on a load cell. The third approach, gaining in acceptance, is to lower the rate of organic acid production via the choice of the primary nutrient energy source, such as the substitution of either fructose or galactose for glucose (see Chapter 5).

9.4.3 Dissolved Oxygen

Providing an adequate supply of oxygen is essential for cell growth in culture. In general, cells tolerate a rather wide optimum for growth, but effects on macromolecule or virus production have not been as widely studied. Kilburn and Webb (1968), Cristofalo and Kritchevsky (1966), and Boraston et al. (1983), working with mouse LS, WI-38, and mouse hybridoma cells, respectively, have shown that varying the partial pressure of oxygen (pO_2) over a range of about 30 to 120 mm Hg has little effect on either the growth rate or the maximal cell density. For pO_2 levels below 10 mm Hg, the cell growth rate and the maximal cell density decreased substantially. Conversely, for pO_2 levels above 300 mm Hg, an oxygen toxicity was generally observed.

The dissolved oxygen concentration can be measured by a number of means. Our personal preference has been for the polarographic electrodes (such as those manufactured by Instrumentation Laboratories). These electrodes are steam sterilizable, accurate to 0.3%, drift less than 2% per week, and show a response time of about 45 sec.

A valuable parameter for process technology that can be obtained using these oxygen electrodes is the oxygen uptake rate of the culture. The exact procedure one could use for the measurement depends on the vessel configuration, as outlined earlier. For stirred-tank designs, one can use the dynamic means assessment (Fleischaker and Sinskey, 1981). In essence, this technique involves interrupting the supply of oxygen to the culture and then measuring the rate at which oxygen is removed from the medium. For column configurations, one can determine the oxygen uptake of the culture if the pO_2 of the medium entering the column is known, as well as the pO_2 of the medium exiting the column (provided it is not zero), and the flow rate of medium through the column.

9.4.4 Other Sensors

Currently available commercially are a number of other sensors for measuring other culture parameters. Among those that can be used in situ include sensors to measure dissolved CO_2, the redox potential of culture media, and culture fluorescence. In my opinion, under cell conditions redox probes largely give a poor measurement of the dissolved oxygen concentration. If we seek the redox potential within the cells, the culture fluorescence probe is better suited to provide that information. This probe operates by measuring the fluorescence of the culture at 460 nm in response to an excitation at 360 nm. This is reported to be largely a measure of the NADH concentration within the cells, and if the cell concentration is known, then an estimate of the intracellular NADH concentration can be made. In addition, if the cells maintain the same internal redox potential (which often happens during the early phases of cell growth), it provides a means of estimating the cell mass. While I believe that this sensor has tremendous potential, my concern is that its utilization in a control scheme is not straightforward. In designing process control, one must decide if the goal is control of the intracellular concentration of a particular chemical species or the turnover rate of that compound. Frequently turnover is important, though in the particular case of NADH both parameters are useful.

In addition to these sensors, techniques are being developed to run a sampling line from the culture vessel to a number of very powerful analytical instruments such as HPLC, FFT infrared analyzers, and automated wet chemical analyzers. I also believe that in the near future we will see developed a number of sensors using fiber optics, electrochemical, and immunological techniques.

9.5 THE USE OF ATP FLUX IN MONITORING CULTURE GROWTH

There are in principle a number of means to interpret the information provided by instrumentation. One which I have used has been the estimated ATP flux (Fleischaker, 1982). Specifically, the rate at which cells generate ATP, presumably for cell growth and maintenance, is calculated by measuring the rate of glycolysis from the rate of lactic acid formation, and the rate of oxidative phosphorylation from the oxygen uptake rate, using the following formula:

$$d(ATP)/dt = 6(O.U.R.) + d(L)/dt$$

where

$$O.U.R. = \text{oxygen uptake rate}$$
$$d(ATP)/dt = \text{total rate of ATP formation}$$
$$d(L)/dt = \text{rate of lactic acid formation.}$$

This treatment assumes that all of the oxygen consumed by the cells was utilized for oxidative phosphorylation. While an equivalence between ATP production and oxygen utilization was not measured, it should be mentioned that an equivalence between oxygen uptake and CO_2 production was demonstrated.

While working with the FS-4 cells (a normal diploid human foreskin fibroblast cell strain), we noted the following:

1. Both the growth curve and the calculated rate of energy formation show a remarkably repeatable profile (see Figure 9–2).
2. One can significantly alter the metabolism of these cells and yet have little effect upon the appraised (calculated) rate at which the cells produce ATP (see Figure 9–3). Specifically, while the FS-4 cells grow equally well on either glucose or galactose as the primary carbohydrate, they show markedly differing metabolisms on these different carbohydrates. Cells grown on glucose typically show elevated rates of glycolysis and depressed rates of oxygen utilization when compared to growth on galactose (see Table 9–1).
3. Most of the ATP generated appears to be used to satisfy the demands for cell maintenance. While the FS-4 cells produce ATP at an elevated rate (about 3 mmoles ATP/g DCW-h) following inoculation onto microcarriers, that rate decreases at 48 h to a steady level of about 1.6–1.8 mmoles ATP/g DCW-h and then remains essentially constant for the rest of the culture period. This change in the observed rate of ATP formation does not correspond to a change in the growth rate, as the cells remain in exponential growth (doubling time, about 66 h) until 100

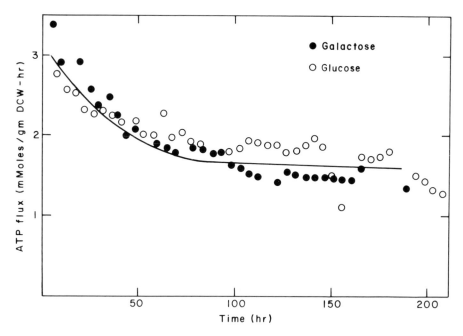

FIGURE 9–2 The calculated ATP flux in FS-4 cells versus fermentation time for FS-4 cells is shown for cultures grown on either glucose or galactose.

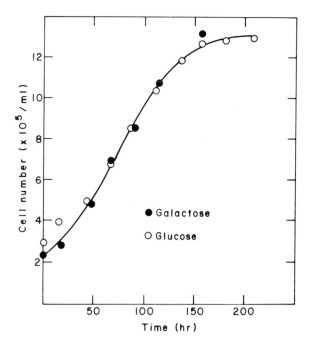

FIGURE 9–3 Comparison of cell growth on glucose versus galactose.

TABLE 9–1   Metabolism of FS-4 Cells Grown on Glucose versus Galactose

Measurement of Metabolism	Glucose	Galactose
Carbohydrate consumption (mmoles/1)	~ 50	7
Lactic acid formation (mmoles/1)	~ 95	6
Oxygen consumption (mmoles/1)	8	22

or 120 h following the inoculation of the culture. In fact, the assumption of a constant maintenance requirement of 1.7 mmoles ATP/g DCW-h is a reasonable predictor of the cell number for FS-4 cells (see Figure 9–4). A word of caution: we saw little growth-associated energy demand* with the FS-4 cells. Ways of thinking about cell energy sources and uses are still in development.

4. Carbohydrates are the major source of energy for these cells—perhaps the most controversial conclusion of our work. Notably, other researchers (Reitzer et al., 1979) have concluded that with HeLa cells, glutamine was the predominant energy source. Specifically, they determined that 98% of the energy utilized by these cells was derived from glutamine when galactose or fructose were the primary carbohydrates. The FS-4 cells, however, behaved very differently, as only about 10% of the energy generated might be attributable to glutamine consumption. Personally, I believe both conclusions are correct and that the apparent discrepancy only emphasizes what can happen to cells (in this case HeLa) after years of adaption to a tissue culture environment containing high amounts of glucose and glutamine.

9.6   CONTROL OF GLUCOSE METABOLISM BY FS-4 CELLS

It may be useful to consider a study in FS-4 cells aimed at achieving process control in cell culture. Specifically, the aim of this work was to utilize the calculated ATP flux to control the metabolism of glucose by the FS-4 cells so that formation of lactic acid was minimized.

---

* In the Piret model (Luedeking and Piret, 1959), the consumption of substrates by microorganisms is partitioned into a growth-associated term and a cell or cell maintenance-associated term:

$$(-1/x)(ds/dt) = [1/(Y_{x/S})](\mu) + m$$

where

$$x = \text{cell number}$$
$$S = \text{substrate}$$
$$Y_{x/S} = \text{yield of X on S}$$
$$\mu = \text{growth rate}$$
$$m = \text{maintenance factor}$$
$$t = \text{time.}$$

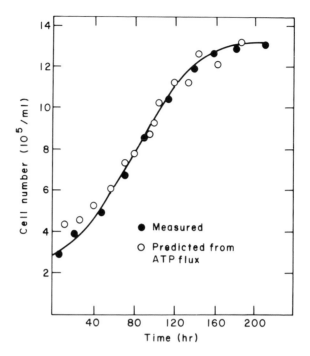

FIGURE 9–4 Use of calculated ATP flux to calculate cell number.

This objective had its inspiration in the work of Rheinwald and Green (1974), who found that by substituting starch and other secondary sources of glucose for glucose itself, glycolysis was greatly diminished. Presumably, these secondary glucose sources serve as a constant but slow source of free glucose. In addition, we observed that if the glucose concentration was allowed to fall below 1–2 mM, glycolysis decreased and oxidative phosphorylation increased.

Thus, in principle it seemed reasonable to assume that glucose could be fed to the cells at a rate that would provide for normal cell growth while keeping the cells at a low level of glycolysis. There was one major snag with this plan, which also made it more interesting: We did not know beforehand at what concentration the glucose level should be maintained. Consequently, the following control scheme was devised (see Figure 9–5). This scheme used three control loops, two feedback and one feedforward. The oxygen uptake rate and the rate of lactic acid formation were used to determine a glucose demand based on a desired ratio of glycolysis to oxidative phosphorylation. To ensure that the glucose concentration would remain within a certain concentration range, a second control loop was implemented. This feedback loop adjusted the glucose feed rate to satisfy unaccounted demand and to prevent adding glucose should the level be above the desired con-

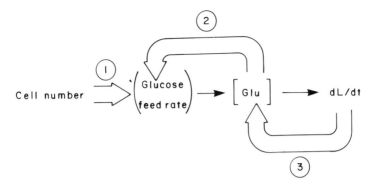

FIGURE 9–5 Outline of scheme used to control the metabolism of glucose by the FS-4 cells. Control loops 1, 2, and 3 are numbered in order of their description in text.

centration. The trade-off in this scheme was that when cells were presented with high glucose concentrations, the cells produced too much lactic acid. Alternatively, too low a level would retard cell growth. This concern was incorporated into the third control loop. Here, we begin by controlling the glucose concentration at a level believed to support growth and a reduced rate of glycolysis. Periodically, the rate of glycolysis was examined and the glucose set points lowered if that rate was determined to be excessive.

The growth and metabolism of the FS-4 cells under the conditions of controlled glucose metabolism are presented in Figure 9–6. In essence, the plot shows that the cells exhibited both normal growth and metabolism. Yet when the specific rate of lactic acid formation is examined, a notable difference between these cells and those grown without control is apparent (see Figure 9–7). The rate of acid formation by these cells (0.2 mmole/g DCW-h versus 1.3 mmole/g DCW-h for cells typically grown in glucose) was substantially reduced after corrective action was taken to lower the glucose set point. The final set point of not greater than 0.1 mM glucose (and more realistically about 50 μM) is strikingly less than the level of glucose present in Dulbecco's modified Eagle's medium (DME), 25 mM.

9.7 CONCLUSION

I have tried to accomplish three things in this chapter: first, to review some of the more commonly used instruments in cell culture, in particular those for temperature, pH, and dissolved oxygen, and their practical limitations; second, to show how some of these sensors can be used to monitor certain physiological processes such as the rate of energy flux through glycolysis and respiration; and third, to give an example of how this kind of information can be applied to process control.

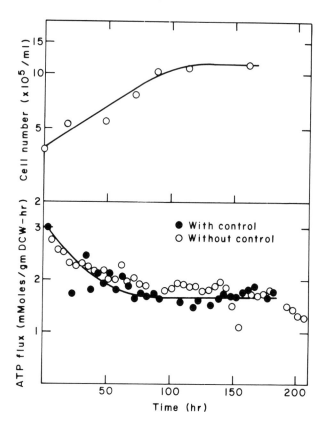

FIGURE 9–6   Plot of cell growth and energy metabolism versus time of fermentation. FS-4 cells were grown in microcarrier culture (5 g/l bead concentration) in a 14-liter fermentor on DME containing only 0.5 mM glucose and buffered with 5 mM tricine and without bicarbonate. The inoculum was prepared using roller bottles. The initial culture volume was 7.5 liters.

REFERENCES

Boraston, R., Thompson, P.W., Garland, S., and Birch, J.R. (1983) *Dev. Biol. Stand.* 55, 103–111.

Cristofalo, V.J., and Kritchevsky, D. (1966) *J. Cell Physiol.* 67, 125–132.

Fleischaker, R.J., Jr. (1982) Ph.D. Thesis, Massachusetts Institute of Technology, Cambridge.

Fleischaker, R.J., Jr., and Sinskey, A.J. (1981) *Eur. J. Appl. Microbiol. Biotechnol.* 12, 193–197.

Kilburn, D.G., and Webb, F.C. (1968) *Biotechnol. Bioeng.* 10, 801–814.

Luedeking, R., and Piret, E.L. (1959) *J. Biochem. Microbiol. Technol. Eng.* 1, 431–459.

Reitzer, L.J., Wice, B.M., and Kennell, D. (1979) *J. Biol. Chem.* 8, 2669–2676.

Rheinwald, J.G., and Green, H. (1974) *Cell* 2, 287–293.

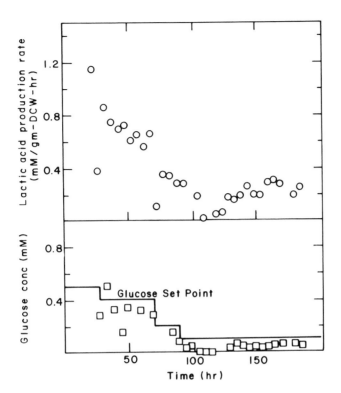

FIGURE 9–7 Glucose set point, glucose concentration, and rate of lactic acid formation by the FS-4 cells versus time of fermentation.